genre *fission*

DBS Arts Library

This book is due for return on or before the last date shown below.

dies

Ꝺℬ

University of Iowa Press,
Iowa City 52242
Copyright © 2000 by the
University of Iowa Press
All rights reserved
Printed in the United States of America
Design by Richard Hendel
http://www.uiowa.edu/~uipress

Printed on acid-free paper

Library of Congress
Cataloging-in-Publication Data
Barr, Marleen S.
  Genre fission: a new discourse practice
  for cultural studies / by Marleen S. Barr.
    p.   cm.
  Includes index.
  ISBN 0-87745-703-4 (pbk.)
    1. American fiction — 20th
  century — History and criticism —
  Theory, etc.   2. Postmodernism
  (Literature) — United States.
  3. United States — Civilization —
  20th century.   4. Postmodernism —
  United States.   5. Discourse analysis,
  Literary.   6. Culture — Philosophy.
  7. Literary form.   I. Title.
  PS374.P64 B37   2000
  814'.54 — dc21   99-058453

00   01   02   03   04   P   5   4   3   2   1

For my beloved father, George Barr, who,

until shortly after I completed this book,

was always present to offer advice and

encouragement in regard to all the pages

of the story of my life. Words cannot express

the depth of my appreciation for this

wonderful man and for all he did for me.

CONTENTS

INTRODUCTION

"The Grand Mix" or Who Wears the White Hats When the Barbie Liberation Organization Strikes Back?

Donna Haraway provided this blurb for my *Lost in Space: Probing Feminist Science Fiction and Beyond*: "[Barr's work] redraws the basic categories of analysis and has an impact on the study of literary practice in general." *Genre Fission: A New Discourse Practice for Cultural Studies* presents nine chapters, written after *Lost in Space*, which exemplify redrawings of basic categorical-analysis rubrics. The chapters illustrate a new critical writing style, a new reading methodology.

The critical community sorely needs a revitalizing discourse practice: *Apollo 13* commander Jim Lovell's understatement, "Houston, we have a problem," has become applicable to literary critics. Some critical methods (such as reiterating current stellar theories and excluding supposedly marginal imaginative texts) are so tedious that university presses are starting to refuse to publish literary criticism. Furthermore, well-known critics are moving from scholarly to popular venues (such as Henry Louis Gates' frequent contributions to the *New Yorker*). The discourse practice I call genre fission can enliven criticism. Genre fission is an idiosyncratic juxtaposition of the categorically disparate which yields new critical or cultural insights. It is an eccentric close encounter undertaken to reveal a thought-provoking third kind.

Lost in Space communicates my efforts to help to pioneer a field; I now name a reading practice which shares much in common with the reader response theory Norman N. Holland champions. Holland says that the reader's response is legitimate: I say that juxtaposing the disparate is a valid critical act. Readers' responses are infinite. Ditto for enabling usually unrelated cultural artifacts to address each other. Some people will take issue with a nonfinite discourse method. I remind them of Roland Barthes' description of "myth": "Everything, then, can be a myth? Yes, I believe this, for the universe is infinitely fertile in suggestions" (109). So, too, everything can be included within genre fission; critics are infinitely fertile regarding interpreting objects orbiting in the cultural universe. Reconstruction (using infinitely fertile suggestions to put dissimilar artifacts together) should follow in the wake of deconstruction.

I wish to counter conditions which cause "Houston, we have a problem" to describe literary criticism. To begin to do so, I point out that recasting James Tiptree, Jr.'s title "Houston, Houston, Do You Read?" can describe criticism. I ask my profession's mission control center, the critical community, "Houston, how do you read?" The answer I propose, a less fixed approach to established generic and discourse categories, is akin to the ideas Bill Nichols articulates in *Blurred Boundaries: Questions of Meaning in Contemporary Culture*.[1] My answer calls for theoretical license, a plasticity of application which rules out nothing from its purview. Yes, it can be argued (for example) that this volume's second chapter, which conflates Jackie Kennedy, *Star Trek*, and Superman to consider the possibilities of women's political agency, is farfetched. But farfetched (I prefer to use "creative") discourse can refresh literary criticism, transforming critics from those who reiterate the previously articulated and categorically sanctioned to artists who freely combine diverse cultural undertakings. Literary critics engaged with genre fission resemble painters who combine different (sometimes clashing) colors to create images which confound categorical expectations. Each chapter in this volume, with J. L. Austin in mind, exemplifies how to do things with genre fission. Each chapter generates questions which extend beyond its particular topic. Should literary critics be more constrained than visual artists? Must literary critics forever be locked in the prisonhouse of their writing conventions? As Marge Piercy notes in "Marleen Barr's Lost and Found" (her introduction to *Lost in Space*), I am a question raiser: Barr "stands outside the elaborate imitation Gothic edifices of academic criticism and says, But Why and How Come and Why Not and Who Says So and Phooey. She keeps asking, but how come you leave out all the fun and really inventive stuff? . . . All cultural artifacts — from art deemed high and awarded Nobel Prizes to television re-runs that secretly form our inner world of common images — are the matter of her discourse" (ix). *Genre Fission* enables me to find and name what has been lost in critical space: a discourse method to practice what I preach — a term for putting together all the fun and really inventive stuff.

Genre Fission logically follows *Lost in Space* and springs from the conclusion to my *Feminist Fabulation: Space / Postmodern Fiction*: that is, from Italo Calvino's description (in "All at One Point") of a woman's maternal language inventing space. When Calvino's protagonist Mrs. Ph(i)NKo speaks in the voice of a noodle-making Italian mother, all existing material — hitherto compressed at one point — expands and the universe is born (Calvino, 46–47; Barr, *Feminist Fabulation*, 258–259). Since the new woman-made universe emanating from the mother's word remains a fiction, *Genre Fission* considers processes of categorical compression to an all-at-one point which can potentially result in expansive new, presently indistinct, meaning systems. I am concerned with merging traditional boundaries to challenge fixed definitions that the hegemony and patriarchy perpetuate. I focus upon forces which bring disparate cultural categories together, forces which enable these categories to exist in the same point or space. Genre fission causes established discourse practices to collapse, to form a new interpretive horizon: genres merge and become new discourses which hide from view old patriarchal and hegemonic master narratives.

Two framed spaces, Judy Chicago's *Through the Flower* (1973) and Lee Bontecou's *Untitled* (1959), picture this newness. Chicago's androgynous circular flower made of phallic petals portrays an undemarcated interchange of feminine and masculine — i.e., it exemplifies genre fission. Her neither completely feminine nor completely masculine flower questions power dynamics between women and men. She portrays specific feminine and masculine matter (and matters) breaking down. Newness results from her picture of gender-distinction collapse: a fragile feminine flower made of phalluses, the penis / petals which connote genre fission.

Bontecou's *Untitled* — a relief construction of welded steel, wire, and cloth which forms the focal point of a Museum of Modern Art exhibit organized by Elizabeth Murray (*Artist's Choice Modern Women*, June 20 – August 22, 1995) — relates discourse to collapsing matter. Murray, in the film which accompanies the exhibit and shares its title, explains that she placed *Untitled* at the exhibition's entrance because this work has an impact upon people: it either pulls them in or scares them away. She also comments that Bontecou's "sexual as opposed to erotic" creation concerns stepping outside the boundaries of reality to "see what you come up with." Murray feels connected to Bontecou's "very powerful" and "very confrontational" image, which conveys the depth of emptiness and the unknown with beautiful dramatic dignity. *Untitled* at once attracts or repels an audience and circumvents categories. Bontecou presents a quilt supported by steel, an example of feminine art covering a nonfeminine structure.

Chicago's penis / petals and Bontecou's patchwork cloth and welded steel are postmodern, utopian interweavings of difference. They picture ideas Tobin Siebers posits in *Heterotopia: Postmodern Utopia and the Body Politic*, ideas which apply to genre fission. Siebers argues that postmodernism is characterized by "the desire to put together things that do not belong together" (4) — and genre fission charts this desire's cultural manifestations. *Genre Fission* — which itself transgresses fixed definitions of category — juxtaposes the disparate, desiring "to collect and to combine as much as possible into a new vision" (Siebers, 8). Hence, my book boldly probes cultural spaces and collects diverse samples which no critic has combined before: textually cross-dressed male authors, the aforementioned Jackie Kennedy Onassis confronting *Star Trek* and patriarchy-as-Superman, contemporary American novelists acting as girl gangs and male clones, prostitutes and gazes, Lorena Bobbitt eyeing the *Saturn 5*, "churtening" (Ursula K. Le Guin's term for stories functioning as spaceship fuel) Hispanic-American writers, Reichstag wrappers and rapping racism, and Holocaust novel authors who play with time. Genre fission is quite congruent with Siebers' description "of mixed places and themes," his vision of "heterotopia" (20).[2] Genre fission concerns a heterotopian goal: to analyze a "postmodern vision of utopia, where community is based on the inclusion of differences, where different forms of talk are allowed to exist simultaneously, and where heterogeneity does not inspire conflict" (Siebers, 20). More simply stated (as this introduction's title indicates), like Siebers, I explore "the grand mix" (Siebers, 32).

Who "ya gonna call" to provide a structure for a book about the grand mix (or category busters)? Categories, of course. Hence, *Genre Fission* is divided into three parts. Part I, "Private Lives: Peaceful Coexistences," discusses private lives in terms of the potential to achieve peaceful coexistences between women and men. Part II, "Public Displays: Sexed Spectacles," positions the public display as an erotic gaze. Part III, "Premier Discourses: First Times," addresses the first time a particular discourse appears.

The first chapter presents Max Apple, Saul Bellow, Edgar Allan Poe, and Lynn Redgrave forming a textual cross-dresser support group. These writers, in their texts which draw upon personal experiences, confront canonicity — the dead white male's continuing influence.

The second chapter discusses that most private of all public figures, Jackie Kennedy Onassis, according to myths of American national identity: Camelot, *Star Trek*, and *Superman*. I read these myths in terms of establishing new roles for women.

The third chapter explains that female novelists (Margaret Atwood, Marilyn French, Joyce Carol Oates, and Marge Piercy) and male novelists (John Barth, John Updike, and Philip Roth) respectively create girl gangs and male clones. After retreating to all-female and all-male corners of the gender battle arena to consider female solidarity and male authorial duplication, these authors, hopefully (after creating protagonists who engage the opposite sex according to rubrics of peaceful coexistence), will emerge from their separated gendered artistic spaces.

The fourth chapter posits that Amsterdam prostitutes displayed in windows represent the looking practices I call utopian and dystopian gazes. I bring Dutch window culture to bear upon viewing framed women, and refer to the artwork of Bill Copley and Claes Oldenburg.

The fifth chapter positions New York and Los Angeles as respectively masculine and feminine public displays. Through my analysis of class distinctions — as well as such disparate entities as the Fifth Avenue Warner Brothers Store, the Guggenheim Museum, and Hollywood movies — I explain how the cities at once differ and converge.

The sixth chapter describes a group of American middle-class men, the Apollo Program astronauts, as participants in an enterprise which views the moon as both Woman and an extension of suburbia. Despite the Apollo Program's macho bravado, the presently rusted *Saturn 5* rockets pose no threat to Lorena Bobbitt.

The seventh chapter explores literary criticism's first pairing of Hispanic-American novels with a science fiction "thought experiment" (Ursula K. Le Guin's term). The novelists I discuss (Ana Castillo, Cristina Garcia, and Julia Alvarez) create characters who "churten" (the word Le Guin coins to describe lack of differentiation between story and science — i.e., between science fiction and spaceship fuel).

The eighth chapter considers the emerging understanding of race and religion as amorphous categories. Drawing upon imaginative texts (written by Aharon Appelfeld, Octavia Butler, Alan Gurganus, Stanislaw Lem, John Updike, Richard Wright, and Pamela Zoline) and critical texts (written by Walter Abish, Salomo Friedlaender, Sander Gilman, Shirlee Taylor Haizlip, Erica Jong, Michael Lerner, Oskar Panizza, and Jack Zipes), I address such new ideas as Lerner's and Gilman's opinion that Jews are not white and the notion that black and white are indistinct racial categories.

The ninth chapter analyzes novels (written between 1990 and 1995 by Martin Amis, E. L. Doctorow, Ellen Galford, Alan Isler, and Tova Reich) which indirectly address the Holocaust and appear at the moment when all eyewitnesses are reaching advanced old age. Citing such novelists and critics as Sheila Finch, Saul Friedlander, Geoffrey Hartman, Lawrence Langer, Sherri Szeman, and George Steiner, I argue that the novels I include are time travel tales which share much in common with science fiction in general and Jack Dann's science fiction in particular.

The epilogue positions the black hole and liberated light as central metaphors for *Genre Fission*.

In the spirit of the traversed generic boundaries pertinent to genre fission, I bring the following paintings (exhibited in Munich's Lenbachaus Museum's Spring 1995 exhibit "The Battle of the Sexes") to bear upon some of my ideas: Gert H. Wollheim's *The Victor*, Hans Thoma's *The Guards in Front of the Love Garden*, and Edvard Munch's *The Scream* and *Encounter in Space*.

Part literary analysis, part cultural studies, part feminist critique flavored with a smattering of science fiction and utopian studies, the chapters address heterotopian convergences of the different. Genre fission, in short, concerns the simultaneous homogeneity and heterogeneity which is the crux of our present postmodern cultural moment.

When discussing this moment, Václav Havel seems to have in mind Siebers' "new vision," the mixing, blending, and plurality characterizing genre fission. Havel states:

> The distinguishing features of transitional periods are a mixing and blending of cultures and a plurality or parallelism of intellectual and spiritual worlds. These are periods when all consistent value systems collapse, when cultures distant in time and space are discovered or rediscovered. New meaning is gradually born from the encounter, or the intersection, of many different elements. . . . The artificial world order of the past decades has collapsed and a new, more just order has not yet emerged. The central political task of the final years of this century, then, is the creation of a new model of co-existence among the various cultures, peoples, races and religious spheres within a single interconnected civilization. (A27)

New meanings will be born from the encounters (or convergences) of the disparate that *Genre Fission* explores. Attempting to establish peaceful co-existences between women and men, understanding public displays as sexed spectacles, and defining race and religion differently are all hopes for heterotopian connections. *Genre Fission* concerns models which emerge from the postmodern melting pot — the collapsed categories and new systems which characterize a new discourse practice.

Our transitional period's popular culture is obsessed with new discourse. For example, consider Westerns. *The Ballad of Little Jo* is a feminist Western in which "women are men" (Verhovek, 1). *Dances with Wolves* insinuates that cavalrymen may become honorary Native Americans. These films indicate that a new Old West now reflects heterotopia and genre fission: "Today, in the new Old West, they [Westerns] pick up the national arguments about racism, sexism, and violence and show a lot of confusion about who wears the white hats" (Verhovek, 5). Who wears the white hats is a less complex version of the question my eighth chapter includes: Who is white?

In addition to blurred racial categories, much confusion presently exists regarding exactly who wears the pants. This gender and power quandary is a less complex version of another current popular culture obsession relating to sex / gender ambiguity. A question of the moment involves who has a penis and who has a vagina. Will Self's *Cock and Bull*, for instance, describes a woman who finds a penis located in her genital area and a man who finds a vagina located behind his knee. The man gives birth. And so, according to *Junior*, does Arnold Schwarzenegger. If these male mothers are sexually harassed, they can read Michael Crichton's *Disclosure*.

Extreme gender role confusion is not limited to films and novels. Lesbian activist Joann Loulan, now involved with a male lover, announces that she is still a lesbian, not a bisexual or a heterosexual.[3] Another example of gender role ambiguity concerning very real people involves the eight Boston men who sued the Jenny Craig weight loss organization. Their charge: while counseling overweight women, they were discriminated against by female chauvinist pig executives. *Time*, when describing the Jenny Craig story, answers this question: do the alleged diet center female chauvinist pigs wear the pants or do they wear white hats? *Time*'s verdict is that the empowered Jenny Craig executive gals are not the bad guys: "All this attention also suggests a man who is sexually harassed has a greater claim on our sympathies — a notion coming this week to a Multiplex near you in *Disclosure*, a movie in which predatory executive Demi Moore accosts sweet, sensitive Michael Douglas. Jenny Craig plaintiff Tracy Tinkham looks more like Joey Buttafuoco than Michael Douglas, but never mind. . . . But before the Jenny Craig Eight pour their heart out to Sally Jessy Raphael, they should check with all the women who have looked up the corporate ladder and seen 10 men for every woman and wondered how they could prove their lack of success was due to some failure in the corporate culture, and not in themselves" (Carlson, 62).

The allegedly sexually harassed Jenny Craig employees resemble Joey Buttafuoco; Barbie sounds like Amy Fisher and GI Joe. Barbie's unexpectedly new voice exists because the Barbie Liberation Organization strikes back. The *New York Times* explains that the BLO is a group of Manhattan East Village performance artists who, in response to Barbie's stated opinion that "math is hard," switch the voices of talking Barbie and GI Joe dolls. The BLO engages in "painstakingly swapping their [the dolls'] voice boxes and then . . . replacing dolls on the shelves of the toy stores in at least two states. The group, which asserts that it has surgically altered 300 dolls, says its aim is to startle the public into thinking about the Stone Age world view that the dolls reflect. The result is a militant colony of Barbies-on-steroids who roar things like 'Attack!' 'Vengeance is mine' and 'Eat lead, Cobra.' The emasculated G. I. Joe's, meanwhile, twitter, 'Will we ever have enough clothes?' and 'Let's plan our dream wedding!'" (Firestone, A12). Joanne Oppenheim, president of the *Oppenheim Toy Portfolio* (a publication which reviews toys), charges that the BLO perpetrates "terrorist acts" (Firestone, A12). Unlike the BLO, Oppenheim, who considers Barbie to be a good guy, would not critique the doll's wedding veil; she would, instead, see it as a benign white hat. The real world, in contrast, less frequently adheres to Oppenheim's view of gender-role status quo. After all, when expressing her feelings for Joey Buttafuoco, Amy Fisher seemed to say "Attack!" — not "Let's plan our dream wedding!"

An emasculated GI Joe speaking in Barbie's different voice signals a new lack of distinction between organic and inorganic matter — another part of the grand mix which includes male vaginas, lesbians who have sex with men, and female chauvinist pigs. When robot Dante II malfunctioned while exploring the interior of Mount Spurr (located eighty miles west of Anchorage), the *New York Times* article about the event was called "Helicopter Rescue Is Planned for Robot." The *Times* told readers that the soon to be rescued robot in distress fell over "after breaking one of its eight legs"; despite this damage, Carnegie Mellon robotics expert John Bares announced that Dante II was "still alive." Luckily, since Dante merely "lost its footing" ("Helicopter," 31), Bares did not have to ask this question: they shoot robots, don't they?

People might lose their footing in regard to negotiating the collapsing categories which merge to form "the grand mix" that *Genre Fission* de-

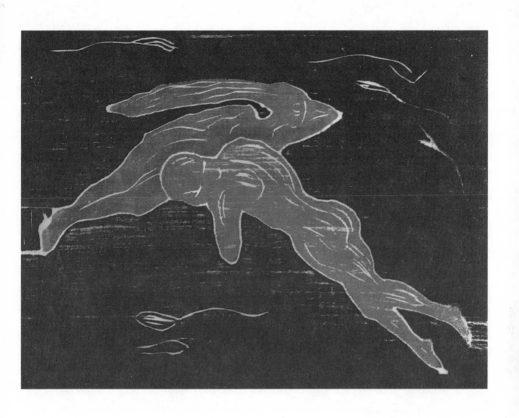

Edvard Munch, Encounter in Space, *1899. Woodcut. Munch Museum, Oslo.*

scribes. In response to this cultural convergence, Havel addresses the effort to achieve stability in a world in flux, a world whose new solid ground does not yet exist: the "'anthropic cosmological principle' brings us to an idea, perhaps as old as humanity itself, that we are not at all just an accidental anomaly, the microscopic caprice of a tiny particle whirling in the endless depths of the universe, we are mirrored in it, just as the entire evolution of the universe is mirrored in us. . . . . The only real hope of people today is probably a renewal of our certainty that we are rooted in the Earth and, at the same time, the cosmos. This awareness endows us with the capacity for self-transcendence" (A27).

Munch's *Encounter in Space* seems to picture Havel's description of capricious tiny particles whirling in the universe as well as the mirrored reciprocity between human and universe. Hence, *Encounter* also seems to picture this introduction. Munch's blue woman and red man are outside human racial categories. Like the sperm images appearing beside them, the figures are ensconced within a black space which may represent the inside of a woman's body. Perhaps the figures are akin to the sperm / protagonists of Woody Allen's *Everything You Always Wanted to Know about Sex But Were Afraid to Ask* and John Barth's "Night-Sea Journey." Perhaps the figures exemplify seeping beyond the category "human"; perhaps the female and male figures are other versions of the sperm Allen and Barth imagine.

Although this relational possibility will remain forever uncertain, I suggest that *Encounter in Space*, created in 1899, more appropriately represents humans at the turn of our century than does the *Pioneer* spacecraft image I discuss at the start of *Feminist Fabulation* (xi–xii). *Pioneer* portrays a communicating man and a subordinate woman. Munch depicts the mouth of man (his communicative orifice) obliterated while seemingly merging with the labia of woman. Man's mouth, not his sperm, interacts with woman. In stark contrast to *Pioneer*'s woman gazing at a man, Munch's female figure (unconcerned with man) looks forward to new directions — directions which will not be born from the old method of sperm meeting egg. New directions might emerge from silenced, faceless man encountering woman looking at an undifferentiated something Other than him. Munch's female and male figures float in ambiguous space — an enveloping blackness, instead of specifically designated outer or inner space. *Encounter in Space* represents the at once close and unexpected encounters I explore in *Genre Fission: A New Discourse Practice for Cultural Studies*.

1 private lives
peaceful coexistences

Edvard Munch, The Scream, *1895. Lithograph. Munch Museum, Oslo.*

1

BRIDGING THE DEAD
FATHER'S CANONICAL DIVIDE

Max Apple, Saul Bellow, Edgar Allan Poe,
and Lynn Redgrave Form a Textual Cross-
Dresser Support Group

As the *New York Times* noted:

> Desperate to end what they thought were attacks from beyond the grave,
> New Englanders once unearthed corpses and performed vampire kill-
> ing rituals, scientists say. . . . [B]odies from 18th- and 19th-century New
> England graves appear to have been dug up within a few months or
> years of death and then mutilated or disrupted. . . . [T]his tampering
> with corpses was prompted by the idea of "killing" the dead to stop
> them from sucking the life force from the living. . . . [F]amily members
> would go into the grave and somehow attempt to kill the person again.
> ("New Englanders 'Killed' Corpses, Experts Say")

In light of dead fathers' propensity for speaking from beyond the grave,
New Englanders who "killed" corpses provide a useful tactic for feminist
critics. I imagine these critics performing "killing" rituals to stop dead fathers' master narratives from sucking the life force from living women's
stories. This chapter points out that male fiction writers who create what I
define as cross-dressed texts also engage in such rituals.

The at once female and male figure in Gert H. Wollheim's *The Victor*, attired as a woman, whose head appears as a genderless blank page, performs
a killing ritual (pointedly accomplished via an arrow) on the male body
(see p. 136). The male body, suspended over the figure's shoulder —
bagged, captured, controlled — acquiesces to the cross-dressed, cross-
bodied figure attired in suspenders crossed between female breasts. The
suspended male who kisses the androgynous victor's hand is in danger of
becoming a dead father.

Ellen G. Friedman might applaud what I see as Wollheim's androgynous
figure's victory over the potential dead father. In "Where Are the Missing

Contents?: (Post)Modernism, Gender, and the Canon," she provides material to support the need to approach Donald Barthelme's *The Dead Father*— the power of the dead father's word that this text represents — by attempting to kill him again. Friedman cites Jean-François Lyotard's notion that Western civilization's master narratives are the "missing contents" in modernist and postmodernist literature. She does so to argue that the sense of loss for these no longer presentable narratives is more pervasive in men's, *rather* than in women's, modern and postmodern texts. Women's texts of modernity look to the future; men's look to the past and, hence, more easily *become* canonized (Friedman, 244). Using Barthelme's *The Dead Father* and Thomas Pynchon's *Vineland* to address Fredric Jameson's response to Lyotard — Jameson's insistence that paternal Western master narratives remain present and powerful — Friedman explains that "the yearning for fathers, for past authority and sure knowledge that can no longer be supported, permeates male texts of modernity. . . . Although he [Barthelme's protagonist, the dead father] is buried, he is not silenced. . . . As Pynchon turns away from the quest for the mother, he suggests that the longing for the lost father is inevitable, because the father's order is the only one that Pynchon can imagine" (240–241). This yearning for the father marks Pynchon and Barthelme as already "'past' [Friedman uses Gertrude Stein's term] and thus classical or, in current terms, canonical" (Friedman, 251; Stein, 514). In contrast, female modernists and postmodernists (such as Stein, Anaïs Nin, and Kathy Acker) look forward and remain "outlaws" located outside the canon (Friedman, 244–251).

With Friedman's points in mind, I position Max Apple's "Bridging" as a woman's text of modernity. In the first section of this chapter (which pays cursory attention to Amos Oz, Norman Rush, and Philip Roth), I argue that "Bridging," which is neither "past" nor classical, does not look backward to master narratives about gender roles. Instead, the story discusses yet to be presented nonpatriarchal roles for men. After describing how "Bridging"— a male-authored women's text — suggests a new order for the father and calls attention to the dead mother's absence, I explain (in the second section) why Poe's science fiction is a precursor to male-authored texts which conform to Friedman's argument. My third section claims that, like "Bridging," Saul Bellow's recent fiction rejects the father's law and looks forward — beyond patriarchal master narratives to the new order which will exist after old categories merge at Calvino's "All at One Point" (discussed in the introduction).

I conclude by focusing upon Lynn Redgrave, a woman who seeks her dead father in terms of her own authority. Redgrave, in *Shakespeare for My Father*, seems to reply to men's efforts to create women's texts when she plays — and, hence, appropriates — her own dead father's role. Apple, Bellow, and Redgrave belong to a textual female cross-dresser's support group that Poe engenders. A question asked by one of the characters in *The Male Cross-Dresser Support Group* by Tama Janowitz is relevant here: "And what does this mean, cross-dress support?" (293). What I call a cross-dressed text is male-authored discourse which conforms to Friedman's notion of a forward-looking woman's text of modernity. Men's cross-dressed texts impersonate the women's texts Friedman defines. They defy categorization.

A TROOP OF MEN WHO PRODUCE CROSS-DRESSED TEXTS

"Bridging" includes a dead mother whose influence reaches beyond the grave: she affects her husband's decision to lead a Girl Scout troop in order to nurture their daughter, Jessica. Instead of exalting the dead father, "Bridging" depicts an unnamed living father who critiques fixed definitions of fatherhood. Language fails to describe his activities: "We had no den father" (Apple, 549). Apple's unnamed protagonist does not emulate a particular dead father familiar to his community: "Mr. Clark was killed in the Korean War. . . . John [Mr. Clark's son] had that hero on the wall, his father in a uniform, dead for reasons John and all the rest of us understood" (549, 551). This protagonist, instead, formulates a new male hero: a leader of uniformed girls, not uniformed male soldiers. He is a living father who replaces the dead mother. Mainstream America does not yet fully welcome a nurturing maternal father, a father who wishes to compensate for "the years in which I paid so little attention to my daughter" (553). Apple creates an antipatriarchal fabulator,[1] a man who wishes to rewrite himself in opposition to patriarchal fictions.

Apple's story defines "bridging" in terms of maturity: "the way Brownies become Girl Scouts" (546). He describes this growth process as a transition from yearning for dead fathers (fallen soldiers like Mr. Clark, for example) to applauding men who become heroes when they act as nurturers. Apple's maternal male protagonist is as heroic as soldiers or other absent fathers who, in regard to their families, had "never been there" (552). Mothering fathers do not receive cultural Brownie points, however; "househusband" lacks the panache of "CEO." Regardless, Apple's protagonist rejects usual male gender roles when he "swoop[s] past five thousand years of stereotypes and accept[s] . . . [his] assistant leader's packet and credentials" (547). This assistant scout leader blazes a trail for future new paternal roles. Unlike Pynchon and Barthelme, Apple portrays a maternal father and describes a dead mother influencing a living father. This father views a dead mother's impact upon him as an "irresistible presence" (Friedman, 240) — or a force. Apple, then, writes in the manner of one of Friedman's female "outlaws."

"I'm learning to be a leader" (554), says Apple's protagonist. Apple himself could lead a troop of contemporary male writers whose texts resemble Friedman's description of women's texts. Instead of longing for the Western narrative tradition, some men now author fictions which cross-dress as female texts. These writers view the dead father's authority as the "'missing contents,'" the "'unpresentable' in the literature of modernity" (Friedman, 240; Lyotard, *The Postmodern Condition*). For example, I refer to Amos Oz and Norman Rush to position them as members of the textual cross-dresser group I describe. In the manner of Apple's attention to the dead mother and his unorthodox approach to fatherhood and heroism, Oz's Yoel Ravid, the protagonist of *To Know a Woman*, nurtures his daughter and mother after his wife dies. Ravid is most heroic when he realizes that his hospital orderly job is more fulfilling than being a master spy. In addition, Norman Rush's *Mating*, another male-authored crossed-dressed text, presents a woman protagonist's critique of a man who fathers an all-female feminist utopia.

Differentiating themselves from the male voice emanating from a female body part depicted by Philip Roth in "The Breast," male authors such as Apple, Oz, and Rush mimic female voices — produce cross-dressed texts. Rejecting such "past" texts of modernity as "The Breast," *Vineland*, and *The Dead Father*, they create a corpus of male-authored women's texts which challenge dead fathers' canonical corpses. These men, holding their own women's texts firmly in hand, thrust themselves upon the contemporary literary scene in a manner which enables them to avoid becoming categorized as the presently "past" practitioners of an impotent literature of exhaustion. They silence dead fathers, using cross-dressed texts to sever ties with the male Western narrative tradition. Poe engendered them. Bellow is now one of them.

Poe and contemporary male creators of cross-dressed texts are scouts — a troop which charts literary paths located beyond worn-out patriarchal paths. Poe and Bellow, who possess many canonical Brownie points, support other men who wish to redefine themselves as makers of women's texts, not dead canonical fathers.

POE AS SCOUT LEADER

In such science fiction stories as "The Unparalleled Adventure of One Hans Pfaall," "The Thousand-and-Second Tale of Scheherazade," "The System of Dr Tarr and Prof. Fether," and "The Facts in the Case of M. Valdemar," Poe creates women's texts and functions as a feminist critic.[2] "Pfaall," for example, critiques the power of city fathers — "the burghers of Rotterdam" (13) — personified by one Burgomaster Mynheer Superbus Von Underduk. The story describes how a balloon functions as a transport bus which enables a text (Pfaall's letter about his moon flight undertaken via balloon) to commute from the moon to Earth. Pfaall's outer space journey and letter enable him to transcend the Rotterdam fathers who position him as underdog and Woman. His departure and the letter he sends via the balloon's return to Earth are "an egregious insult to the good sense of the burghers of Rotterdam" (13). Poe critiques patriarchal reality when he imagines a machine carrying Pfaall above and beyond the burghers' systems.

Pfaall's letter, which is "so fatally subversive of both person and personal dignity to his Excellency, Von Underduk" (16), is a subversive document. Like a feminist critical text, it challenges systems which enable fathers to maintain power. Pfaall, "as poor as a rat" (17) and doomed to fall and fail, invents a means to leave patriarchal power systems when he ignites the balloon which will carry him beyond Earth: "Dropping a lighted cigar on the ground, as if by accident, I [Pfaall] took the opportunity, in stooping to pick it up, of igniting privately the piece of slow match. . . . This manoeuvre was totally unperceived. . . . I shot upwards with inconceivable rapidity" (22). Pfaall places himself on top of patriarchal systems when he very purposefully uses a cigar, that most stereotypical of all phallic symbols, as an explosive device. He literally uses energy derived from igniting a representation of phallic power to escape from the burghers' power systems.

Pfaall, a man the burghers don't see, behaves analogously to the female protagonists of James Tiptree, Jr.'s (Alice Sheldon's) "The Women Men Don't See." Like Tiptree's Ruth and Althea Parsons, Pfaall is Woman-as-immigrant from fathers' repressive systems. In the manner of the Parsons women, Pfaall, to escape oppression, leaves Earth and ventures to an unknown world. He describes his intentions with words that could appropriately apply to Ruth and Althea: he is "determined to depart, yet live — to

leave the world, yet continue to exist . . . to force a passage . . . *to the moon*"
(26). This man who possesses a feminist imagination and describes himself
as a "madman" boldly going "beyond the confines of the possible" (26) resembles a "madwoman" venturing beyond the confines of the attic — Ruth
and Althea begging aliens to enable them to leave Earth.

While floating above confining patriarchal systems, Pfaall can place
Earth and the Rotterdam city fathers' power in a new perspective: "the surface of my mother earth . . . was indeed over my head, and completely hidden by the balloon, while the moon — the moon itself in all its glory — lay
beneath me, and at my feet" (51). Pfaall's balloon, his own construction,
blocks out the patriarchal world he escapes. The usually hidden Earth, in
fact, might represent the newly ineffective patriarchal father, not Pfaall's
mother. His new mother, the moon, appears at his feet. Unlike patriarchal
Earth, the maternal moon will not suppress him. Pfaall's balloon allows
him to render father Earth impotent — to experience alternative social
roles. The balloon hides Earth, positioning it as "a world placed under erasure" (McHale, 99–111). Von Underduk and his fellow burghers themselves realize that pardoning Pfaall "would be of little use" ("Pfaall," 57).
Pfaall's text (his letter) effectively nullifies patriarchal power — causes this
power to become of no use. "The Unparalleled Adventure of One Hans
Pfaall" is a power fantasy for women, a precursor to feminist science
fiction.

A feminist critical voice figures in Poe's "The Thousand-and-Second
Tale of Scheherazade." Scheherazade tells the king stories that obviously
contain lies. In contrast to her other stories, Scheherazade's last tale —
which describes women's loss of subjectivity in patriarchal fictions — is
true (152). This story (which is about women who use bolsters to conform
to a beauty standard in which dromedary-like back protuberances are desirable) seems to cause Naomi Wolf's *The Beauty Myth* to echo Poe's critique of continuously changing femininity requirements. Like feminist science fiction writers, Scheherazade exaggerates to articulate the harmful
impact of patriarchal narratives.

The king describes Scheherazade's insightful story as "your lies" (153).
His interpretation, of course, prevails. The story implies that Scheherazade, who "plays" for time by lying to the king, dies after telling a tale which
articulates a truth in regard to women's lives (153). Although Scheherazade's time is up, Poe makes sure to suggest that it is appropriate to
continue to tell stories which benefit women: "She [Scheherazade] derived,
however, great consolation . . . from the reflection that much of the history

remained still untold" (153). Poe engenders a literary history in which men, instead of silencing women and writing about men's lives, create women's texts. His Scheherazade, who tells tales to entertain a man and to live, ultimately switches to a subversive story about women which the king does not want to hear. Many contemporary male writers follow her example. In the manner of their female colleagues, these men enliven literature; they do not become "past" creators of the literature of exhaustion. Poe's "The Thousand-and-Second Tale of Scheherazade" is more sympathetic to Scheherazade than John Barth's "Dunyazadiad."[3] Poe is a lively dead father of postmodernist literary sons who choose to replenish literature by critiquing patriarchal systems.

Poe, in "The System of Dr Tarr and Prof. Fether," indicates that social systems define more women than men as insane. When the story's narrator visits an asylum, after assuming that the inmates are predominantly female, he is informed that this assumption is false:

> "Oh, no — every one of them men, and stout fellows, too, I can tell you."
>
> "Indeed! I have always understood that the majority of lunatics were of the gentler sex."
>
> "It is generally so, but not always. . . . but, lately, matters have changed very much, as you see." (186)

The narrator's first impression is reasonable. Few men, after all, can relate personally to stories which resemble Scheherazade's beauty myth critique of the dromedary-like women. In literature, men who behave according to analogues of Scheherazade's dromedary scenario inhabit feminist science fiction sex-role reversal novels. In life, patriarchal beauty myth stories cause many women to die from bulimia. I again turn to Apple to link Poe to the contemporary.

Perhaps bulimia kills the dead mother in "Bridging." Readers never know precisely which disease causes her death: "My Jessica had to explain a neurologic disease she couldn't even pronounce, 'I hate it when people ask about Mom,' she says. 'I just tell them she fell off the Empire State Building'" (Apple, 551). Did Jessica's mother enact her own version of Hans Pfaall's departure from patriarchal reality? Did she die from nervousness that the mad housewife role precipitates? Was she a Fay Wray captured by King Kong in the guise of patriarchal master narrative? Readers can fill in the blanks regarding Jessica's absent dead mother, who does not influence the world in the manner of dead fathers. Her story exemplifies "'missing contents,'" "a 'crisis in narrative'" (Friedman, 240; Lyotard, 78–81), a longing for new stories and roles which form alternatives to dead fathers' words. Jessica is unable to pronounce medical terms which communicate the story of her mother's illness. Similarly, American culture cannot yet comfortably articulate words which comprise dead mothers' narratives. Jessica's linguistic difficulty signals that "Bridging" is a female text which "look[s] forward, often beyond culture, beyond patriarchy, into the unknown" (Friedman, 244). Apple pulls readers toward new discourses and paradigms. He creates women's texts — and he evokes Poe.

Apple's protagonist would not pal around with Poe's Burgomaster Von Underduk. In "The Facts in the Case of M. Valdemar," Poe again critiques the patriarchs Von Underduk typifies and describes an alternative to Barthelme's influential dead father protagonist who speaks from beyond the grave. Like Barthelme's protagonist, Valdemar also speaks after death: "the voice seemed to reach our ears — at least mine — from a vast distance, or from some deep cavern within the earth. . . . It was evident that, so far, death (or what is usually termed death) had been arrested by the mesmeric process" ("Valdemar," 200, 202). "Valdemar," however, portrays the dead male voice as ultimately silenced. Valdemar-as-dead-father deconstructs: "his whole frame at once — within the space of a single minute, or even less, shrunk — crumbled — absolutely *rotted* away beneath my hands. Upon the bed, before that whole company, there lay a nearly liquid mass of loathsome — of detestable putridity" (203). He shares much in common with the New Englanders who "kill" corpses.[4] Poe — if I may echo the Raid roach spray commercial — kills the dead father dead. When he depicts Mother Nature prevailing over constructed patriarchal systems that empower dead fathers, Poe emphasizes what any Girl Scout knows: you can't fool Mother Nature. Mother Nature causes dead fathers to rot, to disappear.

BELLOW PRODUCES SOMETHING ELSE TO REMEMBER HIM BY

Bellow's recent work functions in tandem with Apple's "Bridging" and the Poe stories I discuss. Instead of continuing to invent such larger than life men as Henderson, Humbolt, and Augie March, Bellow now creates women's texts which critique patriarchal master narratives. The stories collected in *Something to Remember Me By* indicate that Bellow presently wishes to be remembered as someone who advocates that women's stories should have as much clout as dead fathers' stories. To speak to the possibility of deintensifying people's reverential attitudes toward repressive dead fathers, "The Bellarosa Connection" indicates that sons differ from their fathers — that men change: "We [sons of Jewish immigrants to the United States] grew up under a larger range of influences and thoughts — we were the children of a great democracy, bred to equality, living it up with no pales to confine us" (23–24). Bellow signals that women's stories should not pale beside patriarchal master narratives, that authors should try to remember something other than their nostalgia for these narratives.

Appropriately, then, "The Bellarosa Connection" begins when its narrator, a founder of a memory institute, states that he "would like to *forget* about remembering" (5). Just as Jews cannot forget Holocaust narratives, Western culture cannot forget patriarchal master narratives. Bellow's narrator, who wishes to forget about remembering, tells a story about Harry Fonstein remembering that Billy Rose saved him from the Nazis. Rose views Fonstein's reminiscences according to a fixed definition: he will not permit Fonstein personally to thank him. Like Rose, Bellow embarks upon a rescue mission. Fonstein "was alive today because a little Jewish promoter took it into his queer head to organize a Hollywood-style rescue" (27). Bellow, an eminent Jewish writer, took it into his head to promote women's texts, to rescue them from being eradicated by patriarchal cultural mechanisms. He pulls people toward the Other.

Bellow emphasizes that both Rose and the Nazis were adroit constructors of reality: "Billy Rose wasn't the only one in show biz. So the Germans did it too, and what they staged in Nuremberg was bigger than Billy's rally in Madison Square Garden — the 'We Will Never Die' pageant" (27). Patriarchy stages the idea of its own omnipotence: the "We Will Never Die" pageant is enacted via nostalgia for Western master narratives. Patriarchy is "in show biz" too; in terms of patriarchy, the word "we" in "We Will Never Die" refers to influential dead fathers. Like Nazi propaganda and the entertainment industry, patriarchal fictions can be categorized as "[d]eath and mass fantasy" ("Bellarosa," 28). Patriarchal fictions perpetuate the mass fantasy that dead fathers never die. They prevent graves from entombing (or silencing) dead fathers' voices.

Fonstein's wife, Sorella, uses a woman's text — "Mrs. [Deborah] Hamet's file" ("Bellarosa," 43) — to challenge Rose's narrative production. Hamet, Rose's employee and admirer whom he ignores (hence, she is one of Tiptree's women men don't see), creates a file about him replete with uncomplimentary anecdotes. When Sorella decides to use the file against Rose, she chooses her weapon wisely: "the material [in the file] was explosive, and in the wrong hands it might have been deadly" (44). Hamet is no supportive secretary; Sorella is no meek housewife: "She was an ingenious and powerful woman who devised intricate . . . schemes. What she had in mind was confrontation, a hand-to-hand struggle. . . . the antagonist *was* Broadway Billy Rose" (45). When staging this confrontation, Bellow admonishes his narrator's dismissive response to Hamet's text: the narrator "was sorry now that I hadn't taken the opportunity to read Mrs. Hamet's record" (45). Bellow, when he positions Hamet's file as Rose's foe, stresses that men should not view women's texts as unimportant — as not worth reading. With Sorella's help, Hamet, from her grave, takes revenge upon Rose: "'Dead, is she' [Rose asks Sorella about Hamet]. 'You know she is' [answers Sorella]. . . . So at this moment you [Sorella] come along to take revenge from the grave for a jealous woman" (47, 55). Rose, the male producer of a single-versioned story about Fonstein, is confronted by a text which enables Hamet to wield power. Sorella is well aware of this dead woman's impact: "Deborah recruited me, so I would continue her campaign against him, keep the heat on from the grave" (57). Hamet, no woman enclosed within the grave, is a force.

Sorella, a daughter of Mrs. Hamet-as-dead mother, behaves differently from male scions of dead fathers. Unlike conservative sons who perpetuate dead fathers' texts and eventually themselves become dead fathers, forward-looking daughters approach dead mothers' texts as catalysts for their own creativity. Sorella, for example, inadvertently throws Hamet's text out of a window: "I threw the document at him [Rose]. . . . I aimed Deborah's packet at him. But I'm not much good at throwing, and it went through the open window" (56). Sorella throws the book at Rose's male story and its fixed definitions.

Rose responds by using his economic clout to retrieve Hamet's text; he informs his hotel that "'[a] very important document was dropped from my window. I want it brought up right now. You understand? Immediately. This minute'" (56). Because of its power to diminish him, Rose belatedly attributes importance to this discarded female-authored critique of male power. Bellow, in turn, belatedly attributes importance to women's narratives. Rose rescues Jewish victims of Nazism; Bellow rescues texts which are victims of patriarchal silencing. I would like to thank Saul Bellow for recognizing the power of women's stories. (I hope Bellow would not respond as Rose responds to Fonstein's wish to express appreciation: "'What I did for you, take it and be welcome, but spare me the relationship and all the rest of it'" [50].)

Women are ultimately more powerful than Billy Rose: "My guess was that his defeats by lady Jews were the most deeply wounding of all. He could win against men. Women . . . were too much for him" (40). His antagonists battle someone from a different world: "[s]o this was Billy from the world of the stars" (46). Sorella also appears as a larger than life alien. This obese woman's eyes "were like vents of atmospheric blue, and their backing (the camera obscura) referred you to the black of universal space, where there is no object to reflect the flow of invisible light" (37). Sorella is impervious to the patriarchal camera's gaze and the housewife role. A litany of domestic and feminine accouterments — such as "flatware, wallpapers . . . cosmetics, shoes . . . shopping malls, department stores" — are "things, or forces, or powers [which] could [not] keep a woman like Sorella in subjection" (38). Rose, a producer, cannot stage Sorella. She is Bellow's new larger-than-life female protagonist, a superwoman undaunted by patriarchal power. She can leap over malls in a single bound while wearing high heels. Sorella, a vast feminine, seemingly fantastic space who escapes from demeaning female roles, is as much a survivor as Harry Fonstein. Harry escapes Nazis' stories about Jews; Sorella escapes patriarchy's stories about women.

Bellow does not applaud directors who continue to perpetuate patriarchal stories. Rose is right on the mark when he says "[n]othing is real that isn't a show" (58). Patriarchal stories have exceeded their run in the constructed show called reality. It is time for another opening, another show — new social constructions. It is time for the new realities Le Guin calls "thought experiments" to become alternative social stage sets. Israel, after all, is "the invention of Jewish fantasy" ("Bellarosa," 64). Israel is a Jewish story, a Jewish dream, which becomes reality. Israel is a stage set upon which Jews act as powerful human beings, not alien Others. Sorella and Harry appear on this particular Jewish stage: "And here they were in color, the Judean desert behind them, as husband and wife in a once-upon-a-time Coney Island might have posed against a painted backdrop or sitting on a slice of moon" (70). Israel functions as a Hans Pfaall–like moon for Jews: the country is a new location which affords Jews spaces in which to rise above oppression and fixed definitions. As a rescuer of women's texts, Bellow facilitates the emergence of new Israel-like spaces for women — promised liberatory lands.

Hence, *Something to Remember Me By* indicates that Bellow remembers to describe women's oppression as well as Jewish oppression. He realizes that nostalgia for dead fathers coupled with the notion that dead mothers are not worth remembering results in a lack of female cultural memory. Regressive stage sets, however, change; oppressive producers see their productions become invalidated. For example, all Jews and all Germans are now allowed freely to pass through Berlin's Brandenburg Gate. Although Jewish women and German women may walk beneath this gate together, no one can yet traverse what Sheri S. Tepper calls *The Gate to Women's Country*. Bellow and Apple, and their fellow feminist fabulators, establish foundations for the possible construction of the gate Tepper envisions.

In another example of efforts to strengthen these foundations, by acting as an authorial cross-dresser, Bellow, in "Something to Remember Me By," introduces a male adolescent protagonist who, when he literally cross-dresses, experiences female vulnerability. Billy Rose plans his own memorial; Bellow, by writing "Something to Remember Me By" (a story dedicated to his children and grandchildren), plans not to be memorialized as a dead father who articulates patriarchal fictions.

The young protagonist of "Remember" has a terminally ill mother who "couldn't find the breath to speak. She sometimes made signs" (189–190). This nearly dead mother's voice is ineffective. Here Bellow, like Apple, stresses that dead mothers' stories do not resound through society. Bellow, aware of the very real implications of these usually absent women's stories, describes the boy's thoughts about his mother's chest, which cancer surgery mutilates. Patriarchal stories are somewhat responsible for her "gnarled scar tissue" (197). Patriarchal stories — attitudes which cause women's health care to receive low priority — yield dead mothers.

The boy's attachment to the untitled textual fragment he keeps in his coat pocket addresses the pervasiveness of patriarchal stories. It reads as follows: "*When given to her charge, the human being before us is reduced to dust. . . . The visible world sustains us until life leaves, and then it must utterly destroy us. Where, then, is the world from which the human form comes?*" (193). This text alludes to the dead father's power. When males are reduced to dust — when the visible world destroys them and they become dead fathers — the world from which the human form comes continues to be formed by them. The boy values this text, his "talisman from a fairy tale to open castle gates or carry me to mountain tops" (202); the boy's text fragment seems to describe patriarchal stories, the fairy tales which transport privileged white men to the apex of society. The particular tale the boy tells takes place during 1933, the year of the Fatherland's birth: "Von Hindenburg's choice of Hitler to form a new government" (189). This choice sets the stage for fathers to become war heroes who lead troops differing from the ones that Apple's Girl Scouts form.

The young protagonist participates in the still unresolved war between the sexes. His first battlefield is the sight of "a naked woman lying on the [gynecologist's] examining table" (195). He etherizes her upon this table, anesthetizes her subjectivity, views her according to the patriarchal gaze's fixed definition of woman chapter four addresses (195–196). Literally attached to a patriarchal mechanism — "[w]ires connected her nice wrists to a piece of medical apparatus on a wheeled stand" (196) — the naked woman is a cyborg positioned as sex object and "research project . . . an experimental subject" (196). The boy immediately relegates the woman to his story about her, a component of his sexual fantasy. All her actions are attributed to the story he directs (197–199).

She, at first, appears not to be a Sorella-like transcender of female roles who overcomes shopping malls while wearing high heels: "She was wearing pumps in the snow and placed each step with care" (200). Her careful steps do not signal her frailty, however. When the boy follows her to a room, he becomes part of a story she directs. By informing him that she will go into the bathroom while he undresses (204), she authors the ensuing events. Evoking the aforementioned incident where Hamet's journal falls from a window in "Bellarosa," she throws his clothes out of a window (205); he is an abandoned and failed seducer who hears "her pumps beating double time in the hallway" (205).

Beating pumps indicate that the woman in "Remember" marches to her own rhythm, transcending high heels in a manner worthy of Sorella herself. The boy loses all signs of patriarchal power, especially "the fragment of an untitled book, author unknown" (205). He stands "as naked as the woman herself had been in the doctor's office" (205). Because a woman's clothes are the only garments available for the naked boy to wear, he must face the world dressed as a woman. He emerges from the apartment in "boots, dress, tam, and jacket" (206). He wears boots — not high heels. This male dressed as a female is not permanently in woman's shoes. In the manner of Wollheim's *The Victor*, he is a cross-dresser momentarily exhibiting combined female and male characteristics. Becoming Woman eventually will be something he can only remember.

Bellow, when he depicts the cross-dressed boy experiencing female vulnerability, creates a woman's text. By doing something other than creating he-man protagonists, Bellow stages his own deviation from a genre to which he previously contributed and indicates that he would like to be remembered as someone other than an evoker of nostalgia for narratives about larger than life men. Many American intellectuals are becoming bored with white male he-men. Bellow makes his own work relevant when he describes a male protagonist who knows "how it feels to go around like a woman" ("Remember" 215). Bellow himself cross-dresses — goes around as a male creator of women's texts. His protagonist is "not a man — you've got a dress on" (218); Bellow is not a man who eventually will justifiably be canonized as a one-track dead father.

A little girl in "Something to Remember Me By" is surprised to see the protagonist urinating while he is attired in a woman's garment. She informs him that she views the unexpected: a penis located under a dress (218). In my role as a feminist critic noticing Bellow's female texts, I share much in common with this little girl. She observes a penis beneath a dress; I observe that Bellow's pen produces a woman's text about a boy who wears a dress. Bellow and his protagonist undertake unexpected gender reversals, like the unexpected sight of the cross-dressed boy's penis, The notion that the well-known protagonists of Bellow's novels should not overshadow the woman-centered characteristics of his recent work indicates that men's authorial roles are themselves stories subject to revision.

"Something to Remember Me By" mentions a particular dead father's text etched in stone — John Milton's words inscribed under a library dome: "A GOOD BOOK . . . IS THE PRECIOUS LIFE'S BLOOD OF A MASTER SPIRIT" (220). Bellow's revised authorial role confronts this seemingly everlasting pervasive male text. His personal change emphasizes that dead fathers' master spirits (and master narratives) should not vampirically suck the life's blood from dead mothers' texts. Like the dead father, the dead mother should also wield power from beyond the grave. Her text should not be the Other book excluded from the category "good book." Women's texts which — like Mrs. Hamet's jettisoned journal — have been thrown out of canonical structures should not remain unretrieved. Billy Rose's aforementioned response to Mrs. Hamet's jettisoned text articulates my response to the dead mother's cast out text: "'I want it brought up right now. . . . Immediately" ("Bellarosa," 56).

The conclusion of "Something to Remember Me By" comments upon Bellow's work. The boy avoids his image reflected in a shop window (222); Bellow, in his recent fiction, avoids the images of he-men his previous fiction reflects. Bookshop windows now feature something other than stories about patriarchs. Bellow appears not to want his heroic men to be the only something to remember him by. He seems to desire to cover their influence, their cultural nostalgia for male master narratives.

This desire is apparent in the story's commentary about the Jewish mourning custom of blocking reflections by covering mirrors: "After a death, mirrors were immediately covered. I can't say what this pious superstition means. Will the soul of your dead be reflected in a looking glass, or is this custom a check to the vanity of the living?" (222). Reverence for male master narratives is another pious superstition, a "past" myth about worshipping patriarchal stories. Many members of the literary establishment are now beginning to cover patriarchal stories and recover dead mothers' stories. Bellow's writing no longer solely reflects influences of dead fathers — and no longer positions him as a future dead father. He covers his male vanity, crosses over to women's texts, and, hence, becomes a lively male feminist fabulator by critiquing — rather than creating — patriarchal master narratives. Instead of functioning as yet another male who reflects the long line of dead father narratives, Bellow writes something else to remember him by. Like Apple and Poe, he is a male teller of women's stories.

Apple's narrator "decide[s] to trust the Girl Scouts. First Girl Scouts, then the world" ("Bridging," 549). In this chapter, I decide to trust the Boy Scouts, to argue that Poe blazes the trail that contemporary male authors who create women's texts follow. Postmodern Girl Scouts and Boy Scouts should not be placed in separate, unequal canonical and noncanonical troops. Respected contemporary literature might consist of a new gender-neutral center enveloping two extremes: males who are recognized and "past"- (Friedman, 251, quoting Stein, 514) and "forward"-looking women who are ostracized and relevant. Apple's narrator seems to describe this newness to his daughter Jessica (who likes baseball and refuses to join the Girl Scouts): "But if they have a new center things will be different" ("Bridging," 554). This new center is an "all at one point" from which peaceful coexistences between women and men potentially can emerge.

A WOMAN'S TEXT FOR LYNN REDGRAVE'S DEAD FATHER

In *Shakespeare for My Father* Lynn Redgrave acts the part of a new gender-neutral center when she portrays the canonical dead father's voice in the guise of her own woman's story. A short-haired figure appearing on stage in black slacks and a black shirt, Redgrave is an androgynous presence who evokes her dead father, Michael Redgrave. She might cause Michael's onstage genre to seep into her own. As opposed to the Jewish mirror-covering ritual Bellow mentions ("Remember," 222), she imagines that her father's soul is reflected in a makeup mirror. Lynn emphasizes that Michael seemed to her literally to be Shakespearean texts. As a child, she positioned Michael as the roles he played. "I am the daughter of Mark Antony," young Lynn responds when she is reprimanded for making unwelcome noise while watching Michael perform.

Illness literally causes Michael to become one with his roles. A Parkinson's disease victim during his last years, he only remembers the past and is unable to master new material. *Shakespeare's People*, a reiteration of his former roles, is one of his last projects. Michael, then, is literally frozen in the Shakespearean lines Lynn articulates. Hence, when Lynn quotes Shakespeare, she becomes the dead father she seeks.

The father who, from her perspective, lives in terms of speaking Shakespearean roles almost never speaks to her. Michael's failure to communicate with his daughter becomes a comic element in *Shakespeare for My Father*. Due to this failure, Lynn encounters a dead father while Michael is alive; she encounters "the missing contents." She desperately wants the father who so articulately moves his audiences to speak to her. *Shakespeare for My Father* describes Lynn's desire to find an at once living and dead father. When Lynn utters the same Shakespearean lines Michael uttered, she places her voice in tandem with his. Lynn believed that her father was his Shakespearean characters; she plays these characters' roles; while performing, she becomes her dead father. *Shakespeare for My Father* is a demarcated stage space which pulls Lynn into her father's staged roles.

Lynn's rendition of Shakespeare at once articulates her life story and causes Michael's words to describe her life. *Shakespeare for My Father*, then, positions Michael as another son of Poe: Lynn transforms Michael's words into a cross-dressed woman's text. For example, she equates Hamlet's desire for the ghost to speak to him with her aforementioned wish for her father to speak to her. Lynn bridges the canonical divide between dead fathers and women's texts when she at once becomes her dead father and causes his voice to emerge as a woman's text. Michael's *Shakespeare's People* exemplifies the literature of exhaustion; Lynn's *Shakespeare for My Father* exemplifies the literature of feminist replenishment. Lynn, a daughter clad in the guise of androgyny who positions her dead father's voice as her own female life story, personifies the aforementioned different new center, the "all at one point" Apple describes. Lynn herself bridges the gap between the dead father's authority and marginal women's stories. She becomes the vehicle which enables a woman to speak her own story while echoing the dead father's voice. Lynn, while attired in a black guise of androgyny and mourning, celebrates herself in a manner which affirms that the dead father's pervasive voice does not always silence living women's stories.

The young Lynn desperately wants her father to speak to her. During one of the few occasions when he does so, she fails to listen. She describes phoning her father to seek his advice about whether or not to take the first acting job offered to her. "No," says Michael. Lynn accepts the role. She becomes an "actor," enables the word which resonates so profoundly for her father to itself become a cross-dressed text which refers to a woman's story.

Lynn describes how she made it possible for the word "actor" to describe, in perpetuity, her father's dead father. In the manner of Alice Walker seeking Zora Neale Hurston's grave in the Florida swamp, Lynn locates the grave of her grandfather, Roy Redgrave, in the Australian bush. Following her father's instructions, she purchases a headstone for Roy inscribed "actor." "Actor" describes Michael's dead father; "actor" simultaneously describes Lynn's dead father, her living mother, her sister, her nieces — and herself. When applied to the Redgrave family, "actor" is a woman's text which denotes mothers as well as fathers.

In a scene reminiscent of Poe, Lynn becomes the dead father in action as well as in voice. The trunk located on the stage very obviously represents Roy's grave. To exemplify that the granddaughter and the dead grandfather become one, Lynn flings herself on the trunk — on a representation of her dead father's dead father's grave. Her voice becomes a stand-in for Michael; her body becomes a stand-in for Roy. No self-annihilating Ophelia who jumps into Hamlet's grave, Lynn jumps on the trunk / "Roy's grave" to underscore that her woman's story is not truncated by the dead father's voice. *Shakespeare for My Father* concludes when she drags the trunk offstage. Lynn controls the dead father's grave; she makes his words speak for her. She is the director and producer of the dead father's voice — a Billy Rose who at once saves her father's life for present audiences and reaffirms her own female experience. Lynn Redgrave, a denizen of old England, evokes the New England custom of "killing" the dead to stop them from draining the life force of their living relatives.

Shakespeare for My Father bridges the dead father's canonical voice and woman's story. Lynn Redgrave shares a great deal in common with the line of male authors Poe engenders: like these male textual cross-dressers, she attempts to kill the dead father dead.

2 "ALL GOOD THINGS"

The End of *Star Trek: The Next Generation*,
the End of Camelot, and the End of the Tale
about Woman as Handmaid to Patriarchy-
as-Superman

On May 23, 1994, American television carried two endings:
Jackie Kennedy Onassis' funeral, which seemed to mark the end of
Camelot, and the final episode of *Star Trek: The Next Generation* (called
"All Good Things"), which seemed to mark the end of a popular culture
phenomenon. These endings concern rewriting the cultural tale about
Woman as talented, powerless handmaid to patriarchy-as-Superman. In
this chapter, I explain that *Star Trek: TNG* and Camelot's demise epitomize
American culture struggling to conclude the pervasive story about women
who function as appendages to all-powerful men. The chapter shares
much in common with "The Kennedy Enterprise," David Gerrold's story
which places John F. Kennedy in a new genre.[1] Gerrold imagines that instead of pursuing politics, Kennedy goes to Hollywood, bombs in *Camelot*,
and achieves fame "as Captain Jack Logan of the starship *Enterprise*" (61).
Gerrold repositions John Kennedy as someone who merges two of contemporary American culture's most pervasive narratives: the Kennedy
mystique and the *Star Trek* myth. I undertake a similar repositioning for
Jackie. I argue for a Kennedyesque genre shift when I bring *Star Trek* to
bear upon Jackie's positive role in Camelot.

Hans Thoma's *The Guards in Front of the Love Garden*, to my mind, pictures a critique of this role (see p. 70). The female knight guarding the love
garden / Camelot, the woman in armor holding a phallic symbol, will not
play handmaid to patriarchy-as-Superman. Unlike Jackie, this female
knight is not the feminine standardbearer of Camelot. The other guard, the
lion, shows that something other than John Kennedy, the male hero, can be
king of the jungle.

Jackie resembles the woman inside Thoma's love garden / Camelot, the
beautiful woman presiding over a rarefied space of pleasure, art, leisure,
and wealth. Yet beauty and wealth do not completely explain why Amer-

ica was so moved by the passing of a book editor, mother, and wife. Other wealthy or beautiful women have died without evoking the deep feelings Jackie's death elicited. Marilyn Monroe, for example, was not given a nationally televised funeral. People revere Jackie, I think, because, in addition to acting as a powerless appendage to two Supermen, she became Superman herself. She boarded *Air Force One* clad in her pink, blood-stained uniform, flew over the United States, and functioned as the Wife of Steel — a superhero leading a mourning nation. Since American culture has no place for Woman-as-Superman, Jackie attached herself to a Superman II, Aristotle Onassis. Empowered by the Kennedy name and the Onassis wealth, Jackie, in a single bound, leaped to the top of a tall building, 1040 Fifth Avenue. She was accompanied by Maurice Tempelsman, who, as a Jewish man, can never be Superman. Jackie evokes emotion because she represents truth, justice, and the American way. Yet, of course, wielding governmental power did not cause this courageous and talented woman to become a national myth.

Now that JFK's infidelities have made him become something less than Superman, people might believe that Jackie, a paragon of mothering and nurturing who held the national family together, was something more than a handmaid. Such a desire to respect competent women is reflected in *Star Trek: TNG*, especially in the final episode called "All Good Things." This episode — which places Captain Jean-Luc Picard in the past, present, and future — signals American culture's readiness to recognize that patriarchy is a good thing for men which should come to an end.

STAR TREK, CAMELOT, AND SUPERMAN

During the utopian time that was Camelot, a militarily and economically powerful America applauded a White House which welcomed arts, humanities, and European culture. The country had two saviors ensconced in the White House: JFK, who saved us from the Communists in Cuba and their flying nuclear phalluses, and Jackie, who saved us from cultural barbarism. She was a powerless Superman who came to the rescue. She turned the White House into a *Star Trek* "holodeck" whose programmed vision championed artistic expression and historical reclamation. The nation emulated Jackie's style, her White House as holodeck. Jackie, who neither held public office nor repelled a single missile, constructed cultural reality.

This unmanly respect for art and cultural diversity characterizes another White House, the Starship *Enterprise* commanded by Captain Picard. He is the Frenchman, the feminine man, the antithesis of the all-

American he-man. (Perhaps the Picards are related to the Bouviers.) His *Enterprise* is no penile rocket. Positioned like breasts, two thrusters propel his round, feminine ship, which houses authoritative Others. A nation which is supposedly offended by gays in the military is happy to see a Klingon security officer on the bridge. Perhaps America is ready to empower the outside Other, the woman and the minority.

A Klingon Star Fleet officer exemplifies Linda Hutchison's notion of the postmodern acceptance of the "ex-centric." (The same holds true for the Kennedy family's recent doings. A Jew and an Austrian have both become Kennedys. Despite their own wealth and achievements, when Edwin Schlossberg, Maurice Tempelsman, and Arnold Schwarzenegger penetrated the Kennedy family inner circle, they became male appendages to Kennedy women. They became "wives." Schwarzenegger's Hollywood star does not outshine Maria Shriver.) In the Kennedy White House, as on Picard's *Enterprise*, nurturing and artistic pursuits are as noteworthy as militaristic power displays. On trips abroad, Jackie was often more impressive than JFK; on the bridge, Deanna Troi is often more impressive than Worf. In Camelot and on the *Enterprise*, the patriarchal institution known as marriage does not engender people's best selves. All *Enterprise* officers are single; Jackie was her best self sans husbands.

Star Trek: TNG and Camelot exemplify postmodern reclassifications of fixed definitions. JFK deconstructed cultural stereotypes when he showed that someone Other than Dwight Eisenhower — someone other than an elderly Protestant — could be president. The *Enterprise*, whose task is "to seek out new life and new civilizations," exists to discover and understand the Other. The *Enterprise* is at once a part of Star Fleet Command and outside Star Fleet Command. JFK was at once a part of and, as a Catholic, outside America's political hegemony. Kennedy's Camelot and Picard's *Enterprise* battle the same enemy: the fixed definition. JFK confronted the Russians, the single-minded Communist ideology; Picard confronts the Borg, the single-minded mechanistic communal entity. Picard, who interferes with alien cultures, counters the Prime Directive master narrative. Jackie, who interfered with American cultural isolation, countered an American cultural master narrative: Huck Finn's desire to escape civilization. Jackie and Picard both rewrite cultural master narratives and change social structures.

Picard, the blatantly not macho man, is empowered; JFK, the outsider Catholic, is empowered. But what about another Other — talented women? What about Lt. Uhura and Counselor Troi and Nurse Chapel and

Mrs. Kennedy? As we are all aware, these women are neither captain nor president. Superman can be an edifice as well as a person. The *Enterprise* is Superman. The White House is Superman. American culture has not yet allowed women to control Superman. But the Superman that constitutes the White House and the *Enterprise* is not unitary. These institutions function via power ensconced in mergers of dynamic duos. The White House and the president are a fused cyborg juxtaposition of governmental machine and individual. The *Enterprise* and the crew are a fused cyborg juxtaposition of technological devices and individuals. I describe transcending attributing power to one man — transcending attributing phallic power to one person who possesses a penis.

Many of Picard's crew members exist beyond normal biology. Geordie LaForge's human body is supplemented by a mechanical visual device. Data is a machine who enjoys human culture. Deanna Troi's intuition is Betazoid, not human. And, at the end of Camelot, both JFK and Jackie transcend their human bodies to become myths. "In death, our princess has been returned to us. Now she will be buried next to our prince, and when the television cameras make their periodic respectful visits to the Kennedy grave, the eternal flame will be the powerfully telegenic symbol for them both" (Blair, 25). American culture, which valorizes cyborg *Star Trek* characters and perpetuates mythology about deceased male and female White House inhabitants, seems to be emphasizing the question Le Guin articulates: "Is Gender Necessary?" (*Language*, 135–147). The fact of JFK and Jackie receiving equal prestige as myths sets the stage for a woman president. *Star Trek's* world of reality constructed at will and cyborg imagery sets the stage for a woman captain. "All Good Things" functions as this stage. It articulates this Prime Directive: to separate the he-man from the captain, to jettison American manhood — to characterize Will Riker and Picard as two distinct entities in order to proclaim that someone Other than James T. Kirk can be Superman. *Star Trek: TNG* boldly goes beyond Rikers Island, beyond the prisonhouse of patriarchal language and patriarchal reality. *Star Trek: TNG* implies that women can be Superman.

WHO, APPROPRIATELY, IS SUPERMAN?

This question presently pervades American culture. It is, for example, at the heart of Ted Kennedy's political life. A May 23, 1994, *New Yorker* article, "We're Not in Camelot Anymore," proclaims that Ted Kennedy is definitely not Superman: "[F]or the first time in thirty years, Ted Kennedy is campaigning in a Senate race whose outcome is not already certain"

(Boyer, 39, 40). Far from being Superman, Ted Kennedy himself needs to be saved from the tarnished image of Kennedy manhood. (Chappaquiddick and his nephew William Kennedy Smith's rape trial position Ted Kennedy as Lois Lane.) None other than a woman appears to rescue Ted / Lois: his wife Victoria Reggie, who "became the centerpiece of Ted Kennedy's rehabilitation by marrying him" (Boyer, 44). Boyer continues:

> Vicki Reggie Kennedy is often referred to as "the asset," and one meeting with her explains why. She is attractive, gracious, and smart, and her presence beside Kennedy inspires approval. . . . Alone on the campaign trail, without Vicki, Kennedy might seem nothing but spectacle, all bloat and tremor; with her one senses a flash of new energy. . . . Her visibility may, in fact, be her greatest contribution to her husband's campaign. She is a direct answer to the character issue, living evidence that Kennedy's raucous bachelorhood is over. (Boyer, 44, 45)

Kennedy as tremorous bloat epitomizes the literature of exhaustion (the tired male hero story) revitalized by the literature of replenishment (the presence of a savvy woman). Vicki is Ted's Superman. But, despite her success as his rescuer, she is not running for the Senate.

Luckily, the question regarding who is appropriately Superman applies to a more powerful female half of a prominent couple: Hillary Rodham Clinton. Americans absolutely accept the idea that, although Jackie could never become president, the same does not hold true for Hillary. In fact, the May 23, 1994, cover of the tabloid New York Post, which shows pictures of both Jackie and Hillary, announces this recognition. The headline "Final Farewell to Jackie" is positioned directly above "Pals: Hillary for Prez." The article "Hillary for Prez? Friends Want First Lady in Office" proclaims that "[f]riends of First Lady Hillary Rodham Clinton are plotting for her to become the next commander-in-chief once President Clinton's two-term limit runs out, New Yorker magazine says" (Rauber, 2). Cold War plots that Communist enemies generated have been replaced by Hillary's plotting friends. The anxiety that the Russians are coming, the Russians are coming has been replaced by a new anxiety: a powerful woman is coming, a powerful woman is coming (I do not intend to convey any sexual innuendo). The comfortable title "president" describes Bill; Hillary is called something more threatening: commander-in-chief. The Post headline and article reflect the fear that Hillary, Jackie's White House counterpart, is a woman who can become Superman. Here is what the New Yorker has to say about her potential:

The notion of Hillary Clinton as a Presidential candidate is an interesting one. She is almost an icon for many women today. . . . Hillary is, of course, attempting the feat on a singularly elevated platform in full public view. . . . What seems plain, to me watching Hillary Clinton as First Lady, is that she is always learning, and that the makeover never stops. And, notwithstanding the President's denial, if her goal is, as friends have suggested, to fashion her own place in history, or to become President herself, then that means that for the first time since she decided to throw her lot in with Bill Clinton she is no longer merely an adjunct. There are vestiges of such a role, since at this moment her power is still dependent on and largely protected by his. But the bedrock premise of their partnership may be altered, for what is best for him politically is no longer necessarily best for her. (Bruck, 94)

America is absolutely poised to empower a brilliant woman. Ironically, she might attain power at the expense of someone who is a dead ringer for Superman. President Clinton denies that Hillary Rodham Clinton would even think of upstaging Al Gore: "'But I also think she didn't think about that sort of thing, in no small measure because she has an enormous regard for Al Gore, and for what he's done here, and how much of a difference he's made to our common endeavors'" (Bruck, 93–94).

American popular culture, then, now reflects the question about who, appropriately, is Superman, posed in regard to power relations between hegemony and Other. For example, Richard Goldstein, writing in the *Village Voice*, positions Oskar Schindler as Superman: "And then there is the question of the righteous Christian in the movie [*Schindler's List*], the Superman figure, who flies in and saves Lois Lane, the Jew" (Goldstein, 27). As I have explained, like Oskar Schindler, Vicki Reggie is Superman; Ted Kennedy and Schindler Jews are Lois Lane. Vicki and Ted, Schindler and Schindler Jews, and Hillary and Bill are teams who benefit from each other's presence. Although Superman does not need Lois, these pairs need each other — and the Camelot myth needs Jackie ("But what put JFK over the top on television — and arguably won him the election — was his wife" [Blair, 25]). Hence, teamwork between the empowered and the disempowered, the powerful man and the talented woman, is currently a pervasive cultural topic. We have President Billary Clinton. We have a Jewish Kennedy family member. The point is that Lois / Jew is currently often positive and powerful.

Negative comments are made neither about Schlossberg nor about

Tempelsman. Lois is always a positively portrayed single career woman rescued by Superman when she bravely goes beyond her professional call of duty. And she is a woman of the nineties. This decade's Superman television show is called *Lois and Clark*— not Superman; Lois is given top billing. Another television show, *Dr. Quinn, Medicine Woman*, portrays a brilliant woman who becomes Superman via her scientific expertise. Sulley, Dr. Quinn's woodsman he-man lover, does rescue her from the woods. But Sulley, when he is ill, becomes Lois rescued by Dr. Quinn / Superman. *Lois and Clark* reflects Hillary and Bill. Dr. Quinn reflects America contemplating electing Hillary, rewriting the tale of the talented woman acting as handmaid to a man.

Star Trek: TNG— and "All Good Things" in particular — signals that Ronald Reagan and George Bush are not Superman. *Star Trek: TNG* points out that America is tired of Superman and that America wants women and men to work together as a team. America wants women and men to behave like Lois and Clark. Reagan and Bush have given way to Bill Clinton. Captain Kirk and Commander Riker have given way to Captain Picard. "All Good Things" tells its audience that even Captain Picard is not Superman. The last *Star Trek: TNG* episode asks this question: what do talented women who are forced to act as handmaids to Superman want? And the episode provides an answer: women want a new tale, an alternative to the patriarchal story about who has the right stuff to be Superman. "All Good Things" retrieves Tasha Yar — the woman ejected from *Star Trek: TNG* because she was too powerful.

PATRIARCHY IS NOT A GOOD THING

"All Good Things" convinces me that Deanna Troi reflects Jackie Kennedy and that Dr. Beverly Crusher reflects Hillary Clinton. Deanna is a dark-haired, charismatic beauty, a sexy and elegant possessor of superhuman insight, the respected bringer of reason and decorum to the *Enterprise*. Like Jackie, Deanna is "fascinating, not competitive; gracious, not ambitious; poised, not strategic . . . graceful, sympathetic, a marvelous listener. All of which Jacqueline Kennedy [and Deanna Troi] did better than anyone else ever" (Blair, 1). In "All Good Things" Deanna, the love object of two powerful men (Riker / Kennedy and Worf / Onassis), dies prematurely — is not part of the future.

Beverly Crusher, on the other hand, commands in that future. Hillary might become President Clinton; Beverly does become Captain Picard. When I saw Beverly answer to the name "Captain Picard," I reacted as if I were hit by a photon torpedo. Dr. Crusher, the former Mrs. Picard who becomes Captain Picard, gives the aged Jean-Luc the command seat "for old time's sake." When Riker and Worf refuse to help Jean-Luc, she, in addition, provides the ship he needs. For the benefit of humanity, the woman captain cooperates with the formerly powerful man. The good-old-boys network no longer functions; Beverly and Jean-Luc's teamwork is effective. "All Good Things" shows that male supremacy and solidarity can come to an end. The final *TNG* episode is a postmodern, rewritten *A Christmas Carol*—a vision of Picard's past, present, and future which asserts that patriarchy is Scrooge.

Crew members' language reflects this point. A female officer calls Captain Beverly Picard "sir." Another example: Beverly informs Jean-Luc that, even though he is her ex-husband and ex-captain, he is verbally out of line. And, in the past, Tasha Yar echoes Beverly's assertiveness. When these women question male authority, they reflect the current cultural penchant to act in kind. In addition to what the women have to say, the aged Picard's word choice underscores his lack of credibility: charged with diffusing an anomaly which threatens human existence, the former captain, who might suffer from a brain-impairing illness, refers to the threat as "my mommy." Beverly appropriately treats the infantilized Picard like a child. As opposed to the sleek, pajama-like Star Fleet uniform which connotes power, Picard now appears in colorless, loose-fitting pajamas; Shakespearean actor Patrick Stewart seems to be playing King Lear. The captain, whose competence and verbal utterances were never questioned, is reduced to saying, "I'm not stupid." He is told to go back to bed. Picard represents patriarchy as being passé and childish.

But even a future in which Beverly becomes captain and Jean-Luc becomes Lear on the heath fails to keep a woman in command. Captain Beverly Picard, who upbraids and sedates the former Captain Jean-Luc Picard, commands a ship which is about to explode. Beverly immediately goes from commanding to becoming Lois Lane rescued by Superman (in the form of the *Enterprise* commanded by Admiral Will Riker). Beverly was Superman for one brief shining moment. Her exploding ship burns brighter than her time as a captain.

"All Good Things" conveys mixed messages: it at once questions patriarchal power and is unable to continue depicting a woman wielding power. After Beverly's ship explodes, the critique of patriarchy continues, though. Picard's nemesis Q judges him while seated on an ornate chair whose two outstretched protuberances resemble gynecological stirrups. Q, who proclaims that the human race is an inferior entity, examines and judges humanity in the manner in which patriarchy examines and judges women. Q sounds like a woman who has just spent the day listening to the Anita Hill / Clarence Thomas Senate hearings. "You don't get it, Jean-Luc," he says. He challenges Picard to expand his mind — to chart, instead of stars, unknown possibilities. Q critiques patriarchy by advocating alternatives to the male-oriented science responsible for the *Enterprise* itself. Q would have more respect for Deanna Troi, pioneer of inner existence, than for Captain Kirk, he-man star mapper. Q would have more respect for Jackie, pioneer of inner aesthetic space, than for JFK, responder to *Sputnik*, repeller of missiles. Picard answers Q's verbal challenge by saying, "I'll get back to bed. I can use some sleep." This former male commander is extremely tired; Q articulates the need for new possibilities to a symbol of the male commander as exhausted story.

An image of a precursor to rebirth also communicates this need. In order to nullify the anomaly, *Enterprises* from three time periods meet and create a "stellar warp shell" which can accomplish the "disengagement of a tachyon pulse." The three *Enterprises*, in the manner of sperm, gather to penetrate a round anomaly. Picard, who, as I have mentioned, calls the anomaly "my mommy," fathers a method in which starships / sperm nullify a pulse which makes it possible for the anomaly's threat to humanity to exist. The future Picard, then, is a good nurturing father rather than a dead father who perpetuates patriarchal imperatives. The anomaly — the "antitime" which is larger in the past — might represent patriarchy itself. New uses of macho, the current decline of the he-man's prestige, are represented by the sperm / ships which nullify the anomaly and, hence, nurture humanity. This decline creates space for talented women effectively to wield power. I imagine this real world counterpart to the "stellar warp shell": men who are not militaristic he-men (Alan Alda and Kim Stanley Robinson, for example) enter (i.e., penetrate) the Pentagon and diffuse all the missile launching apparatuses. While this sabotage is ensuing, Diane Feinstein, Janet Reno, Madeleine Albright, and Ruth Bader Ginsberg meet with Hillary Clinton in the White House in a room Jackie decorated.

Male power games, after all, have changed; women can now play. Riker and Worf, two male antagonists, cast aside their he-man stance to give each other a cooperative "hand." They sit down at a card table with Deanna, Beverly, Data, and Geordie to play "five card stud nothing wild, the sky is the limit." He-man, black man, woman, Betazoid, android, and Klingon play a new (and very multicultural) inclusive game in which the stud is tamed, in which those who are Other to all-American manhood vastly out-number the he-man.

Like the ship / sperm surrounding the round anomaly, the crew — sperm-like entities about to create a new something — surround the round card table. The new something is a sense of an ending, the sense that patriarchal power can be terminated. The present Captain Picard, the non-macho male authority figure, finally sits at the table to play with his subordinates. This card game depicts an end to patriarchal power games. The round card table is the Round Table. In postmodern America, Camelot and *Star Trek* never end. The same does not hold true for the patriarchal story which demands that talented women serve as handmaids to male Supermen. Dr. Crusher and Dr. Quinn, women who have been Superman, pave the way for President Hillary Clinton.

THE KENNEDYS: THE NEXT GENERATION

Star Trek never ends. Camelot never ends. And neither does the Kennedy family. Unfortunately, Kennedy *TNG* is not as progressive as *Star Trek: TNG*. John, not Caroline, stood at the entrance of 1040 Fifth Avenue to describe Jackie's death. After his announcement, television news commentators called John, not Caroline, the next President Kennedy. John was no clone of the Cold War heroic he-man who emanated from the site of the dead mother. The particular examples of popular culture that I have discussed indicate that the next generation of Americans does not wish to resurrect the dead father, the Cold War presidential hero.

Americans are, instead, ready to follow Q's injunction to expand their minds. The next generation can accept a new possibility. Now that it is no longer possible to try to mirror the past by electing JFK's son as another President John Kennedy, we might, instead, opt for President Caroline Kennedy. Perhaps the concluding episode of *Star Trek: Voyager* will not involve a female captain who is rescued by a he-man admiral. Perhaps this last episode will not involve an intuitive feminine crew member who dies due to the actions of he-men who vie for her attentions. There is hope for creating new master narratives, alternatives to the predominating social stories about women acting as handmaids to male Supermen. Jackie changed. Tempelsman, the last man in her life, was an invisible man and, in the discourse of her funeral, Aristotle Onassis became an invisible man too. Jackie "became less identified with the man she was with. . . . [M]uch of American learned about him [Tempelsman] only when she died. . . . Aristotle Onassis, the wicked intruder in our national fairy tale, has been nearly erased. In network coverage of her funeral . . . commentators barely mentioned her second husband's name" (Blair, 25). The he-man is passé; the Other is at the heart of the present and the future. (Toni Morrison, for example, is currently more popular and respected than Ernest Hemingway.) As JFK proved, the Other can be president.

And it is the Other who respects the alternative to public prominence that Jackie epitomizes. When I went to Grand Central Station to sign the book the Municipal Art Society placed there to commemorate Jackie, I noticed that those standing in line were predominantly women and blacks. The men in business suits who routinely rush through Grand Central Station were not clamoring to sign. Perhaps the women, the blacks, and the casually dressed young men desired to sign a declaration of independence from men in business suits. My observation about the Grand Central Station line also holds true for the May 21, 1994, front page *New York Times* picture of the crowd standing outside 1040 Fifth Avenue. Again, women, blacks, and informal young men (and a lone feminist science fiction critic) are in evidence. The men in business suits, Jackie's neighbors, were not paying their respects outside their front door. The Others gathered to mourn someone who, despite her great wealth, is, in relation to presidential power politics, one of their own.

As we are all aware, men in business suits also do not appear on the Starship *Enterprise*. Anna Quindlen, however, comments that the 1992 New York Democratic National Convention looks like the *Enterprise*: "Late at night, bleached by the street lights, Madison Square Garden looked like the Starship *Enterprise*, the satellite dishes pale moons at its perimeter" (17). The Starship *Enterprise* crew looks like America. May the American government act like the *Enterprise* crew playing cards at the Round Table. In the near future, may the American president look like Beverly Crusher, Geordie LaForge — or even Maurice Tempelsman. For the moment, we, at least, realize that the Russians are not Klingons — and Hillary's cookie baking is an anomaly from the past.

As the next version of the Starship *Enterprise* / Superman flies across television screens in America / Camelot, we can rest assured that all good things do not necessarily come to an end. On May 23, 1994, two Kennedy family members named Rose were living in America. Caroline's daughter Rose can become president of Camelot / America — and, while ensconced in the White House, she can watch a version of the *Star Trek* myth which speaks to her generation's cultural reality. While sitting in a room Jackie decorated, President Rose Schlossberg might watch a *Star Trek* episode about Admiral Tasha Yar.

President Rose Schlossberg might initiate my reading of the new frontier David Gerrold describes: "What is the new frontier? . . . The new frontier isn't out there. It's in here. In the heart. It's in us. . . . If it's not in here, it's not anywhere" (67–68). The new frontier involves ensconcing a new myth — the story of strong women leaders — within America's inner space, within its heart. The new frontier involves imbuing this inner discourse with the devotion we shower upon the *Star Trek* myth and the Kennedy saga. The new frontier involves casting the White House as a domicile which can pull a woman leader within its "in here."

3

SHUTTING THE
BESTIAL MOUTH

Confessions of Male Clones
and Girl Gangs

Environmental biologist John Cairns, Jr.'s term "coevolution" addresses the North American novels (all published between 1993 and 1994) I discuss here. Cairns defines coevolution as "the simultaneous development of adaptations in two or more populations, spaces or other categories that interact so closely that each is a strong selective force on the other" (4). Cairns states that, in ecology, coevolution describes paired changes applicable to, among other categories, predator and prey (4–5). He further explains that coevolution is characterized by "interacting entities" which "serve as selective forces on each other and that changes enhance the survival of each partner" (Cairns, 5). Cairns' distinction between "benign" and "hostile" coevolution (26) is reflected by the novels this chapter addresses. Seven authors — Margaret Atwood, Marilyn French, Joyce Carol Oates, Marge Piercy, John Barth, Philip Roth, and John Updike — consider the consciousness-raising steps needed before benign coevolution can occur. Sherry Gottlieb's Love Bite and Paul Theroux's Chicago Loop portray the result of hostile coevolution.

Gottlieb and Theroux respectively describe vampirism and cannibalism, real and fantastic ways in which women and men relate as predator and prey. Since the literal ingestion of the opposite sex that they depict is not a good thing, before the sexes can accomplish benign coevolution via mutual interaction, they must pause and separate. The seven novels I read here depict this pause. Retreating from vampiric modes, Atwood's The Robber Bride, Oates' Foxfire: Confessions of a Girl Gang, French's Our Father, Piercy's The Longings of Women, Barth's Once upon a Time: A Floating Opera, Roth's Operation Shylock: A Confession, and Updike's Memories of the Ford Administration offer a textual "time out" from tensions regarding interactions between two populations: women and men. While Gottlieb and Theroux portray these tensions, their seven colleagues break up the fight, allowing women and men to retreat to their own corners before they begin benign coevolution. The protagonists Atwood, French, Oates, and Piercy present evoke the woman-centered orientation of Mary McCarthy's *The Group* and Wendy Wasserstein's *Uncommon Women*. Following the example of Robert Louis Stevenson's *Dr. Jekyll and Mr. Hyde*, Barth, Roth, and Updike portray men contemplating their differing selves, men trying to be Jekyll sans Hyde. The seven authors, responding to the problem of women's and men's predator / prey relationship currently so pervasively articulated in art and life (Gottlieb's and Theroux's novels are but two examples of this pervasive articulation), make the point that, in order to survive, women and men need to adapt, to become something other than predator and prey.

First, a few words about the predator / prey problem and America's close attention to it. Anita Hill has informed us about the least life-threatening manifestation of this relationship: men sexually harassing women in the workplace. The O. J. Simpson case epitomizes the worst outcome of men's predatory actions. As Lorena Bobbitt and *Thelma and Louise* make clear, women are not above avenging themselves against their male antagonists. If change does not occur, individual women and men will not survive. Change, however, is still in process; women and men have not yet adapted to new social roles and rules. Gottlieb and Theroux, in remarkably similar ways, portray hostile female / male interaction, a problem which presently lacks a solution.

Chicago Loop is a contemporary rewritten version of *Dr. Jekyll and Mr. Hyde*. Successful business and family man Parker Jagoda, Theroux's protagonist, turns into a monstrous version of himself who places personal ads to attract female victims. After Jagoda murders a woman named Sharon, he cross-dresses to become her. Like Jekyll, Jagoda expires. In an extreme burlesque act, he strips off his female attire while plunging from the top of the Sears Tower, the phallic symbol which towers over Chicago. Jagoda "was sure he was flying" (Theroux, 200). Although I have written that Thelma and Louise might survive their plunge into the Grand Canyon,[1] I do not claim this reprieve for Jagoda. Is this any way to run an airline? Is this any way for a man to relate to women? Theroux and Stevenson portray dysfunctional relationships between women and men—hostile coevolution in the form of men relating to women by reverting to their bestial selves. Barth, Roth, and Updike, in contrast, depict pre-benign coevolution. Their protagonists, other versions of the authors' selves, contemplate further selves. These various "counterselves" (Barth's term) are prerequisites to the naissance of a new future male self, a male who neither masks nor enacts his desire to prey upon women. Again, I describe Jekyll hiding — and ultimately obliterating — Hyde.

Taking advantage of the fact that female protagonists of fantastic novels can become vampires, Gottlieb portrays a woman in revenge mode. Risha Cadigan, Gottlieb's protagonist, changes into a vampire according to the usual method. After her transformation, she uses personal ads to attract male victims. She feeds upon men who would sexually prey upon her. Some of the dates she dines upon (instead of with) might — in the manner of Sharon's fate at the hands of Jagoda — have murdered her. Readers do not feel sympathy for Risha's victims.

In Gottlieb's and Theroux's fictional worlds, the personal ad becomes a textual means of entrapment. Hostile coevolution occurs when Jagoda appears as a woman and Risha becomes a vampire. These role reversals between predator and prey do not portend well for women's and men's potential for survival as partners. People must abandon the predator / prey genre, coevolving into other more suitable roles. The fact that both Gottlieb and Theroux portray police officers as survivors might show that they have hope that civilized law will not go the way of the dodo bird — that women and men will coevolve and develop better ways to relate to each other.

Both Gottlieb and Theroux focus upon the mouth to communicate their views about female / male interaction. Jagoda is a Hannibal Lecter who murders Sharon by biting her to death. She "was so badly chewed and mutilated that he had quickened his violence" (Theroux, 119). Risha the vampire, as is to be expected, also bites her victims to kill them. Diana Fuss' analysis of the Jeffrey Dahmer case and *The Silence of the Lambs* is helpful here. Fuss explains that the "face, the surface upon which subjectivity is figured, is also the zone of bestiality and primordial hunger" (Fuss, 191). Interestingly, in the 1932 film version of *Dr. Jekyll and Mr. Hyde*, transformation is portrayed via a close-up of Fredric March's face.[2] His mouth, which becomes wider and acquires jagged spaced teeth, is the most apparent sign that man has become beast. Like the film's photographer, Karl Struss, Gottlieb and Theroux also use the face, especially the mouth, to show women and men engaging as predator and prey, interacting within a zone of bestiality. Fuss can be called upon to illuminate the behavior of Gottlieb's and Theroux's protagonists. When Risha sinks her teeth into her male victims, she exemplifies "the subject's primal urge to avenge itself on the object by sinking its teeth into it and devouring it" (Fuss, 188). Jagoda the cross-dresser, in turn, desires "to cannibalize the other who inhabits the place . . . [he] longs to occupy" (Fuss, 192).

Gottlieb and Theroux, as well as the current plethora of "real and fictional accounts of sexually motivated murders who methodically stalk, torture, mutilate and sometimes eat their victims" (Fuss, 199), show that benign coevolution is an immediate necessity in regard to female / male interaction. The seven novelists, recognizing this necessity, portray the pause and discussion which must ensue before benign coevolution occurs. In regard to female and male relationships, human civilization is presently extremely discontented. Popular culture and fiction are the canaries announcing a crisis in which people use their mouths to relate to each other as beasts. (Hostile verbal interactions qualify as bestial behavior.) Hannibal Lecter, like Jagoda and Risha, "covets and feeds on human flesh in one of the most serious transgressions against the social prohibition separating the inedible from the edible, the human from the animal, the cultural from the natural" (Fuss, 195). The seven authors try to return women and men to civilization. To accomplish this return, like Gottlieb and Theroux, they focus upon the mouth. The groups of women that the female authors create talk to each other. The male authors, who clone themselves in their texts, talk about differing versions of themselves. These male authors shut the bestial mouth in terms of spoken and written language and hence pave the way for ultimately embracing woman in the spirit of peaceful coexistence.

This peaceful coexistence is now only a potential act, however. For the moment, the male authors I discuss are too involved with speaking among themselves to pay rapt attention to the opposite sex; their protagonists would never place personal ads in order to prey upon the female responders. These authors do write a different sort of personal ad, however. Their novels-as-personal-ads function as benign rather than hostile texts. In the manner of personal ad writers, Barth, Roth, and Updike use their novels to describe themselves. Atwood's, French's, Oates', and Piercy's women, who band together and speak to each other, are uninterested in responding to men's textual self-descriptions. My image of shutting the bestial mouth, of replacing the bestial mouth with the civilized mouth, shows women and men speaking differently: the civilized male mouth talks about itself and the civilized female mouth talks to other women. For example, while Roth's confession is about cloning himself, the confessions that Oates' protagonist Maddy authors are about forming female community.

The seven authors desire to change the situation Gottlieb and Theroux describe. Reading the differing plots that Gottlieb, Theroux, and the seven authors present constitutes a progression from the bestial mouth to the civilized mouth, from women and men ingesting each other to men talking about themselves and women talking among themselves. The authors' emphasis upon the mouth shows that women and men have yet to achieve psychological as well as physiological maturity vis-à-vis their sexual relationships. As Fuss reminds us, Freud "insists that as organs of sexual desire, mouth and anus must be 'abandoned' in favor of genitalia if the subject is to attain sexual maturity" (184). Although women and men in the novels I explore do engage in heterosexual intercourse, genitalia are neither the authors' nor the characters' primary focus. Instead, the mouth is all important. While Gottlieb and Theroux emphasize people who ingest each other, the seven authors emphasize people who talk to and about members of their own sex. A civilized means for women and men comfortably to relate to each other personally and professionally might emerge from these discussions. Recently published novels, in the manner of the Hill / Thomas hearings, are giving women and men food for thought. We are all thinking and discussing — and waiting to see what changes will ultimately emerge in the conversations' wake. Since men who act bestially toward women face the possibility of having their penises chopped off, it is in their best interest to change their behavior. Regarding this change (regarding, in other words, women's new assertive position and men's new contemplative position), we are at the moment of beginning the transition stage. The mouth is an orifice from which new generic roles for women and men can emerge.

MALE SELVES AS FEEDBACK LOOP
OR JEKYLL SANS HYDE: BARTH'S BARTH,
ROTH'S ROTH AND ROTH, AND UPDIKE'S ALF

In *Invisible Cities*, Italo Calvino describes cities which replicate themselves and their citizens. He imagines Eusapia, whose "inhabitants have constructed an identical copy of their city, underground" (109). Laudomia, a second city that Calvino categorizes as "cities and the dead," "has at its side another city whose inhabitants are called by the same names: it is the Laudomia of the dead, the cemetery" (14). In Laudomia "the living population pays a visit to the dead and they decipher their own names on their stone slabs. . . . And to feel sure of itself, the living Laudomia has to seek in the Laudomia of the dead the explanation of itself" (140). Barth, Roth, and Updike — who hold fame and generational ties in common — also share an affinity with Eusapia and Laudomia. These men who have entered their sixties, perhaps out of fear of becoming "dead white males," copy themselves.

Alfred Clayton, the protagonist of Updike's *Memories of the Ford Administration*, writes a life of James Buchanan, the subject of Updike's play *Buchanan Dying* (published in 1979, the year Gerald Ford became president). Clayton (called Alf) and Updike both re-create Buchanan. In addition, Updike's novel *S* evokes Nathaniel Hawthorne and *The Scarlet Letter*. So does Alf's Buchanan manuscript. Alf, then, mirrors Updike. Similarly, in *Once upon a Time*, John Barth writes about John Barth. And Philip Roth, in *Operation Shylock*, encounters characters named Philip Roth. These aging authors clone themselves, re-create themselves, and use their texts to endure. As they face cemeteries containing dead white males, they use the same names and decipher their own names, trying to explain themselves and feel sure of themselves. The living of Laudomia pose "questions [that] are asked in silence; and it is always about themselves that the living ask, not about those who are to come" (Calvino, *Invisible Cities*, 141). Alf asks, "But what did Ford do?" (Updike, *Memories*, 354). I imagine Barth, Roth, and Updike asking this question: "What do celebrity white male writers do when white men's writing is chastised?"

They ask this question to answer the "those who are to come" who will call them dead white men. Would their answer echo the words that Alf's student Jennifer utters: "Phallic isn't all bad" (Updike, *Memories*, 86)? How else to respond to those who dismiss "the full canon of Western masterpieces, every one of them . . . a relic of centuries of white male oppression, to be touched as gingerly as radioactive garbage" (53–54) and who decry "the white male power of bygone generations" (54)? Barth, Roth, and Updike, self-conscious because they are powerful white male creators of the present literary canon, are the selves future generations will decry. They respond by rewriting themselves, creating counterselves. During a time when white male power is being questioned, these white men question themselves. Via textuality, they create a same which is different, authorial selves which reach beyond the boundaries of themselves. This move allows them to discard the oneness of being an oppressor—to imagine future critics who will not look back and dismiss them. As Alf explains, "When all this fuss about sexism is over, we'll be able to sit down together and see that men and women are just like Tweedledee and Tweedledum. With what Jacques Derrida calls a *différence*" (Updike, *Memories*, 88). Now (when the fuss about sexism is far from over) Barth, Roth, and Updike cast themselves — not women and men — as Tweedledee and Tweedledum.

These authors and their characters — John Barth: John Barth; Philip Roth: Philip Roth and Philip Roth; and John Updike: Alf Clayton and James Buchanan — are the same with a *différence*.

All this fuss about sexism certainly has an impact upon male writers such as Barth, Roth, and Updike. How can they continue to tell their male stories while they are well aware that many people wish to equate the white male canon with radioactive garbage? Alf notes that, during Buchanan's time, "prosperous men, white, Protestant, and land-owning, rolled across lesser lives like barrels loaded to the bursting of their staves with a self-righteousness thick as molasses" (Updike, *Memories*, 108). Updike knows that little has changed. How, then, can he continue to write his own experience, the experience of the oppressor, the privileged white Protestant man? Alf, who is "cripplingly struck by the hopelessness, in an era when history has turned away from tales of kings to the common heroes of everyday life" (242), exemplifies Updike's answer: he turns Buchanan, an American king, into himself, a common hero of everyday life. Alf's Buchanan is not Buchanan; he is, instead, a rewritten version of Alf: "After my break with Genevieve, I realized that my attempt to complete my [Buchanan] book and my attempt to marry her had been aspects of a single vain effort to change my life" (303). Alf's attempts address why John Barth writes about John Barth and why Philip Roth writes about Philip Roth and Philip Roth. Crippled by the hopelessness of the fact that the heroic white man has become a despised protagonist, the authors turn to stories of their counterselves, casting themselves as characters in politically correct stories. They position themselves as the common heroes of everyday life in tales which are not about oppressors, tales which future critics will not call radioactive garbage. Buchanan's story is Alf's story, which, in turn, reflects Updike's re-creations of Buchanan and Hawthorne.

In the manner of feminist historians who generate the new scholarship about women, Alf and Updike turn away from tales of kings. Alf's narrative about Buchanan and his vice-president William R. D. King is certainly not the story of America's most heroic executive branch leadership. Alf's wife, Norma, feels that Buchanan is "too dreary" (Updike, *Memories*, 14). Alf responds: "'He's *not* dreary . . . I *love* him" (14). Buchanan, the "only bachelor President" (13), is loved by Alf, a man separated from his wife and unable to form a permanent relationship with a married woman (Genevieve Mueller). Alf bonds with Buchanan, not with a woman. Here Updike creates a new version of Leslie Fiedler's notion that American literature's white male heroes embrace the dark-skinned Other. Updike's common hero of everyday life loves the Other in the form of the nonheroic hero, the "dreary" president. And, like Alf, Updike picks a dreary president too: "For that matter, was there ever a Ford Administration? Evidence for its existence seems to be scanty" (76). Gerald Ford, the attractive all-American WASP man, is, in retrospect, boring.

Alf's Buchanan story and Updike's Ford story nullify the despised "tale of kings." Buchanan's relationship with his vice-president, King, is certainly not a canonical narrative. Updike chooses a president who literally would not be king: Ford "was the only President to preside with a name completely different from the one he was given at birth — Lesley King, Jr. 'President King' would have been an awkward oxymoron" (Updike, *Memories*, 354). Gerald Ford, the nonheroic man who is neither a kingly president nor President Leslie King, is, in terms of the new version of Fiedler's insight I describe, a fitting protagonist for Updike to create. The white male author is reduced to a common hero of everyday life, placed in the same category as "the women and slaves patriarchal historians had hitherto consigned to the shadowy margins of their establishment-prone accountings" (242); Updike's and Alf's books are about the president as antihero. (Ford, in fact, is so much the president as antihero that, when he spoke at the 1996 Republican National Convention, the network coverage I watched switched from the speaker's podium to a reporter's comments.) The male author's counterself acts as a lead shield to protect him from the charge of writing radioactive garbage.

Memories begins with images of patriarchy itself reacting as if August 1974 in America might be a counterpart of August 1945 in Japan:

> I remember I was sitting among my abandoned children watching television when Nixon resigned. My wife was out on a date, and had asked me to baby-sit. We had been separated since June. This was, of course, August. Nixon, with his bulgy face and his menacing, slipped-cog manner, seemed about to cry. The children and I had never seen a President resign before; nobody in the history of the United States had ever seen that. (3)

In the Clayton home and America at large, patriarchy, the law of the father, resembles a bombed-out shell. The Claytons are no longer a nuclear family. The commander-in-chief, the country's father figure, is (in the manner of my previous chapter's discussion of Captain Picard) infantilized, not in a position to launch phallic missiles. Updike's solution is to give the president a counterself, changing the president's usual genre. Hence, Alf advises his student to think "about what I said about Presidents as mothers" (88). Alf would like his students to explore "effeminacy in the Presidency — the President as national mother. Like LBJ — he loved us all in sorrow, protest though we did. The *most* motherly, of course, was the one who sent the most American boys to their deaths — Lincoln" (86). No king, no oppressor, the presidential wielder of napalm and canon is categorized as "mother." And so is the white male author: Alf's Buchanan manuscript is "a bouncing book . . . [a] feebly kicking old fetus" (14).

Alf gives birth to his counterself, Buchanan. Alf, who simultaneously authors his own past and positions Buchanan as another version of himself, is a constructor — and he is the "mortal foe" (250) of his deconstructionist colleague Brent Mueller. Deconstruction is the enemy of a male author who articulates his self via making a text. Deconstruction, for Alf, is rather like death. His rival Mueller "would have deconstructed . . . [him] without a pang" (250). Deconstruction functions as the nuclear bomb in Alf's and Mueller's personal war. Alf, in contrast, reconstructs himself by re-creating Buchanan's male mind. Updike, in turn, re-creates the Ford era by constructing Alf. Present male selves, in both instances, become another self, a past self articulated via a historical personage who is another version of the author.

Alf places deconstruction in the radioactive garbage dump reserved for the Western canon that male oppressors create. Mueller is "contaminated by his anti-canon deconstructionist chic, which flattened everything eloquent, beautiful, and awesome to propaganda baled for the trashman" (201). Deconstruction is Alf's enemy: he is so close to his Buchanan text that he "began to fall in love with" (136) Buchanan's love, Ann Coleman. The most torrid relationship *Memories* describes is not the affair between Alf and Genevieve Mueller — it is Alf's love for Buchanan, the male author's devotion to the counterself he engenders. Perhaps Updike feels similarly about Alf, his creation who shares his respect for Buchanan and Hawthorne.

Alf / Buchanan / Updike is one entity connected by the energy textuality generates. Nothing, no aspect of their personality, is lost in the lack of order which results from merging three individuals — Alf, Buchanan, and Updike — into versions of the same self. The merged version, Alf / Buchanan / Updike, no longer fits within these separate categories: author, character, and real historical figure. "Truly, our lives are like the universe: nothing is lost, only transformed, in the slide toward disorder" (251), Alf believes. The protagonist of the sitcom *Alf*, the cute outer-space alien puppet, signals that Alf Clayton is appropriately viewed in terms of the universe. After enjoying sex "in the warps of erotic space" while floating "in love's hyperspace" (Updike, *Memories*, 19), Alf explains that, during the Ford administration, body fluids were not potentially lethal: "[O]ne dabbled and frolicked in them without trying to picture the microscopic galaxies within, the squadrons of spherical space ships knobby with keys for fatally unlocking our cell walls" (22). Further describing sexuality in terms of space imagery, Alf advises a student that "women don't need to banish men out to another planet to achieve personhood" (87). Until men perfect the nonsexist counterself, banishment will be justifiable. Feminist science fiction writers do not need, just yet, to abandon their thought experiments about separatist planets.

Male authors re-create themselves; feminist science fiction writers re-create the world by imagining worlds without men. In "Amor Vincit Foeminam: The Battle of the Sexes in Science Fiction," Joanna Russ describes a war ensuing between sex-role reversal novels. This war is abating. Male authors' counterselves are created in response to their discomfort regarding women who are "squeezed on all sides by patriarchal prohibitions and directives" (Updike, *Memories*, 112). When Alf first hears about one of these directives, sexual harassment, he reacts by thinking that this term is "novel, the idea alien" (248). The male authors' counterselves resemble astronauts training to become welcomed citizens of feminist utopian planets. In other words, now that "sexual harassment" is neither novel nor alien, men want to portray themselves as something other than harassers. Updike's Alf, Barth's Barth, and Roth's Roth and Roth would never, if they happened to land on Russ' feminist separatist planet Whileaway, denigrate women.

Although patriarchal prohibitions and directives have not expired, they are now named and deemed unacceptable (for example, universities presently act against male college professors who define having sexual relationships with female undergraduates as a "perk" [Updike, *Memories*, 248].) Society now quells the sexist behavior it has previously defined. "Each era simultaneously holds, in the personalities of its citizens, an absorption into mainstream life of previous social frontiers and an exhaustion of the energy that propelled recent breakthroughs and defiances" (18). Defining the term "male chauvinist" is an exhausted form of social energy. Male chauvinists, like smokers, are socially unacceptable. In response to this situation, male authors create counterselves to place themselves outside the genre "male chauvinist pig." They expend energy discerning how the newly enlightened male will function in a society which liberates women from the sex object role. The male counterself is able to conform to the counter-patriarchy. In this new world, unlike "that far-off Ford era," colleges no longer have "no announced policy on fornication between faculty and students" (82). Energy not spent on enacting patriarchal imperatives (male professors seducing female undergraduates, for example) must have a new outlet. Hence, the male counterself appears in some male-authored contemporary novels. He is the transformed energy resulting from newly designating the male chauvinist pig to be a pariah.

The retreat from patriarchal imperatives absorbs the energy former chauvinist pigs used to expend. Despite men's positive efforts to try to establish new generic classifications for themselves, Alf takes a dim view of human energy: "[A]ll that earth and oxygen and airspace to give *Homo sapiens sapiens* [*sic*] room to breed and eat and starve. . . . you see that the human race is just one immense waste of energy. The lifeless surface of Mars and Io must sigh in relief" (Updike, *Memories*, 366). Alf would believe that this waste of energy could appropriately be pulled within the counterpart to Calvino's imagined city, Beersheba. This counter city, this other Beersheba, is a fecal city: "its substance is dark and malleable and thick, like the pitch that pours down from the sewers, prolonging the route of the human bowels, from black hole to black hole, until it splatters against the lowest subterranean floor, and from the lazy, encircled bubbles below, layer upon layer, a fecal city rises, with twisted spires" (Calvino, *Invisible Cities*, 111–112). Updike signals that he is willing to throw *Memories* into Beersheba's fecal matter.

His decision reflects his awareness that some readers will call *Memories* a novel whose unitary male voice is created by a male author (an entity viewed as radioactive garbage or, even worse, as defecation: here — Updike's novel *S* notwithstanding — the "s" word is no scarlet letter). As I have mentioned, Mueller would gladly deconstruct Alf — and Updike accommodates him by causing Alf to deconstruct himself. Alf's last words: "The more I think about the Ford Administration, the more it seems I remember nothing" (369). So much for Updike's 369-page novel about male memories and counterselves. Updike, with the radioactive garbage accusation in mind, explodes his novel. Alf, a male character who abhors deconstruction but is deconstructed by his creator, experiences genre fission.

Alf states that "[t]here comes a moment when we cease creating ourselves" (360). This moment is certainly not the prevailing one for male authors. While feminist utopias are thought experiments about changing patriarchy, the male counterself is a thought experiment for well-meaning men who must invent new selves to function within a changing society. Many female feminist authors take steps to make a new world; many male authors try to reconfigure their selves to adjust to this newness.

Barth, teller of the retold tale par excellence, participates in this activity by retelling himself in *Once upon a Time*. He confronts women's unequal opportunities by comparing himself to his twin sister, Jill. He copes with his membership in the category "prosperous men, white, Protestant" (Updike, *Memories*, 108) through what I regard as his efforts to embrace Jewish culture. He creates Jay Wordsworth Scribner, his counterself, whose own counterself, Jerome Schreiber, might be Jewish.

The "water-messages" (43) comprising *Once upon a Time* are retold tales of Barth's life story, tales which epitomize genre fission involving wife and husband, sister and brother, and Protestant and Jew. Barth floated in his mother's womb as a biological other half of Jill. He floats on his boat, named *Us*, as a matrimonial other half to Shelly Rosenberg Barth, his Jewish second wife. Forever unable to cope with his twin or to become a true insider in relation to his wife's Jewish culture, Barth, another male author writing at a time when men must cope with a less misogynistic world, creates other selves to function as his guide through outer space darkness: "Indeed, we stand now in a blackness illuminated only by our projected selves, as in some avant-garde stage set or outer space" (64).

Placing himself and his writing out into the universe, Barth listens for signals: he monitors his "new and old jottings like those radio astronomers listening for intelligent extraterrestrial signals against the low buzz of the expanding universe — except that these are my signals, my mutterings" (12). He hears "the background noise of one's personal universe, whether expanding or contracting, against which one listens, listens for the Signal" (13). The male writer is the alien. The myths at the heart of *Once* are not the stories of Scheherazade and Perseus, myths Barth retells in *Chimera*. Rather, *Once* stresses the notion that the necessity of patriarchal supremacy is newly revealed to be a myth. In light of this revelation, Barth presents his own life as "a story" (8), a factual fiction, a "futuristic, time-travel fiction: a journey in the unknown like all our journeys" (18–19). His chronological interminglings signal that, in regard to new appropriate interchanges between women and men defined since the Ford administration, the formerly known has become unknown — i.e., alien.

Barth, well aware of the connection between "*pen* and *penis*" (*Once*, 267), to signal his generation's loss of manhood, has his protagonist lose the pen he used for years. Barth's new pen becomes a time machine: "[i]n its

Ready position, Time's arrow streaks forward through the past" (142). Jay explains that this pen possesses its own counterself: "It *looks* like your precious pen, right? It may even *write* like your precious pen. But what we have here . . . is a super-high-tech, made-in-Japan *replica* of your precious pen. Or maybe it's your precious pen itself, sea-changed into a solid-state, hypertech, multiform remote" (128). At a time when it is no longer kosher for penises (circumcised or not) boldly to go where no penises have gone before (into vaginas of virgin undergraduates, for example), the counterself of the male author's pen becomes a simulacrum.[3]

A pen which represents itself is a fitting communicative instrument for a male writer who, as a boy, questions the lauding of the white Protestant phallus. Young Barth ponders "the range of actions permitted to the Lone Ranger but not to Tonto" (187); Barth now writes at a moment when men of his ilk are chastised for oppressing Tonto and treating women as squaws. Both Barths confront the same quandary: "the ordeal that the Main Character must surmount if he is to remain the hero of his own story" (187). Barth (and other men of his generation) faces the ordeal of the white male who is no longer the sole main character. Furthermore, the white male as main character, as hero of his own story, is no longer considered to be heroic. Hence, male authors populate their own stories with counterselves, stunt men who substitute for the original when the charge "oppressor" appears.

In *Once*, Updike's Alf/Buchanan seems to appear as Jay Scribner/ Jerome Schreiber (the counterselves of John Barth), who is John Barth's counterself. The relationship between self and counterself articulated in terms of pen and penis appears in both *Memories* and *Once*. Alf "intended to model Buchanan's love for King upon . . . [his] for Genevieve" (Updike, *Memories*, 242). Jay informs Barth that "you've internalized me. I'm onto you and into you" (Barth, *Once*, 300). Alf uses his pen to assert his sexuality. Barth pens Jay, the counterself who is "into" John Barth, the counterself who relates to the author as a penis. Jay might appear as the potentially Jewish Jerome because Barth, who as a boy suffered from phimosis ("an infection of the prepuce" [*Once*, 247]), would want his counterself-as-penis to be circumcised.

Although, as I have said, I cannot be certain that Jerome Schreiber is Jewish, Jay Wordsworth Scribner is Protestant. Barth emulates Scribner's juxtaposition with someone whose religion he potentially does not share. I think that this potential seepage between religions reflects Barth's desire to become even closer to his beloved Shelly by embracing Jewish culture.

Barth seems to want to extend himself toward Judaism, to have a Jewish counterself or twin. Jerome becomes Jay because of "coincidence of surnames and first initials" (*Once*, 258). Another *J* is relevant here: the first letter of the word "Jew." Barth would like to re-create himself as a Jewish John (more appropriately called his childhood name, Jack). The letter *B*, "the Hebrew letter of creation" (349), is also important. Jerome Schreiber sends Barth a postcard whose message "consisted of a large block-Capital B initiating a column of proper names, thus: Buffalo, Borges, Baltimore B(rawlbrat)" (323). The letters *J* and *B* clue readers that John Barth seeks another counterself: to recast himself as Jewish Boy.

Unlike Jerome Schreiber, some of the language appearing in *Once* evokes Jewishness. Referring to the personal ads Gottlieb's and Theroux's protagonists are so fond of, Barth describes himself as a "divorced White *Goyische* Male" (*Once*, 377). I echo the title *Real Men Don't Eat Quiche* when I proclaim that a real *goy* does not call himself a *goy*. And what *goyische* male has a mother who is "*schlepping* those kettles of soup for the store" (153)? Barth might wish that chicken soup with matzoh balls was in demand in his hometown, East Cambridge, Maryland. Non-*goyische* language pervades Barth's personal declarations: his first literary efforts are "cockamamie Dorchester Tales" (276); his first drink with Shelly results in the toast "*so l'chaim*" (370); he comments on the conclusion of *Once*: "Oy veh is mir, no Act Three" (386). Neither John Updike nor Alf Clayton (nor, for that matter, President Buchanan) would ever say "*Oy veh is mir.*" They also would not mention the Jewish holiday Simchas Torah (Barth 265). Only really real Jews mention Simchas Torah.

Barth's use of Yiddish might relate to the fact that he was born with a "*congenitally constricted foreskin*" (*Once*, 247). He notes: "Had I been born Jewish, for example, this circumstance would never have come to light. . . . I lacked that advantage . . . as circumcision of the goyim would not become the pediatric norm in America until the Spockish 1950's" (247). His faulty foreskin has an impact upon his work— and his entire life: "Ought you not to remark in passing, Freudischers, that among his [Barth's] first undergraduate, postcircumcisory literary efforts was — surprisingly, from a parochial sophomore — an ode to Rosh Hashanah, and that his first published fiction was of a Jewish character as well, as if his elective surgical foreskin-excision had both eased some constriction with his muse and prompted an 'elective affinity' with the Chosen People. . . . Have you not explained, in a word (the word . . . *phimosis*) . . . his essential personality and the entire course of his life and work?" (250).

Barth is of German ancestry. Ironically, at the very time when young Barth's foreskin was having a psychological impact upon him, his Jewish counterselves (circumcised males) residing in Germany were denied life. Barth, who psychologically connects his pen to his penis, uses his pen to evoke Jewish culture, which forbids foreskins. Barth, who views his youth in terms of a flawed foreskin, shares an affinity with another counterself, Solomon Perel, the protagonist of Agnieszka Holland's *Europa, Europa*. Perel, a Jew masquerading as a German in Nazi Germany, continually faces life-threatening situations because he is circumcised, because he possesses a penis which is defined as faulty. Perel suffers from a true phallic lack. Barth and Perel form another counterself to Barth's pen and its relationship to time travel: men who are marked by their penises.

Itzhak Stern, the accountant in Steven Spielberg's *Schindler's List*, states that "the list is life." In other words, a text is life and a writing implement creates life. When again bemoaning the loss of his pen, Barth says "that pen *was* the Elixir" (*Once*, 319). This evocation of the pen "used" and "abused" (319), of the penis and pen which, in Barth's case, are related to his foreskin, his lack of Jewishness, is followed by a question: "That the key to the treasure *is* the treasure?" (319). I relegate this question — which echoes a statement appearing in *Chimera* and, hence, also possesses a counterself — to categorical potential Jewishness, like the name Jerome Schreiber. To my ear, the question is posed with a linguistic cadence which routinely emerges from the mouths of Jewish New "Yawkers." This question, then, is a Jewish linguistically rewritten version of its counterself articulated in *Chimera*. Its tone is part of the crux of *Once*. Barth re-creates himself as a Jewish counterself. The pens, words, and protagonists appearing in *Once* all have counterselves; the same is true for the novel as a whole. *Once upon a Time* could appropriately reappear as *Barthnoy's Complaint*. Perhaps Barth wishes that Philip Roth was his counterself. After all, it is impossible for the real Barth to become a *real* Jew.

Once describes another near impossibility: women of Barth's generation becoming and being recognized as postmodern writers. *Once*, then, also rewrites Virginia Woolf's narrative about Judith Shakespeare. Barth echoes Updike's concern about how a man who is enlightened about patriarchal oppression can continue to generate male stories. While Shakespeare did not have the female counterself Woolf imagines, the same does not hold true for Barth. The differences characterizing Jill Barth's and her brother Jack's life stories epitomize the different paths open to women and men. Aware of this situation, Barth includes a lengthy satirical rendition of the

"Jack and Jill" nursery rhyme (210–220) which questions why Jack precedes Jill in their journey up the hill. *Once* charts Barth's life journey in terms of a chronological ebb and flow (which can be called "temporal present one") where the novel's creation occurs two years behind its plot ("temporal present two"). Temporal present one eventually meets and passes temporal present two (its counterpresent).

While the John Barths float upon this ebbing and flowing time frame, like the nursery rhyme protagonist Jill, Jill Barth and the women of her generation are never first to fetch a pail of water, to attain the "[u]niversal solvent, without-which-not of life, *water*" (*Once*, 215). Although Jill was born first and received better elementary school grades than John, in the floating opera of the Barth twins' lives, Jill—who does not possess the right stuff to undertake the night sea journey of a "spermatozoon" (252)—sinks while John swims. John uses the helm of his boat, a symbol of his affluence, as a diving board. Jill, positioned as Other than the gender given the best chance to attain the nursery rhyme crown, tumbles after Jack. Jack attends Johns Hopkins and Jill attends secretarial school: "When puberty and high school mercifully broke up the nursery-rhyme duo, Jill accepted her tracking in the 'commercial' curriculum and thence to secretarial school in Delaware, although her high-school academic record had been consistently better than mine. While I studied Latin and Spanish and literature and trigonometry in the 'Academic' curriculum and aspired to some undefined future distinction, she studied typing and shorthand and bookkeeping and aspired to secretaryship. Neither of us had enough imagination . . . to protest this arrangement, common practice at the time" (161).

Jill is no counterself of Jack. Jill leads an unimaginative professional life; Jack becomes a famous imaginer whose career is launched with *The End of the Road*. Barth describes this novel's protagonist, Jake Horner, as a "moral vacuum of a protagonist, this ontological Black Hole (back then we didn't have *that* term, either)" (*Once*, 286). Unlike Barth (who at first teaches at Penn State), Horner is employed by a local teachers' college. Barth explains that this teacher's college resembles the one his first wife, a counterself to Jill, attended (286). His former wife finished "her two-year degree at that Eastern shore state college . . . [and] she entered a downtown secretarial school in the fall to learn office skills. Her ambition, like my sister's, did not exceed those typical of American women before the 1960s: some marketable competency like school teaching, nursing, or stenography" (263). Jill and Jack, "erstwhile wombmates" (263) share nothing in common. Jill and her true counterself, Jack's first wife, are analogous to wombmates—

twins floating through life in the vacuum of focusing upon vacuum cleaners, the ontological black hole (the enclosed space which cancels women's aspirations) which engulfed American women before the 1960s. Before 1960, American women reached maturity positioned at the end of the road.

Barth can write "*oy veh is mir,*" "*goyische,*" and "*schlepping*" until he contracts carpal tunnel syndrome. Despite his efforts, however, no one will include him on lists of Jewish writers. Women who make the effort to appear on lists of postmodern writers face a similar situation. Women of Barth's generation were not positioned to be the founders of postmodernism. According to Barth's Barth, Jay Scribner coined the term: "I even made up a word last night for what I think you and some of your contemporaries are doing: Postmodernism" (*Once*, 300). The "doing" contemporaries are men, the "guys" who, as Scribner announces, will "finish inventing Postmodernism" (311). The "girls" of Barth's time never had the chance to start postmodernism. Women who are younger than Barth — I think of Lynne Tillman, the late Kathy Acker, and the late Angela Carter — could only lag behind, could only be the secondary Jill to the primary Jack in relation to constructing the postmodern textual hill. Despite these women's efforts, their names are not included with those of Barth, Donald Barthelme, Robert Coover, William Gass, and Kurt Vonnegut. Women's efforts to write themselves as postmodern guys ring as hollow as Barth's efforts to write himself as something other than a *goy*. Because of women's late start, their illocutionary status as founding postmodern writers is as unconvincing as Barth's use of Yiddish.

Despite his sensitivity to his sister's and first wife's dearth of professional opportunities, Barth is blind to his male advantage. I refer to his personal relationship with Shelly Rosenberg, a member of the Acker / Carter / Tillman generation. Rosenberg, Barth's former student at Penn State, who is thirteen years his junior, made it her business to attract his attention. Nowhere does Barth state that 27-year-old men do not usually throw themselves at 40-year-old women. *Once* is a retold tale of how Barth threw away (or dumped) his first wife and acquired a new one. Men's age advantage has not changed (for example, the 1994 film *Wolf*— which Theroux's Jagoda might find interesting— couples Michele Pfeiffer with Jack Nicholson). Barth blithely accepts his access to a social funhouse from which women are still barred. *Once* describes how Barth's wives are lost in that funhouse. Women have been excluded from inaugurating postmodern fiction; *Once* excludes Barth's wives from textually re-creating themselves. I have mentioned that Updike's Alf states that it is sometimes necessary to cease re-creating oneself. Regarding the published material about the Barth family, his wives have not been given the chance even to begin.

Barth offers no description of how his first wife responded to being dumped. My sole source for descriptions of Shelly Barth is the information John Barth provides. His *Harper's* piece "Teacher: The Making of a Good One" lauds her intellect and pedagogical skill. This is how he describes her reaction to becoming Mrs. Barth: "She had become Mrs. Barth in two aspects: it pleased her to append her husband's last name to her own (to be called 'Mrs. John Barth,' however, rightly rankles her; she is herself, not Mrs. Me), and she had become the pedagogical phenomenon her students refer to among themselves as Barth" (64). Shelly Barth is discussed in *Harper's* merely because she is Mrs. John Barth. Sans her connection to him, her accomplishments would not be included in a national magazine. John Barth, then, in addition to creating his counterself, authors his wife's public self. In relation to his texts which describe her, she is most certainly not herself. She is deconstructed; she *is* Mrs. John Barth. Students who refer to her as "Barth" obliterate a sign of her Jewish cultural background. Real *goyim* are not named Rosenberg.

Barth concludes his *Harper's* piece by motivating readers to discuss teachers. "Talk about teachers! Let's." ("Teacher," 65). Okay. I will talk about teachers, counterselves, and the State University of New York at Buffalo, the institution which granted my Ph.D. Barth describes it as "[t]he Ellis Island of Academe, we new-immigrant faculty called it, also with some pride; so many of us were intellectual heretics, refugees from constrained professional or domestic circumstances, academic fortune-hunters in Governor Nelson Rockefeller's promised land" ("Teacher," 60). Barth fails to mention that the Buffalo immigrants, the heretic academic boat people who comprised the Buffalo English department, were men. When I arrived there in 1977, a few years after Barth's departure, there were no nationally known women professors to serve as my role models. There were no women for me to emulate, to position as my future counterself, to mother / mentor me, to form an *Us*— the foundation for my efforts not to drown as I attempted to seep into patriarchal academic professional currents. To my ear, *Once upon a Time* sings of women's constrained professional and domestic circumstances. As a male, Barth sails to the promised land of male professional and personal privilege. There is no such promised land for women. Woman's counterjourney to *Once upon a Time: A*

Floating Opera could be called *Gilligan's Island*. She sets sail, and the seas get rough; she is marooned. She becomes ordinary Mary Ann or Ginger, the vacuous actress — not the captain or the professor.

Yes, as R. H. W. Dillard states, *Once* "is a celebration of the power of narrative, of the questions it must ask and can answer" (13). The women in Barth's life are not celebrated, though. Women do not yet have equal access to the power of narrative. Women, who are not the "guys" who invent postmodern fiction, are now redirecting the course, rephrasing the questions postmodern fiction asks and answers.

Philip Roth, in *Operation Shylock*, celebrates the power of narrative as a means to communicate and to cope with what happened to Jews once upon a time. Roth positions the Holocaust as a text; he places Jews as characters in a story Nazis authored and he retells their tale. *Shylock*, like *Memories* and *Once*, alters genre classifications. And, although Barth's Yiddish does not ring true, Roth does sound very much like Barth (and Jorge Luis Borges): "Amazing, that something as tiny, really, as a self should contain contending subselves — and that these subselves should themselves be constructed of subselves, and on and on and on. . . . Multiple selves have been on my mind for months now" (*Shylock*, 152). Roth's subselves, analogues of Barth's counterselves, evoke Borges' concern with the infinite.

Reviewers of *Shylock* have difficulty contending with all of Roth's selves which appear in the novel. Updike (a real *goy*!), for example, states: "The myths of personal history have replaced those of a people's history. . . . Somewhere after Philip I sleeps with Jinx, the novel stops pretending to coherence and becomes a dumping ground, it seems, for everything in Roth's copious file on Jewishness" ("Recruiting," 111, 112). Updike does not get it. He fails to see that Roth creates a Jewish countertale to confront another version of the radioactive garbage *Memories* describes. Roth asserts that, due to tales and texts (Hitler's copious files on Jewishness), Nazis defined Jews as toxic material to be disposed of in dumping grounds. Roth uses re-created personal history, makes more Philip Roths, to describe Jews' recent history. *Shylock* can be understood in terms of the conclusion to *Schindler's List*. Spielberg pictures more than one version of an individual Jew when he places real survivors next to the actors who played them. He counters Hitler's "operation extermination" by blurring art and life, by creating different versions of the same person, by replacing extermination with multiplication.

So does Roth — and reviewer Michiko Kakutani misses this point. She writes: "From time to time *Operation Shylock* feels as though it might break out of this old pattern of defensive self scrubbing and truly engage other issues, but each time the novel begins to do this, it's pulled back in by the centrifugal force of its narrative self-absorption" (17). She misunderstands the direction of the novel's energy force. The energy of its narrative self-absorption is focused upon itself as a text which responds to Hitler's story of how properly to absorb Jews. Spielberg pictures this absorption method in one of the most memorable images in *Schindler's List*: the shot of the child who hides in the concentration camp latrine. The child epitomizes Hitler's intention to absorb all Jews under the category defecation. Roth describes Jewish response fifty years after Hitler defined all Jews as (to use the *s* word again) shit.

When Roth encounters his double in Israel, he evokes the Jewish need to be defensive in that very defense-conscious country. *Shylock* is a defensive countertale: Hitler's texts eradicated Jews; Roth's text clones Jews: "there would have been another *fifty* little Jewish boys of our age growing up to look like us if it hadn't been for certain tragic events that occurred in Europe between 1939 and 1945. And is it impossible that half a dozen of them might not have been Roths? Is our family name that rare? . . . You . . . may think it's horrible that there are two of us and that you are not unique. From my Jewish perspective, I have to say I think it's horrible that *only* two are left" (79–80). Roth even addresses anti-Semites who attack dead Jews by desecrating Jewish cemeteries: the Roth clone's penile implant functions after his death. Roth's dead Jew is still potent. In the face of exaggerated extermination (persecuting the dead), Roth insists upon exaggerated reproduction (a corpse capable of achieving an erection).

Roth describes the direction of his novel's energy: "I'm not trying to confuse you. Look, let me tell you something that a lot of people have trouble believing. This happened. I stepped into a strange hole, which I don't understand to this day" (Fein, 13). "This happened" currently pertains to the Holocaust itself. We all know about the revisionists who manufacture confusion by questioning the Holocaust's authenticity. Roth unmasks the purposefulness of this confusion by generating and denying his own purposeful confusion. *Shylock is* confusing.

What else can be said about a plot involving two, possibly three, protagonists named Philip Roth, one of whom engages in an espionage mission which might or might not have been undertaken by the real Philip Roth? In addition, *Shylock*, which is called a "confession," describes the John Demjanjuk trial's reality and points to the fact that Demjanjuk never confessed. "This confession is false" (399), announces the note to the reader that Roth places at his novel's conclusion. This note indicates the absence of another text: the Demjanjuk confession. *Shylock*, in turn, points to Hitler's plan to use words and texts (his written and articulated statements that Jews are vermin) to create an environment which would result in the absence of Jews. Roth's novel shows that Hitler's story of Jews, not the Holocaust which resulted from it, is the fiction. *Shylock* is a narrative which portrays the Holocaust as reality stemming from Hitler's narrative fiction.

The Holocaust is Hitler's *Operation Shylock*, his successful effort to use narrative (propaganda) to equate an entire people with Shylock's stereotypically negative characteristics. Hitler textualized the Jews, transforming them into Shylock, an evil individual who demands his pound of flesh. Genre fission characterizes the Holocaust: all Jews became Shylock; all Jews became shit. *Shylock* focuses on the power of narrative by defining the Holocaust as Hitler's preposterous tale which became real. As the reviewers I cite fail to understand, the narrative energy propelling *Shylock* focuses upon understanding a particular "strange hole" (Fein, 13) — the ovens which almost absorbed an entire culture. To try to come to terms with the real preposterous story which is the Holocaust, Roth provides *Shylock* — his preposterous story of the counterselves he insists are real. Roth's narrative reveals that Hitler's insistence upon validating and actualizing his story of Jews is an Operation Shylock: Hitler's successful effort to turn Jews into Shylock's twin. Hitler textualizes Jews; Roth textualizes himself.

Comments that Roth attributes to Aharon Appelfeld illuminate his own intention:

> The things that are most true are easily falsified. Reality, as you know, is always stronger than the human imagination. Not only that, reality can permit itself to be unbelievable, inexplicable, out of all proportion. The created work, to my regret, cannot permit itself all that. The reality of the Holocaust surpassed any imagination. If I remained true to the facts, no one would believe me. But the moment I chose a girl [to be the protagonist of his novel *Tzili*] . . . I removed 'the story of my life' from the mighty grip of memory and gave it over to the creative laboratory. . . . The exceptional is permissible only if it is part of an overall structure. (*Shylock*, 86)

To equate his firsthand experience with the unbelievable and inexplicable, Appelfeld positions a female protagonist as a thought experiment; Roth uses his clone to achieve the same result. Both authors engage the exceptional to respond to the Holocaust. Appelfeld communicates his story of being a survivor. Roth, an American Jew living fifty years after the Holocaust, turns to the exceptional as a means to confront Hitler's method of constructing the Jew as Shylock. *Shylock* reveals that Hitler was an author who rewrote a tale: Hitler turned the story of Shylock's insistence upon three thousand ducats into millions of Jews incinerated in ovens. In Roth's words: "I studied those three words by which the savage, repellent, and villainous Jew, deformed by hatred and revenge, entered as our doppelgänger into the consciousness of the enlightened West. The three words encompassing all that is hateful in the Jew. . . . You remember Shylock's opening line? . . . 'Three thousand ducats'" (274). Shylock is the doppelgänger of every Jew; Hitler retold Shakespeare's tale in an exaggerated manner; Roth elicits comprehension by creating doppelgängers of himself.

When creating these doppelgängers, Roth, in turn, retells another tale: Ira Levin's *The Boys from Brazil*. Levin clones Hitler; Roth twice clones a Jew — Philip Roth. And, like Roth, Levin describes the relationship between Jews and Nazis in terms of textuality. Levin's Nazi hunter Ezra Lieberman burns Josef Mengele's list of Hitler's clones. I stress that Lieberman burns the list, not the people, because he defines the clones as humans, as "children." Echoing Schindler's accountant Stern, in the hands of Lieberman, Mengele's list *is* life. Roth asks, "What *is* the real life of man?" (*Shylock*, 29). The burning list pictured at the conclusion of the film version of *Boys* provides an answer: the real life of man is contingent upon those who have the power to define life. Nazis burn Jews whose names appear on their transport lists; Lieberman, in contrast, burns the list of Hitlers, making the lives of ninety-four Hitlers possible.

Lieberman learns about the clones when he converses with a biology professor. His conversation addresses Roth's agenda in *Shylock*. The film portrays Lieberman saying, "Excuse me, doctor, but what is impossible? What is impossible, doctor?" The professor responds by saying that "mononuclear reproduction, cloning," is very possible. Both Roth and Levin describe possible impossibilities. Cloning is possible (and has occurred). So is encountering one's double. So is Hitler's plan to turn all Jews into Shylock.

The point is that no scheme, no "operation," is too implausible, too ludicrous to implement. Roth communicates this idea when he describes "Diasporism," a plan to send Israeli Jews back to Europe. Like Alf's biography and Barth's differing time frames, Diasporism is a counternarrative, a counterplot, a plot counter to Hitler's "plot" (used here as a synonym for "operation"): "Diasporism! Diasporism is a plot for a Marx

Brothers movie. . . . Groucho selling Jews to Chancellor Kohl!" (*Shylock*, 221). Diasporism is a counteroperation to the Final Solution. Hitler wanted to eradicate European Jewry; Roth's double wants to send them back. As humorous and ludicrous as Diasporism sounds, it is not impossible. Diasporism has its counterpart in the United States. Blacks, as the *New York Times* reports, are returning to the South:

> And in a nation where the news on race often seems unremittingly sour, the South is offering a different picture.
>
> Seeking jobs and fleeing urban slums, blacks have been leaving Northern states in large numbers since the 1970's reversing the historic migration patterns of midcentury. But in the 1980's, the favored destination changed from California to the South. Between 1985 and 1990, Georgia, largely because of Atlanta, had a net in-migration of 80,000 blacks, leading the nation by far. (Applebome, 20)

The Holocaust is real; Diasporism is real. No operation is too ludicrous to occur. Israel itself provides a case in point. Roth's double justifies Diasporism by "comparing his supposedly unattainable dream to the Herzlian plan for a Jewish state, which, in its own time, struck Herzl's numerous Jewish critics as contemptibly ludicrous, if not insane" (*Shylock*, 239–240). Herzl's ludicrous, insane — and real — Operation Israel is a response to Hitler's ludicrous, insane — and real — Operation Shylock.

In *Shylock* texts as well as the author have counterselves. The entire plot of *Shylock* is a ludicrous / real response to the ludicrous reality of Nazism. Roth states that his story "so far's frivolously plotted, overplotted . . . too freakishly plotted, with outlandish events so wildly careening around every corner that there is nowhere for intelligence to establish a foothold and develop a perspective" (245). So too for Hitler's narrative of Jews that became the Holocaust. Hitler's freakishly plotted, careening Holocaust story, however, leaves many silences in its aftermath. Demjanjuk's lack of a confession is one such silence. Roth responds with a countersilence. *Shylock* does not contain an eleventh chapter (which was supposed to describe Roth's Mossad espionage assignment). This narrative absence exists because an Israeli intelligence officer informs Roth that the omission will eliminate "a lot of *tsuras*" (389).

"*Tsuras*" (trouble) understatedly describes the deadly power of narrative. Roth includes a lengthy anti-Semitic diatribe (253–260), the latest version of anti-Semitism, words currently being written and spoken. The diatribe contains a comment about Auschwitz survivors' books: "Here's the line on Auschwitz, *write it!*" (260). This is sound advice. Narrative is dangerous. Dangerous narrative must be met head on by counternarrative: "THE TEN TENETS OF ANTI-SEMITES ANONYMOUS" (101), for example. These tenets are not ludicrous; they are a needed document in the contemporary world. Again, Hitler authored the Holocaust. And — like Barth, Roth, and Updike — those who survived the reality Hitler's texts inspired also have doubles. Roth's double "looked like the after to my before in the plastic surgeon's advertisement" (72). All survivors can also be described in terms of "before" and "after" — the before and after of themselves in relation to the event, before and after the "operation," the plastic surgery performed on universal Jewish identity that is Hitler's Operation Shylock.

Barth connects pen and penis. Roth's subject matter calls for a different juxtaposition: narrative and gun. He explains, "When I was younger my Jewish betters used to accuse me of writing short stories that endangered Jewish lives—would that I could! A narrative as deadly as a gun!" (186). Hitler's narrative, his story which equates all Jews with Shylock, is as deadly as a nuclear bomb. And what can be used to diffuse this bomb? Certainly not the real bomb the Israelis are rumored to possess. The diffusion device is not Moshe Dayan's army but, rather, Irving Berlin's words. "God gave Moses the Ten Commandments and then He gave to Irving Berlin 'Easter Parade' and 'White Christmas.' The two holidays that celebrate the divinity of Christ . . . and what does Irving Berlin brilliantly do? He de-christs them both! Easter he turns into a fashion show and Christmas into a holiday about snow . . . down with the crucifix and up with the bonnet! *He turns their religion into schlock.* . . . If schlockified Christianity is Christianity cleansed of Jew hatred, then three cheers for schlock. . . . I . . . found more security in 'White Christmas' than in the Israeli nuclear reactor" (157–58).

Hitler authors Operation Shylock; Irving Berlin authors Operation Schlock. "White Christmas" and "Easter Parade" are countertexts to *Mein Kampf.* Irving Berlin, not Hitler, authors the texts most appropriate to the end of the twentieth century. While all Jews have not been turned into ashes, many human endeavors (especially in America) have been reduced to the inconsequential, turned into schlock. Schlock is the black hole into which everything is now pulled. Roth calls this force Pipikism, and his description evokes Vonnegut's trademark satiric tone: "Pipik is the product of perhaps most powerful of all senseless influences on human affairs and that is *Pipikism*, the antitragic force that inconsequentializes everything —

farcicalizes everything — our sufferings as Jews not excluded" (38). Even the Holocaust itself has been trivialized. The late twentieth century foundation of Calvino's city of defecation is informed by Pipikism, not Nazism. No one is now incarcerated in Auschwitz; everyone in America wallows in schlock (or shit). Operation Shlock pervades Western civilization.

Patriarchy itself is now categorized as schlock. In the face of this new definition, in the face of attacks upon the white male canon, male writers clone themselves within their novels. Barth, Roth, and Updike realize that it has become politically incorrect to dream solely of a white Christmas. What is the white male author's response to the Easter bonnet? I refer readers to the discussion of cross-dressing in chapter 1.

WHILEAWAY SANS OUTER SPACE: ATWOOD, FRENCH, OATES, AND PIERCY ECHO MCCARTHY'S *THE GROUP*

No clones of themselves, the women authors I discuss depict characters who survive by forming supportive female groups. Atwood, French, Oates, and Piercy might, in fact, have written the same novel. *The Robber Bride, Our Father, Foxfire,* and *The Longings of Women,* all published between 1993 and 1994, function as different chapters of the same story. The protagonists dissolve the borders of their particular text, break out, resonate as characters in novels other than their own. Their seemingly interconnected groups consist of Piercy's Leila Landsman, Becky Burgess, and Mary Burke; Oates' girl gang, whose most notable members are Margaret Ann Sadovsky (called Legs) and Madeleine Faith Wirtz (called Maddy Monkey); French's Upton sisters, Elizabeth, Alex, Mary, and Ronnie; Atwood's college dormitory mates Antonia (called Tony), Rosalind (called Roz), and Karen (called Charis), who encounter the evil Zenia. The groups all use texts as weapons to confront patriarchy. Rather than single-handedly placing personal ads in order to devour male victims in the manner of vampire Risha Cadigan, they generate textual strategies after consulting with each other. Because they act like lichen, the focus of Ronnie Upton's graduate studies, their battles are effective. Ronnie explains that lichen is "made up of two different species that need each other to exist. It survives by cooperating, not conflict. It can live where nothing else can live . . . and it is a frontier plant. . . . it creates" (French, *Father,* 427). Lichen represents the need for benign coevolution that the formation of these female groups signals.

The individual members of these groups, not women and men, are the differing species the novels highlight. For example, Piercy's Leila, a college professor, has little in common with Mary, a homeless woman. Atwood's Tony, another college professor, differs markedly from Charis, a "head shop" salesperson. And French's Elizabeth Upton, a government financier, inhabits a different world than Ronnie, her impoverished Mexican-American half-sister. Despite their differences, all the group members recognize that, to survive, they need to band together. Acting according to benign coevolution, they transform their conflicts into cooperation. Pioneers who create new women-centered spaces, they demolish race, class, and personality boundaries to survive in the face of the marginality that all women share. They survive together within the space patriarchy reserves for women, what James Tiptree, Jr. (Alice Sheldon) calls the "chink" in the "world machine" where women barely survive ("Women," 154). "Women survived as they could" (Piercy, *Longings*, 374), says Mary.

These tales of group female survival are power fantasies for women. Mary Upton describes one such fantasy when she addresses her dying father, Stephen Upton, influential patriarch incarnate: "The point is, Father, what you did to us. We have never had any recourse for your terrible crime against us. . . . and we still don't really have legal recourse. But we do have power. Over you" (French, *Father*, 294). Abandoning the usual systems that deny them recourse, the Upton sisters create their own when they put their father, a paralyzed stroke victim, on trial — force him to face their accusations. The sisters literally kill him with words. Oates' and Piercy's girl gangs also use words to nullify powerful men. Becky Burgess, by lying to her young lover Sam, convinces him to help her kill her loutish husband, Terry. Similarly, Legs, due to her lies, is able to kidnap wealthy businessman Whitney Kellogg, Jr. Zenia also lies. No real person, she is a force — patriarchy in drag — who infiltrates, by telling false stories, the lives of Charis, Roz, and Tony. When these women become impervious to her fabrications, Zenia self-destructs.

Elizabeth Upton's comments about self-preservation and security explain why it is necessary for the protagonists to form groups: "There is no safe place, that's an illusion, there is no security even though people struggle for their whole lives long as if it existed. . . . We are constantly besieged, threatened, life is a constant struggle, the best you can do is to claw your way to some temporary security, some island . . . and try for dear life to hold on" (French, *Father*, 426). The struggle is, of course, more difficult for women. The women's groups help them to achieve some temporary security — to construct islands. They try to protect themselves from threatening outside space, what Elizabeth calls "out there." She describes the "empty space with exploding stars, black holes, planets of methane ice, comets, and now there's a hole in the ozone layer, and acid rain, and god knows what else threatening us" (426). The space constituting the patriarchal planet called Earth poses the greatest threat to the women.

To seek shelter from this earthly hostile space, the women construct protective islands, using each other as building material. The group pulls the individual woman in for her own benefit. Each group has a leader who serves as the force which repels the other women away from the threatening outside. Legs creates and dominates the girl gang she calls FOXFIRE; Leila literally writes Becky's life and figuratively rewrites Mary's life; Ronnie is the domestic anchor who positions the Upton house as a permanent gathering place for her sisters; Charis, Roz, and Tony band together to protect themselves from Zenia. These women epitomize genre seepage. Their life situations ooze out of individuality to encompass each other. Like the borders of their novels, their lives appear to lack boundaries.

These realistic novels reach out toward embracing feminist utopia. They may, in fact, belong to the literary category Carol Farley Kessler calls the "pragmatopia," achievable feminist utopia. Atwood, French, Oates, and Piercy create women who define utopia as attaining one coveted object: Mary Burke wishes to have Leila's son's sleeping bag; Maddy desires the typewriter which will facilitate her ability to keep the FOXFIRE record; Ronnie wants to study lichens; Charis, Roz, and Tony seek a means to nullify Zenia. This quest for utopia is described by Piercy's title *The Longings of Women*. All of this novel's protagonists realize the objectives they equate with utopia, attaining their desires: Mary finds a home; Becky enters the middle class; Leila completes her book and learns to live satisfactorily without her unsatisfactory husband. The authors create characters who learn to define their most cherished possession as each other, their group which shelters them from threatening outside patriarchal space.

Let me say more about how the protagonists topple boundaries between the novels. Elizabeth Upton's mother, a poor secretary who marries her wealthy boss, epitomizes Becky Burgess' model for success. Clare, a male economist who does not return Elizabeth's love, tells her that to achieve success it is necessary to read people: "Getting to know a professional world, getting familiar with faces and names *and* the language, the manners — these things are everything, believe me. I want you to learn them. Talk to people, establish a connection with them" (French, *Father*, 187). This sophisticated professional describes the system Becky Burgess uses as a model. Becky "never gave up studying How Things

Should Be. . . . Becky quietly accumulated a mental dossier on [office man-ager] Mrs. O'Neill" (Piercy, *Longings*, 136, 209). Becky, who reads middle-class women in order to become one (91), is a character in Clare's story of how Elizabeth should achieve professional upward mobility.

Leila, in turn, writes a book which describes Becky. And, her personal life is akin to Becky's means of achieving upward mobility. In bed with her new lover, Nick, Leila "felt oddly detached, as if she were studying each ges-ture, each kiss" (Piercy, *Longings*, 146). Becky too equates studying and reading people with the personal: "She felt she had mastered most of the complex program that was pleasing Terry" (175). Becky, who collapses dis-tinctions between words and reality, models herself after fashion magazine texts. She studies Terry, approaches him as "a course she was taking, and she planned to ace it" (140).

To survive, Mary Burke must study people and the terrain they inhabit. She learns when she can occupy the homes she cleans and how to mask her presence within them. Like Becky and Leila, she studies. During her first days in the home of Leila's sister Debby, Mary "watched for clues as to what she should make herself appear to be, so that she could stay. So that they would want to keep her" (Piercy, *Longings*, 415). These women are good students. They study, graduate, and emerge as something other than their original selves.

Mary — who shares much in common with the two stray cats Leila adopts — epitomizes the reason why these women must study so hard. And she has another unexpected counterpart: jetsetter Mary Upton. Like Mary Burke, Mary Upton is victimized by divorce: "When he left me, I got this great settlement in court, everybody thinks I have oodles of money, but I never saw a dime of it. Not a dime! I understand what these women go through, the ones in the paper on welfare whose husbands don't support the children after they get divorced, I know all about it" (French, *Father*, 196). The Marys suffer in kind, if not extent. Both mask the fact that they do not possess the resources they appear to possess. No one would think that Mary Burke is homeless. This is her situation despite the fact that she "had been a good wife and mother" (Piercy, *Longings*, 133), despite the fact that she obeys the rules about women's roles. The similarities between the Marys underscore that Everyhousewife, every woman who depends upon a husband's financial support, can become homeless. As Mary Burke ex-plains, "Any woman could end up on the street" (193). The boundary sep-arating Everyhousewife from street women is very thin. Everyhousewife can become part of the genre called homeless woman.

Mary Burke is Mary Upton with less money. Becky is Leila with less education: "Becky was Leila without books, without the resources of the library to open a world beyond the tube" (Piercy, *Longings*, 331). This merger of individuals, couplings existing outside the boundaries of self, indicates that patriarchy relegates all women to some form of Mary Burke's "outside" role. In order not to become outsiders, the protagonists place themselves inside a group of nurturing women. Mary as Everyhousewife is saved when she is pulled within Leila's orbit. Mary, in turn, extends herself toward Beverly, a fellow homeless woman who is even more imperiled than she is. Beverly and Mary "had a bond perhaps stronger than blood" (265). This bond compensates for the fact that Mary's children abandon her.

Bonds marked by blood flow between the novels. The Upton sisters, like the FOXFIRE members, make "a pact" to "mingle blood" (French, *Father*, 183). Even though their interests and social statuses differ, the sisters join forces. Class distinctions manifest themselves as differences regarding their relation to the Upton mansion. Alex, upon entering the Nursery Wing, notes that Ronnie, the servant's daughter, never played there. She imagines Stephen Upton insisting that Ronnie's presence in the nursery "would blur distinctions, which always leads to disaster" (183). Not so: the Upton sisters triumph when they eradicate distinctions and achieve cohesion. Together the sisters rewrite patriarchal codes, roles, and rules.

Their revisions appear as each sister's effort to embrace what she views as Other. The Upton Thanksgiving dinner consists of Mary's quenelles as well as Ronnie's beans and rice (French, *Father*, 144). Ronnie insists, "We have to honor my traditions too. Like pricking our fingers and mingling our blood" (144). She mentions the blood ritual that the sophisticated Upton sisters hold in common with the FOXFIRE girls. *Foxfire* shows that when women ritualistically mingle their blood, their action is far from childish. The FOXFIRE girls, who wield real power, are younger versions of the Upton sisters.

The modest house Legs purchases and the Upton mansion function as clubhouses for girl gangs. When Elizabeth mentions buying a house "for all of us" (Piercy, *Longings*, 414) she speaks with Legs' voice. No law of the father exists within these clubhouses. The dying Stephen Upton ensconced within the mansion is unable to speak. Nor does the patriarchal voice flourish in Leila's house or in McClung Hall, the spawning ground of the Charis, Roz, and Tony group. From within her McClung office, Tony disavows male-centered scholarship, interpreting war in her own female manner. Leila, who always accommodates her husband, casts him out. Her interaction with Becky and Mary leads her to "find it satisfying to work with other women who have been pushed out the door to find a little of their own. . . . there is no one I want to accommodate. At last I am my own woman" (455). Within their respective clubhouses, the sisterhoods cast patriarchy out from their spaces.

The clubhouses are feminist utopias, real versions of feminist science fiction's feminist planets. In 1993 and 1994, Atwood, French, Oates, and Piercy retell a 1977 tale: French's *The Women's Room*, in which Mira, the protagonist, finds her own identity. Almost twenty years later, her counterparts find each other. Two genres of women's fiction currently merge: the realistic novel and feminist utopian fiction. *Foxfire, Longings, Robber Bride,* and *Our Father* are the daughters of a parthenogenic union: *The Women's Room* coupled with Joanna Russ' "When It Changed." Oates, Piercy, Atwood, and French announce that feminist utopia can be transported from Russ' Whileaway to Earth, that Whileaway is now the women's room inhabited by a sisterhood. Piercy's Connie Ramos becomes French's Ronnie Upton. Atwood's handmaid becomes Piercy's Mary Burke as Everyhousewife subject to abuse. The FOXFIRE girls would be more at home on Whileaway than on Earth. Armed with the story feminists told in the 1970s, the very same tellers present a new version of that story in which women, in the manner of feminist science fiction protagonists, join together. Whileaway is now the women's room. When feminist science fiction and feminist realism merge, feminist utopia becomes viable.

The novels themselves signal this new generic combination. Ronnie articulates her situation in terms of space imagery: she is "alone in this house, in the world, in the universe, like a fragment broken off from a star that long ago whirled in orbit, alone in the dark cold silence forever and forever" (French, *Father*, 355). Ronnie, who is not lost in patriarchal space, forms part of the whole star representing the reconvergence of her sisters. Stephen Upton, the dead father, can no longer act as a science fiction force which diminishes the energy of the sisterhood. Sans the father as energy absorber, the sisters become a single body enjoying its own orbit. They are, however, threatened by blood which does not coincide with bond: Mary's daughter Marie-Laure. "The girl was a dark hole, gradually sucking them in" (408). She regards the sisters as if "observing an alien species" (409). Marie-Laure, an outside energy-draining force, is a counterpart of Zenia.

Legs Sodovsky is Zenia's opposite. Like Leila, Legs provides the energy for women to converge, for solidarity to occur. Legs herself epitomizes the place where the real and unreal merge. Maddy describes some of the FOX-

FIRE planning Legs construes: "wasn't real" (Oates, *Foxfire*, 290). In the same breath, Maddy contradicts herself: "Legs had a way of surprising you with things that did turn out *real*—like renting their house" (290). Legs is a real world science fiction hero: "'Sheena' flying through the jungle" (11). This real Sheena is Russ' Jael talking about gender war. To fight, Legs creates a new genre: the girl gang located in a town whose gangs are male. She establishes a positive receptacle space: the FOXFIRE homestead, "a luminous pit of a kind into which our efforts, singly and together, might be emptied without end" (221). Maddy chronicles this positive space.

The adult Maddy becomes an astronomer's assistant. She is, however, a full-fledged astronomer vis-à-vis her position as the assembler of the FOXFIRE story. As an astronomer's assistant, she analyzes photographs through a microscope while looking at "the solar system, deep into space and back into time. Sometimes I grow vertiginous, flying through space and time" (Oates, *Foxfire*, 326). Maddy herself connects her role as storyteller looking back into time to her role as an astronomer: "I have the proper telescope instrument for examining *look-back time*, that I hadn't had before" (327). When she looks back, she recalls that the real merged with the unreal, that she flew through space. While smoking marijuana with Legs, "suddenly, unexpectedly, the top of her tight little skull gives way! moonlight enters freely! Maddy's eyes fly open as Maddy is floating Maddy is airborne Maddy-Monkey is laughing she's overcome gravity *So this is it*! *so easy!*" (193). Maddy is Wendy Darling encountering Peter Pan. She epitomizes the convergence of the real and the unreal, the fantastic and the mundane. She is the girl gang member / assistant astronomer / feminist science fiction character. Her flight marks the spot of genre fission in feminist fiction. As I have indicated, realistic feminist writers currently borrow feminist science fiction tropes to draw blueprints for building feminist utopia on Earth. Their construction plan is a familiar text: sisterhood is powerful. Atwood, French, Oates, and Piercy proclaim that science fiction's power fantasies for women can become real.

Legs as "Sheena of the jungle" rewrites and attributes power to real women's stories. As the gun-wielding kidnapper of powerful businessman Whitney Kellogg, Jr., she is Patty Hearst controlling the gang. When her getaway car plummets off a bridge, she is Mary Jo Kopechne sitting in the driver's seat. (Here Oates rewrites *Blackwater*, her retold Chappaquiddick tale.) While, as I said above, Theroux's Jagoda is not granted the reprieve Thelma and Louise might enjoy, the same does not hold true for Legs. When Legs and gang member V. V. careen from a bridge while seated in their car and are "never sighted again" (Oates, *Foxfire*, 316), they join Thelma and Louise in a fantastic realm. The patriarchal world cannot encompass women like Thelma and Louise and Legs and V. V. These women inhabit extraterrestrial space, exist in fantastic time, journey to a cosmos of their own. "[C]elestial bodies, Legs and Maddy . . . [are] in an ellipsis of Time after FOXFIRE was taking its form" (100). Forever lost in space, Legs may transcend time itself: "*are* you, Legs — in any Time at all?" (327).

Feminist authors, former creators of separate real and fantastic modes, now merge the real and the fantastic within a single novel. They do so to signal that women who join together can change the world. Piercy, for example, merges the real and the unreal when she tells Becky's story. Becky, the woman who compels her very young lover to help her murder her husband, is drawn from a composite of real women who commit violent criminal acts usually reserved for men.[4] While Piercy rewrites real world events as fiction, Atwood's realistic characters transcend reality. Her protagonists resemble shape-shifters who change, at will, their names and personalities. French also writes in this vein. Her Steven Upton is more an essence of patriarchy than a person. He might be another incarnation of Zenia.

Oates pulls her fantastic description of chronology back to the real. FOXFIRE's inception occurs at "a time of violence against girls and women but we didn't have the language to talk about it then" (Oates, 100). We now have this language due, in part, to the novels Atwood, French, Oates, and Piercy created twenty years ago. It is fitting, then, that these authors position word and text as the chief means by which their girl gangs win the day.

As I have explained, Maddy defines her typewriter as a utopian object. It helps her to describe how, by using texts as weapons, Legs wages gender war. FOXFIRE nullifies a harassing teacher by placing a description of his actions on his car for the entire town to read (Oates, 31). The girls again use a sign to reveal a pet store owner's cruelty to animals (92). Legs does not fail to include a ransom note in her kidnapping exploit. FOXFIRE, like an animal marking its territory, places its sign — a red five-foot flame tattoo — all over town. The town responds by acting like a Greek chorus consisting of literary critics: "'What *is* that?' . . . 'Is it supposed to mean something? — what's it supposed to *mean*?'" (80 – 81). FOXFIRE's sign means that women are banding together to attain power. "[A]ll five were one in FOXFIRE and FOXFIRE was one in all" (41). The FOXFIRE gang rewrites the motto "All for one and one for all." At a time when teenagers were becoming Mouseketeers, the FOXFIRE girls became Musketeers; they wield an effective pen-as-sword. FOXFIRE is not Mickey Mouse.

I have also explained how the Upton sisters wield a sword of verbiage —
and how they use it to transform "our father" into the dead father. They
gather together, stage a trial, and sentence their father to death (French, *Father*, 300). Stephen Upton dies due to the force of narrative, the impact of
his daughters' accusations.

Text also assumes life and death proportions in *Longings*. Mary reads
her clients' mail in order to discern when she can seek the aforementioned
shelter in their vacated houses. Becky accomplishes the murder of her husband because she is able to convince her young lover that lies, false texts,
are true. Hence, Becky commits murder by acting as an author. Leila the
author records Becky's life. Leila is Piercy's counterself. Leila / Piercy reads
about Becky / female criminal composites in newspapers. These composites, at once real and fictitious women, blur distinctions between art and
life. To survive, these women master written instructions and emerge as cyborg women, combinations of body and inorganic object. Mary becomes
"trash" (447) and manages to regain her human form. Leila becomes a text
in the form of the words on the poster announcing her lecture which Deb-
bie and Mary read. Becky literally becomes the media she so desperately
emulates. These cyborg women are sisters of Yod, the cyborg protagonist of
Piercy's *He, She and It*. It is essential for these women to use texts to attach
themselves to other women.

Leila is a force of connection; Zenia is a force of disconnection. Zenia
emanates from a retold tale: Roz's twins' insistence that *The Robber Bridegroom* should become *The Robber Bride* (Atwood, 292). No flesh-and-
blood woman, Zenia is evil incarnate — a force who tells stories to enter
and disrupt other women's lives. She is initially successful because Charis,
Roz, and Tony want to be her sister, to assist her, to welcome her within
their girl gang. Atwood tells a story about how a woman who is an evil intruder holds a group together. Zenia breaks out of the "girl gang member
as nurturer" genre. Zenia, who "could be a man in a dress" (432), who possesses fake breasts, who dies twice, is no human. She is, instead, patriarchy
in drag, another Parker Jagoda, another Stephen Upton. "Soulless" (19)
Zenia, like Risha Cadigan, is a vampire; she "has drunk" (425) the lives of
women who want to befriend her. She attaches herself to women she transforms into her creature / characters. Zenia dies and reappears. Charis, Roz,
and Tony — as their name changes suggest — also metamorphose before
readers' eyes. Zenia's actions emphasize that evil stories, especially evil patriarchal stories, hurt people. Unlike Steven Upton, patriarchy is not dead.

And, at the inception of *Robber Bride*, neither is Zenia. Roz imagines that Zenia is a man (396).

Robber Bride proclaims that still-prevalent patriarchal stories, because women write new stories and rewrite old stories, lose some of their illocutionary force. *The Robber Bridegroom*, for example, becomes *The Robber Bride*. But women who mirror men do not provide useful alternatives to old patriarchal stories. Hence girl gang members, women who cohere with other women, do not act like men. Within the widening gyre of feminist narrative revision, many patriarchal things fall apart. Feminists, however, do not have the power completely to put them back together again. In *Robber Bride*, language and images reflect this situation. Tony has a penchant for saying words backward. Her altered, or new, language is not a useful means to communicate. Atwood's main images in *Robber Bride*, eggs and war, respectively signal female reproduction and male destruction. The eggs are broken; war is an academic subject, Tony's scholarly field. No new life emanates from the eggs, and war is not being fought. Alternative new roles do not yet replace dysfunctional female and male roles, the broken eggs and academic wars. We are now only on the verge of such newness. The girl gangs signal that we stand on the brink of change.

Zenia is patriarchy's response to this changing situation — to white men's loss of power in a world that pays increasing attention to multiculturalism. "Zenia is pure freewheeling malevolence; she wants wreckage, she wants scorched earth, she wants broken glass" (Atwood, *Robber Bride*, 410). And Charis, the flower child, can become her: "Zenia's edges dissolve like a watercolour in the rain and Charis merges into her" (394). Charis seeps into Zenia. This merger, this transgression of individual boundaries, speaks against fixed definitions, the old feminist story that all men are the enemy. In Roz's words, "According to the feminists, the ones in the overalls, in the early years, the only good man was a dead man . . . Roz continues to wish her friends joy of them, these men who are supposed to be so bad for you" (387). Charis, Roz, and Tony do meet good men. And, despite the beneficial aspects of women's groups, not all women are good group members. People are not evil because they can be categorized according to a fixed definition of gender. The overalls Roz describes are obsolete. And so is patriarchy itself. Atwood's characters emerge from within the borders of *Robber Bride* to become characters in the larger story of social change.

This overflow touches the female groups French, Oates, and Piercy describe. Charis, Roz, and Tony could be members of these groups. Zenia is a wolf in sheep's clothing; the old patriarchal story disguised as girl gang recruit. She signals that this old story is at war with the new story of female solidarity. Zenia infiltrates the clubhouse. She is the newly weakened patriarchy which now must become subversive itself to survive. Because the women's group is a potent force, patriarchy must be on guard; patriarchy must send Zenia to act as a double agent on its behalf.

Robber Bride retells itself. Zenia disrupts each of the women's lives once — and she returns to do it again. She is unsuccessful the second time, though. Charis, Roz, and Tony no longer believe her. They nullify Zenia-as-negative-force, repelling her power to take them in. "Another way of succumbing would be believing her, letting her in the door, letting her take them in, letting her tear them apart" (439). The second time around, Zenia dies — "again" (445). Charis foresees Zenia's death in candlelight (440). Her alternative woman's vision, woman's way of seeing differently, comes true.

Robber Bride explodes fixed definitions. In the end, Zenia, an evil force, receives Roz's "gratitude" (463). Zenia, who dies twice, "continues to exist" (460). Charis, Roz, and Tony — the good guys — might resemble the bad guy named Zenia. Good and bad overlap in *Robber Bride*. "The fences once so firmly in place around the gender corrals are just a bunch of rusty old wire" (450). As I state in chapter 6, the *Saturn 5* rockets are rusting. And, again, overall-clad feminists are obsolete. Good-guy men, such as Tony's husband, West, have a place within the feminist OK Corral. Gender war has become genre fission. Women, responding to this newness (in the manner of Charis, Roz, and Tony at the conclusion of *Robber Bride*), gather together to tell stories. They are, following the lead of Le Guin, "churtening" (discussed in chapter 7).

Their stories are funny. The feminist sans sense of humor is as dated as the feminist wearing overalls. Unlike their predecessors — *The Handmaid's Tale, Them, Woman on the Edge of Time,* and *The Women's Room* — the new novels by Atwood, Oates, Piercy, and French are humorous. Zenia, the havoc-producing poltergeist, has a light side. Neither Robber Bride nor Robber Bridegroom, due to her fake breasts, she is, according to Roz, "The Rubber Broad" (Atwood, 293). The Rubber Broad who dies twice bounces back. Humor in the novels I focus upon functions via overkill which literally involves death. Zenia's death and subsequent reappearance are more akin to the dead Bobby Ewing's return to *Dallas* than to Joan Delacourt's serious decision to stage her own death in Atwood's *Lady Oracle.* Steven Upton's overacted dying also most certainly fails to evoke readers' tears.

His body's final motions strike this reader as rather analogous to the twitching antennae of a roach about to succumb in the Raid commercial's denouement. Readers are also not sympathetic toward the kidnapped Whitney Kellogg, Jr. Legs would not like to think that the text she scrawls at the bottom of her ransom note — "*we mean business*" (Oates, *Foxfire*, 302) — is more humorous than threatening. Legs seems to have composed an advertising jingle: a businessman's kidnappers mean business. Such equating of violence with humor is also a part of *Longings*. Even when he is being bludgeoned to death, readers do not mourn Becky's husband, Terry. Becky, who so adroitly becomes media, is convicted because her accomplice fails properly to dispose of a television and VCR. Although early 1990s feminist novels depict male chauvinists facing death, their humor is very much alive. If the only good man is no longer a dead one, the new message is that male louts are expendable. Humor counters the deadpan mood usually associated with the genre called "feminist novel."

These at once funny and serious novels emphasize that women's words can have an impact on and become reality. Maddy states that making jokes about the state prison and mental hospital located near her hometown is "like making jokes about Death" (Oates, *Foxfire*, 133). Atwood, French, Oates, and Piercy do make jokes about death — and they make readers laugh. They challenge and topple expectations about "the joke about death" genre. And, when doing so, they challenge and topple expectations about the "women's proper role" genre. The authors portray women nurturing each other instead of their husbands and families. Maddy describes how words spoken in court "got transcribed and made real" (133). The same can hold true for the thoughts transcribed into the words which comprise 1990s feminist novels. These novels, texts which merge characteristics of feminist science fiction with feminist realistic literature, portray possible realities. Victimized women who form groups can become powerful. Girl gangs are at once utopian and real.

Both the female and male authors I discuss, as I have argued, present the self as a widening gyre. This expansion, however, takes a different form in respect to women's and men's choices about how to portray multiple versions of the same self. The male authors describe divided single selves; the female authors describe female individuals joining with other women. The authors, by creating counterselves for their protagonists, take steps toward re-creating stereotypical feminine and masculine roles. Although their female characters remain nurturers, they nurture each other. Although their male characters remain solitary heroes lighting out to the territories, the territories have become their own identities. These heroes, like the cowboy whose horse serves as his most intimate confidant, are still not engaging in dialogues with women. (As I have stressed, for example, Shelly Barth does not describe herself in *Once upon a Time.*) The women write about groups of women; the men write about themselves.

Barth describes *Once* as "a memoir bottled in a novel" (Barth reading). Although this description mixes the categories "memoir" and "novel," the resulting hybrid text is self-contained. The male message in a bottle is encased within a phallic structure and shielded from feminine fluid water. But if the female and male protagonists remain more concerned with themselves than with each other, they are, at least, engaged in the same activity: they transcend categories. The memories, confession, and floating opera that Updike, Roth, and Barth respectively create merge fact and fiction. In Barth's words, "the categories are less important than the result" (Barth reading). But the result signals that American men of letters flow in diverse ways. Mark Twain's Mississippi River, a fixed definition, a body of water that travels in one direction (from source to mouth), has given way to Barth's tidewater, a body of water that lacks a single direction, that ebbs and flows, that is no fixed definition. When the tidewater replaces the Mississippi, the bestial mouth — the source of water moving as a fixed definition — is shut. Perhaps, in the future, women and men will form a tributary together, flow together into Salman Rushdie's "ocean of stories." Women and men could then sing together in a floating opera of shared stories about equality. After all, like feminists who wear overalls, people heard only by like-minded people are obsolete.

Women and men will benefit from using their mouths to sing together in the floating opera which is civilized discourse and interaction. Toward this end, the seven authors I discuss portray women and men attempting to achieve the inception of coevolution, attempting to change from beasts into humans. John Cairns, Jr., adds that this attempt is furthered by the "increasing environmental literacy [which] may also affect human behavior" (23). The seven authors create texts of environmental literacy in regard to changing men's and women's predator / prey relationship. If the girl gangs and male clones fail to embrace each other, the resulting hostile coevolution may give rise to sharing the planet with "domesticated species and a few other extremely tolerant and persistent species that have defied human management efforts, i.e., pests" (Cairns, 26).

As I have indicated, the problem is that many women defy patriarchal management efforts; patriarchy sees these women as pests. "Any new pest . . . could cause severe fluctuation in food crop yields or pest control" (Cairns, 26). To control the new pests — in literature, popular culture, and life — women and men sometimes use their mouths to ingest each other. The seven authors, to approach this problem, emphasize the civilized rather than the bestial mouth. If their version of environmental literacy fails to foster change, if hostile coevolution continues to occur, instead of people, "little more than weeds, flies, cockroaches and starlings may be left" (Cairns, 12). When benign coevolution takes place, heterosexuals will live as contented versions of Updike's *Couples*.

Hans Thoma, The Guards in Front of the Love Garden, *1890. Kupferstichkabinett
—Sammlung der Zeichnungen und Druckgraphik—Staaliche Museen zu Berlin,
Preussischer Kulturbesitz, Nationalgalerie. Kat./Inv.-Nr. A III 403, Fotoarchiv: 25511.*

II public displays

sexed spectacles

4 NIGHT WATCH IN AMSTERDAM'S RED LIGHT DISTRICT

Prostitutes / Dutch Windows / Utopian and Dystopian Gazes

Feminist film theorists such as Laura Mulvey and Mary Ann Doane and linguist Deborah Tannen (in her description of "marking") firmly establish that the patriarchal gaze transforms every woman into the same entity: object. I contribute to this discussion by asserting that the gaze possesses both utopian and dystopian characteristics. I take a cultural studies approach to describe the pervasive dystopian gaze in terms of viewing Amsterdam prostitutes (the women in windows). And I locate the yet to be established alternative utopian gaze on canvases created by Claes Oldenburg and Bill Copley. My argument — in addition to including Doane, Mulvey, and Tannen — is informed by sociologist Hernán Vera's "On Dutch Windows," an analysis of cultural codes regarding looking into and out of large, uncovered Dutch windows. This chapter, then, focuses upon bringing feminist and utopian / dystopian studies discourse to bear upon framed, or enclosed, interior spaces.

According to Vera, looking is an informational game which reflects Dutch conceptions of privacy: "the Dutch window . . . is a statement on the Dutch sense of the boundary between public and private. . . . Capitalism brought a dramatic change in existing notions of the private and the public, of what is individual and what is communal. Could the windows offending my learned notions of privacy be traced back to the same 'cultural force' that resulted in the invention of capitalism?" (Vera, 217). My first section applies Vera's ideas about Dutch windows to the Amsterdam Red Light District's women in windows. The prostitute, the commodified woman on view, transgresses Dutch window culture games regarding public and private, individual and communal. Since Dutch rules regarding looking into uncovered windows are not applicable to women in windows, these women become commodities violated by the eyes of all observers; they are raped by a dystopian gaze. In the second section, I explain how paintings housed in Amsterdam's Stedelijk Museum — Bill Copley's *Untitled* (1974) and *I Am Curious . . .* (1973) and Claes Oldenburg's *Sketch of a 3-Way Plug* (1965) — depict alternative looks, utopian views of nonsexist gazing.

DYSTOPIAN GAZES: FRAMED FEMALE OBJECTS

All women are framed (betrayed as well as enclosed) by the patriarchal gaze. The Amsterdam prostitute who is literally framed by her window merely exaggerates the condition of Everywoman. She underscores the point that the "subjectivity assigned to femininity within patriarchal systems is inevitably bound up with the structure of the look and the localization of the eye as authority. . . . [T]he woman's experience of subjugation to the ever-present eye of the other comes back to haunt her. . . . The dilemma of difference is assigned to the woman by a patriarchal system — it is a double bind which serves to 'keep her in her place'" (Doane, Mellencamp, and Williams, 14). In the presence of the male gaze, all women converge. All women become one framed entity whose place is within the frame the male eye establishes. Since the Amsterdam prostitute exaggerates the visual objectification Everywoman suffers, enabling us better to see Everywoman's visual objectification, it is important to understand her subjugation.

Vera, however, does not apply his analysis of Dutch "window culture" to Amsterdam Red Light District prostitutes. In other words, he does not explain what the women in windows mean. My visit to the district, accompanied by American men who were my fellow participants at an international literature and psychology conference, clarified this meaning for me. These male colleagues very obviously desired to look at the women — and they enjoyed doing so. They got something (a chance to commodify the female body, an opportunity to look and to satisfy their curiosity) for nothing. While the men's reaction is predictable, my own response surprised me. I was curious too.

Taking advantage of the jarring and rare opportunity directly to stare at scantily clad women, I looked at the prostitutes dead on. My female gaze did not differ from the men's looking; it did not conform to the "split" Laura Mulvey describes: "[I]n a world ordered by sexual imbalance, pleasure in looking has been split between active/male and passive/female. The determining male gaze projects its phantasy on to the female figure which is styled accordingly" (Mulvey, 11). My pleasure in regard to an unusual opportunity to stare directly at a woman is as active as the men's. I looked at the woman with a determining male gaze; I noticed the degree to which her body conformed to male beauty standards. Like the men, I manifested a voyeuristic scopophilic look. Both the men's looking and my own involved the power to stare, not the power to experience sexual gratification. We transgressed cultural codes involving looking, not sexuality. Hence, multitudinous gazes dehumanize prostitutes in Dutch windows more than individual paying customers do. This is especially true in light of social codes which apply to Dutch window culture. As Vera explains, "I was taught by several [Dutch] friends that the observation of interiors should be done only in the most tactful ways. . . . By no means should one stand squarely in front of the window. In trying to do so, I alarmed and embarrassed my walking companions" (Vera, 223).

In Holland, standing squarely in front of windows to stare at prostitutes is a greater taboo than paying for sexual acts. For the Dutch, this direct looking is transgressive to the extent of becoming culturally unbearable: "An American visiting professor of social psychology at Groningen had assigned his students the field experiment of standing squarely in front of windows. The students refused" (Vera, 233). The Red Light District offers a looking orgy for all "comers." Even though prohibitions against very obviously looking into windows inhibit Americans as well as the Dutch (albeit to a much lesser extent), the male conferees and I indulged. Like these men, I wanted to experience the newness of directly staring at someone standing squarely in front of me.

My gaze, in a country where windows imbue people with humanity, dehumanizes the prostitutes positioned behind windows. Vera explains that decorating Dutch household windows with such items as curtains, plants, and handicrafts "gives the occupants of a house an opportunity for individual and familial self-expression" (Vera, 216). Red Light District windows, in contrast, "are seldom decorated and are kept closed except when their proprietor is open for business" (Vera, 219). The lack of Red Light District window ornamentation signals that prostitutes are deprived of individual and familial self-expression. The prostitute herself becomes a dehumanized window ornament — a statuette, a handicraft, a poster of patriarchy representing Woman as sexual commodity. Closed, curtained Red Light District windows contrast sharply with the see-through windows so integral to Dutch culture. The closed window, like the Nazi appropriation of the yellow star of David, is a sign which places people outside usual social codes. The curtained window marks the prostitute. When the curtains are open, her window becomes a billboard which proclaims the openness of her orifices to all who meet her price.

The Amsterdam prostitute who is "open for business" is no sexual slave. Although her job is very disagreeable, it is regulated by law. (Her lot is better than that of her American counterparts.) I argue that the prostitute — like all women — is enslaved by the patriarchal gaze's ability to turn women into texts: signs about degrees of sexual availability that gazers read. Deborah Tannen calls this particular sexual semiotics "marking" and argues that no woman can be unmarked:

> The term "marked" is a staple of linguistic theory. It refers to the way language alters the base meaning of a word by adding a linguistic particle that has no meaning on its own. The unmarked form of a word carries the meaning that goes without saying — what you think of when you're not thinking anything special. . . . The unmarked forms of most English words also convey "male." Being male is the unmarked case. . . . Each woman at the conference had to make decisions about hair, clothing, makeup and accessories and each decision carried meaning. Every style available to us was marked. . . . Men can choose styles that are marked, but they don't have to. . . . Unlike the women they [men] had the option of being unmarked. . . . I asked myself what style we women could have adopted that would have been unmarked, like the men's. The answer was none. There is no unmarked woman. . . . [W]e women didn't have the freedom to be unmarked that the men sitting next to us had. Some days you just want to get dressed and go about your business. But if you're a woman, you can't, because there is no unmarked woman. (18, 52, 54)

The Amsterdam prostitute, then, merely underscores women's daily victimization. She is an exaggeratedly marked woman, an extreme indicator of the fact that women cannot escape from the patriarchal gaze and its mark. I have given much thought to my unprecedented direct staring, my act of dehumanizing the prostitutes. Men, in contrast, routinely stare unabashedly at women.

As I write while seated in the Stedelijk Museum Cafe, a man is staring at my breasts. His gaze debases me. Such debasement is relative. I am less diminished than prostitutes behind windows. I would, however, be less sexually marked if, instead of a T-shirt, I wore business attire (a jacket, for example). My point is that all women are always more or less debased by the patriarchal gaze; all women are analogous to prostitutes behind windows. Patriarchal gazes are communication games which deny power to women; the night watch in Amsterdam's Red Light District permeates all public spaces. Patriarchal gazes eradicate the dividing line between women's public and private territory. (A man's gaze transformed me, a scholar writing in a public place, into a sexual object appropriately located in a bedroom.) Tannen says all women are marked; I say all women who appear in public stand in Red Light District windows.

"These communication games and the way their rules are enforced must be understood as a method of rebuilding public tolerance of the private realm and private acceptance of the public domain. In this context, the Dutch window can be understood to achieve its sensory qualities by constituting the dividing line between two types of territory" (Vera, 224). The sexual stare men usually direct at women, like the exaggerated gazing which occurs in the Red Light District, relegates a woman's public domain to the private realm. The male gaze is a socially acceptable communicative rule which deprives women of power — turns their public presence into private sexual marking by blurring distinctions between the appropriately public and appropriately private. In terms of this blurring, Red Light District windows are not Dutch windows; they are exceptions to the looking rules that Vera describes.

Vera states that "in the [Dutch] occupied house, this opening [the window] becomes a sort of blank canvas for self and familial expression. This expression requires a large amount of care and energy to keep the glass spotless, the plants trimmed and watered, the curtains washed, the decorative objects dusted" (Vera, 231). The women in Red Light District windows function as blank canvases for paid sexual expression and for the patriarchal gaze running rampant. Like the prostitute's vagina, the opening which is her window also satisfies. Prostitutes, and all women, satisfy the male eye and are degraded by the male eye. Prostitutes, and all women, are slaves who serve the patriarchal gaze. According to a metamorphosis that communicative rules governing the femininity game make possible, all people who possess vaginas can be changed into blank selves, blank canvases for men's lascivious looking. These rules stipulate that the male gaze places women's power in jeopardy. The price is always right for men. Gazing is always free of charge for men — and always extracts a large toll from women in regard to power and public self-expression.

Utopian gazing can arise from returning frames to their proper place: located around material art objects, not around living female sex objects. The framed / betrayed woman must be unframed, seen differently. In other words, there is a need to wrench "the 'look'. . . from . . . previous structures. And chief among these goals must be that of seeing difference differently, re-vising the old apprehension of sexual difference and making it possible to multiply differences, to move away from homogeneity, away from the same" (Doane, Mellencamp, and Williams, 14–15). Such goals are attainable. Although women are always marked (are always, as I have mentioned, a blank canvas for male sexual self-expression), it is nonetheless possible to create new views, to re-see difference. Bill Copley's *Untitled* and *I Am Curious . . .* depict these new views. Copley pictures nonsexist looking — utopian alternatives to the patriarchal gaze.

The woman in *Untitled* is attired in a manner appropriate for an Amsterdam prostitute. Her anal and vaginal orifices are not covered. Although these orifices are open to penile penetration, they are not visible; hence, the male gaze cannot appropriate them. Her legs engulfed in gartered stockings are as mechanical as the legs which support the camera Copley paints. Instead of protecting her from the male gaze, the stockings satisfy it. Power, however, can be attributed to the purple cloth covering her head. Even though obliterating a woman's head is a common pornographic trope, the cloth shields her head from the male gaze.

This woman, no woman in purdah, might be looking into the camera while contemplating alternatives to patriarchal gazes. Her eye attached to the camera can picture (i.e., record) those gazes. Her hands control the phallic silver camera lever attached to the camera stand; she can use her hands to satisfy her own artistic desires. She is no prostitute who must use her hands to satisfy men. She controls a means of production to manipulate new, nonsexist gazes. This Everywoman marked as the object of the male gaze can think of and picture alternatives to enslavement manifested via this pervasive gaze. She signals that women can themselves gaze and record their new views—that the metaphorical garters holding up the foundations of patriarchal looking rules can become unfastened. Perhaps the squares which form the background of Copley's painting represent the constructed building blocks of society. Perhaps the photo the woman is taking is an art form which will stimulate new views and new social constructions. Since *Untitled* is located in a public Dutch museum—not behind a Dutch private home's window — I can stare at it directly and think so.

Bill Copley, Untitled, *1974. Stedelijk Museum, Amsterdam.*

I can also apply Doane's ideas about the relationship of the gaze and the camera to Copley's *Untitled*. Doane explains that the camera controls the gaze: "The gaze . . . is the possession of the camera, and through identification with that camera, the spectating subject. Hence, it is not at all surprising that this gaze should be further characterized . . . as precisely controlled in the service of voyeurism and fetishism — its subject male, its object female" (Doane, *Femmes Fatales*, 82). Copley's painting challenges this statement: it shows the gaze controlled by a female photographer, attired in the service of voyeurism and fetishism, positioned to determine the gazing camera's subject.

Doane seems to explain why the woman photographer's covered head implies power: the "gaze situated outside, the subject necessarily becomes a part of the picture, assimilated by its own surroundings. Differentiation is lost and, with it, subjectivity as a category" (Doane, *Femmes Fatales*, 84). The female photographer's gaze is situated inside, under the cloth. Her gaze is not a part of the picture and is assimilated neither by the surroundings in the picture nor by the eye of the viewer. Her differentiation from the category subject of the male gaze is, thus, retained. However, women who extensively cover their bodies to try not to become further disempowered do not, obviously, supply a solution that I advocate.

Copley addresses the impossibility of woman appearing outside the male gaze's control as well as the fact that obliterating opportunities to see women, rendering women invisible, constitutes a problem. Copley, in other words, pictures Doane's notion that from "the point of view of apparatus theory . . . the subject is both there and not there, maintained and annihilated. There is a certain tension between the positioning of the subject as point, control, unity . . . and the temptation of space, of losing oneself in a process of de-individualization and the corresponding annihilation of subjectivity" (Doane, *Femmes Fatales*, 85–86). The female photographer is both present and absent. She is a controller of the gaze who is lost in the temptation to try to depict utopian, nonpatriarchal viewing space.

Copley's painting *I Am Curious . . .* eliminates all gender markers — including the femme fatale, who "is not the subject of feminism but a symptom of male fears about feminism" (Doane, *Femmes Fatales*, 2–3). *I Am Curious . . .* at once eliminates this symptom and announces that as "soon as the relation between vision and knowledge becomes unstable or deceptive, the potential for a disruption of the given sexual logic appears" (Doane, *Femmes Fatales*, 14). By disrupting the relation between vision and seeing gender markers, Copley creates space for alternative sexual looking

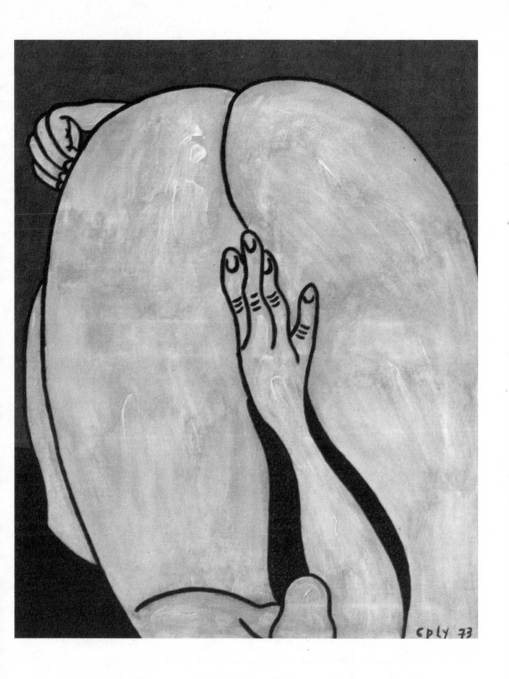

Bill Copley, I Am Curious . . . , *1973. Stedelijk Museum, Amsterdam.*

rules. He eradicates the means of production for the visual truth about women that Doane describes: "Sexuality becomes the site of questions about what can and cannot be known. . . . Both cinematic and theoretical claims to truth about women rely to a striking extent on judgments about vision and its stability or instability" (1). Unmarked (or unstable) sexuality leads to new questions, new ways to know about women, new truths about women.

I Am Curious . . . depicts the anti-*Femmes Fatales*: sex devoid of any contrivances (such as garter belts) worn to attract the male gaze. It is not clear whether or not the picture portrays two sexual partners or one person touching her / himself. The object placed in the bottom middle of the canvas could represent either a solitary person's foot or a sexual partner's penis. *I Am Curious . . .* defies portraying sexuality in terms of power and gender roles. It causes the male gaze to become impotent. The anus, an organ identical in both sexes, cannot be seen. Copley nullifies the male gaze — causes it to lose power when a human body's sex cannot immediately be discerned. The finger probes the inner space of the anus, a hidden place of sameness in both sexes. The patriarchal gaze cannot penetrate the anus, Copley's canvas suggests. *I Am Curious . . .* offers a new utopian, nonsexist view which the photographer in *Untitled* could appropriately picture. Although such new views are needed vis-à-vis looking games, eradicating the patriarchal gaze's control over women is as unlikely as Dutch people electing to cover their windows to end the looking which controls community.

"Dutch windows call our attention to the need of conceiving material culture in terms of the purposive acts we accomplish by adapting objects to our practical and expressive human needs" (Vera, 232). Analyzing the Red Light District windows in terms of his insights about domestic Dutch windows, and applying Copley's work to this analysis, underscores that women are not objects adapted to meeting men's practical and expressive sexual needs. Claes Oldenburg's *Sketch of a 3-Way Plug* functions in kind.

To my eye, the two protrusions located at the bottom of Oldenburg's canvas resemble penises; the four black lines representing sockets resemble vaginal openings. (This interpretation was generated while I attended the aforementioned literature and psychology conference.) *Sketch* attributes power to women and, in the manner of Copley's work, suggests new views. The suggested socket openings are, like Dutch windows and prostitutes in windows, forever open to the eyes of observers. But, although observers are free to look at the lines / sockets, unlike the prostitute's customer, the penis / prongs (frozen on the canvas) cannot penetrate these openings, vio-

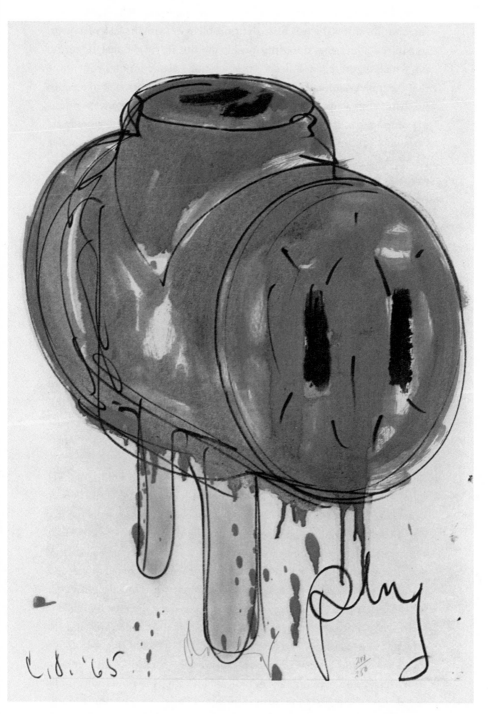

Claes Oldenburg, Sketch of a 3-way Plug, *1965. Stedelijk Museum, Amsterdam.*

lating the space within them. The painted immobile penis which never ventures within solves the psychoanalytic problem of woman's lack of a penis.

Mulvey comments upon this problem: "But in psychoanalytic terms, the female figure poses a deeper problem. She also connotes something that the look continually circles around but disavows: her lack of a penis, implying a threat of castration and hence unpleasure. Ultimately, the meaning of woman is sexual difference, the absence of the penis as visually ascertainable, the material evidence on which is based the castration complex essential for the organization of entrance to the symbolic order and the law of the father. Thus the woman as icon, displayed for the gaze and enjoyment of men, the active controllers of the look" (13). Oldenburg's depiction of nonpenetration removes woman from icon status. The viewer of his vision of castration sees the look lose its power.

The space located between the prongs and the slits is a location of new meaning for woman to be understood as something other than an object. The penis / prongs hang like udders; hence, they are feminized. The female opening is positioned on top of these feminized penises — and the vaginas outnumber the penises. "Plug" is marked on the picture; "sex object" is marked on all women. Oldenburg, like the photographer Copley paints, suggests a new utopian picture, new cultural games / codes in regard to men viewing women. This new picture is an unseen opening. Like Copley's images of the photographer's hidden head and the nonvisible anus, this opening is hidden from gazers. It is the impossible, nonexistent, unmarked female — a third kind: the female outside the patriarchal gaze. It is a new genre.

What would a close encounter with this unseen third kind look like? I am curious. I think the implied unmarked female suggests the deconstructed patriarchal gaze, utopian looking which does not obstruct the free flow of female fluidity. This new utopian vision unplugs the system in which patriarchy determines women's identity. It ends the pervasive social practice in which only patriarchy has the proper currency to define real and imagined sexual exchanges between women and men. This suggestion has yet to be pictured. Oldenburg is unable to let us see it directly.

In the manner of staring at Red Light District prostitutes, we can look directly at the paintings I discuss and imagine short-circuiting patriarchal social games and gazes. The paintings, after all, share much in common with Mulvey's observations about radical film's ability to undermine traditional views: "The first blow against the monolithic accumulation of traditional film conventions (already undertaken by radical film-makers) is to free the look of the camera into its materiality in time and space and the look of the audience into dialectics, passionate detachment. There is no doubt that this destroys the satisfaction, pleasure and privilege of the 'invisible guest,' and highlights how film has depended on voyeuristic active / passive mechanisms" (18). Two male artists paint the first blow against the monolithic male gaze's desire to see the painted and framed woman. They imagine a utopian space in which women, in time, will be free from dystopian voyeuristic looks. They imagine toppling the male watch tower which imprisons Everywoman in the guise of whore.

5

LOS YORK / NEW ANGELES
"New York, New York, a Helluva Town" Sings
"I Wish They All Could Be California Girls"

What does this chapter's title mean? I approach the question by citing another question: Tobin Siebers, in the introduction to his critical anthology *Heteropia: Postmodern Utopia and the Body Politic*, asks, "What does postmodernism want?" His answer (which figures in my introduction): postmodernism has "the desire to put together things that do not belong together" (Siebers, 4). This chapter desires the same for itself. Hence, its focus upon connections and disconnections between New York and Los Angeles includes these disparate entities: suburbia, urban suburbia, the Fifth Avenue Warner Brothers Studio Store, the Guggenheim Museum, Broadway theater, Hollywood movies and sitcoms, and the exodus from Los Angeles.

How do the chapter's disparate subjects cohere? Edward Soja says that "everything seems to come together in Los Angeles" (248). As for this chapter, in the end, everything seems to come together in Johannesburg. To reach this end, I begin by discussing suburbia as a dystopic landscape in which everything seems not to come together.

AMERICA AS HOMODYSTOPIA

James Howard Kunstler's *The Geography of Nowhere: The Rise and Decline of America's Man-made Landscape* explains why the American landscape is constructed in extreme opposition to Sieber's notion of postmodern desire. Kunstler deplores suburbia's "separation of uses" (117), in which individuals move between boxes — from television set, to garage door, to car. While Siebers views postmodern desire as "the romance of community" (8), Kunstler stresses that the American landscape epitomizes a loss of community in which people — and even buildings — are disconnected (266). Public forays usually consist of "physical discontinuity" (Kunstler,

148) in which people, alone in their cars, drive by parking lots which separate Holiday Inns from Pizza Huts.

My parents' response to Gulf Boulevard, the wide multilane street located in front of their Madeira Beach, Florida, condo, exemplifies Kunstler's argument that the American landscape, which is made for cars rather than for people, obliterates community by separating people from public space — hence, retarding the merging of the disparate. Gulf Boulevard stands between my parents' residence along the beach front and a commercial strip. Afraid to cope with the traffic on foot, they use their car to cross Gulf Boulevard. Since my mother does not drive, she must depend upon my father to ferry her to the stores located directly across the boulevard. My parents, usually reasonable people, routinely enter their car, drive across the street, shop, and drive back across the street. (Here I must interrupt my critical voice to allow a voice from another genre, my autobiographical fiction, to slip into this text. When I visit my parents, they say, "Marleen, don't cross the street." Telling a woman in her forties that she is not allowed to cross the street is extreme — even for a Jewish family. However, in light of the real danger Gulf Boulevard presents to pedestrians, I must admit that my parents' concern and response is justified.) Kunstler's version of my anecdote: "[W]e have lost our knowledge of how physically to connect things in our everyday world, except by car and telephone. . . . Living in places where nothing is connected properly, we have forgotten that connections are important" (246). Kunstler's "tyranny of the car" (82) is an evil American empire which crashes into Siebers' "romance of community." Postmodern America houses its citizens and commerce within modern architecture dedicated to "sweeping away . . . all romantic impulses, and to jamming all human aspiration into a plain box" (Kunstler, 67). The American geography of nowhere is no utopia.

Contemporary American space is a tension, a contradiction between architectural disconnection and a postmodern utopian harmony uniting disparate elements. Unable to escape from failed modern architecture, Americans express a postmodern desire to connect the different via their dissatisfaction with lack of community, isolation, and the deified car. We use cars to vote with our feet: hating where we live, we move to another place — and we are unable to love the new location, which resembles the place we sought to escape. Kunstler says that "we choose to live in Noplace" (173). American modernism's worship of technology and suburban individual isolation is a failed effort to achieve utopia.

Siebers' view of the relation between postmodernism and utopia indicates that Americans who desire to be elsewhere than within their pervasive homogeneous suburban landscapes are postmodern and utopian. He explains that utopianism "is not about being 'no where'; it is about desiring to be elsewhere . . . it yearns for happiness but only because it is so unhappy with the existing world. . . . Postmodernists, then, are utopian . . . because they know they want something else" (Siebers, 3). American utopia is not the geography of nowhere, the suburbia that is almost identical from Long Beach, New York, to Long Beach, California. American utopianism is about being elsewhere than within the isolating American suburban terrain. Unhappy within their environments, Americans yearn for somewhere else, for an elsewhere which does not exist in American reality. Hence, we find our something else within fantasy—what America does best, America's most successful export. We escape by watching television, going to movies, and driving to Disney World.

We who inhabit the antithesis of postmodern utopia escape by seeking fantasy versions of postmodern utopia, by creating Disney Main Street USA community and Epcot Center heterogeneity. Community and heterogeneity are the key elements of Siebers' postmodern vision of utopia, his version of the term "heterotopia." Siebers describes heterogeneity as "the dominant characteristic of postmodern utopian thinking. . . . Postmodernists . . . try to include diversity and chaos in their planning, having learned from the failures of modernism that they cannot be eliminated from any model" (20, 27). The American landscape is a model for the failure of modernism.

Americans lack an immediate real-world escape from suburban environments dedicated to excluding diversity and chaos, dedicated to eradicating the heterotopian "desire to assemble people and things that do not normally go together" (Siebers, 25). (As my discussions of New York and Los Angeles below indicate, urban America is very suburban. Suburbia even infiltrates Manhattan.) Juxtaposing Siebers and Kunstler, two thinkers who would not normally be placed together, leads to characterizing the American landscape as what I call a homodystopia — a homogeneous suburbia which breeds dissatisfaction. I then go on to read Kunstler closely with an eye toward describing homodystopia as endlessly absorbing individual energy and public resources.

Kunstler cites Lewis Mumford's comment about post–World War II development: "'the end product is an encapsulated life, spent more and more either in a motor car or within the cabin of darkness before a television set.'

The whole wicked, sprawling, megalopolitan mess, he gloomily predicted, would completely demoralize mankind and lead to nuclear holocaust" (10). Individuals pulled within, encapsulated inside cars and in front of television sets, could cause social explosion. Teenagers below driving age who gather "in furtive little holes — bedrooms and basements" (Kunstler, 14) are prone to such potential explosion. Eventually, with drivers' licenses in hand, these young people can try to counter the "vacuum at the center of American life" by venturing out to "a bunch of concrete and glass boxes set among parking lots" (Kunstler, 119, 118). Americans encounter multitudinous holes, both Mumford's "cabin of darkness" and parking lot and strip mall clones. Kunstler calls one of these clones "a block-long hole in the pattern of downtown Saratoga, a big noplace" (140). America as homodystopia is an incessantly repeated big noplace.

Christopher Alexander, the University of California, Berkeley architect who thought that the elements of the architectural landscape (streets, buildings, etc.) had to be viewed as parts of connecting relationships (rather than as separate objects), offered an alternative to the suburban hole as vacuum which pulls America into dystopia — or toward Mumford's nuclear explosion. He and his followers believed that all aspects of the architectural landscape should be viewed as "connecting relationships" (quoted in Kunstler, 249). Alexander, then, advocated heterotopia, connections between the different. He wanted house fronts to be postmodern heterotopian holes — "not just a wall with holes in it, but . . . a connection between the house and the street" (Kunstler, 249–250). Alexander's ideas about connection, of course, did not prevail. The suburban house's front window is usually a homodystopian hole which fails to relate to the street. What I call a homodystopian hole is Kunstler's hole in the wall: "By viewing a window as an isolated *thing* we turned it into a mere hole in the wall. . . . This was precisely why the windows on suburban houses were so boring and banal, why many office buildings seemed to have no windows at all — why, in short, we live surrounded by failed building relationships" (250). I point out below that the absence of holes in walls shows that we live surrounded by failed social relationships.

The boring or absent architectural hole can also be understood as a failed linguistic relationship rather analogous to Betty Friedan's definition of sexism as the problem which has no name. People do not know how to name — or even how to recognize — the problem that is suburbia. Kunstler describes this problem as a "deficit" (245), a word most people would not associate with suburbia. When linked to suburbia, this word rings hollow, becoming an empty linguistic space. Kunstler's friends are among those who do not connect "suburbia" with "deficit." They respond to his ideas as if they are unearthly, the stuff of science fiction: "they say, 'Huh . . . ?' as though I were describing life on another planet" (Kunstler, 274; ellipsis in original). They fail to see that, like astronauts, suburbanites are encapsulated. Space vehicles explode. As Los Angeles and New York riot victims know, so do separate and unequal living spaces.

Slums in these cities exploded because they are situated outside supposed suburban utopia. All American neighborhoods, however, are located outside utopia. The promise that industry and technology would bring utopia to America in the twentieth century is a lie (Kunstler, 60). What arrived with the mid-twentieth century was homodystopia, a monocultural, homogeneous approach to housing, transportation, and farming which is out of sync with late-twentieth-century multiculturalism and heterogeneity. Instead of utopia, suburbia and cars arrived. While Robert Moses' colleagues defined mass transit as "a bottomless pit" (Kunstler, 110), the true bottomless pits are the houses and cars that absorb human and natural resources. Ditto for corporations which (in the manner of Wal-Mart) absorb local economies. No utopia, the suburban house resembles a garage surrounded by a parking lot: "garages have moved to the front of the house in America. . . . Saratoga, like virtually every other town in America, has become one big automobile storage depot that incidentally contains other things" (Kunstler, 135). During the fifties, science fiction films presented monsters emanating from black lagoons to eat, for example, Cleveland. The real monster is suburban Cleveland — the house as garage, the neighborhood as parking lot, the Burger King that ate America.

This monster can be stopped in its suburban tracts. Doing so requires transforming homodystopia into heterotopia, creating landscapes which combine differences. Kunstler echoes Siebers when he views a town as "a living organism composed of different parts that work together to make the whole greater than the sum of its parts — that is, a community . . . [which is] a living organism based on a web of interdependencies . . . connectedness" (Kunstler, 147, 186). Heterogeneous webs are alternatives to homogeneous enclaves. How to remove Cleveland's suburbs from the mouth of the devouring monstrous Burger King? How to shut this particular bestial mouth? The answer is Cleveland itself — the urban culture of the city. It is necessary to desist from venerating suburban monoculture built in opposition to urban heterogeneity. (It is necessary to stop locating mall stores and malls in Manhattan.)

Kunstler describes the difference between the urban and the suburban: "the motive force behind suburbia has been the exaltation of privacy and the elimination of the public realm. Where city life optimizes the possibility of contact between people, and especially different kinds of people, the suburb strives to eliminate precisely that kind of human contact. And so my argument throughout this book has been that the city in some form, and at some scale, is necessary" (189). While (as I explain below) Los Angeles' new downtown functions as a suburb, popular culture echoes Kunstler when the cast of *On the Town* sings, "New York, New York, a helluva town, the Bronx is up but the Battery's down, and people ride in a hole in the ground." The New York subway — a whole composed of the originally differing BMT, IND, and IRT lines — encapsulates the city's diversity and, hence, is a heterotopian enclosed space. Many of my fellow New Yorkers would respond to positioning the subway as a utopian solution to suburban uniformity by echoing the "huh" Kunstler's friends expressed. Regardless, I'll take Manhattan.[1]

THE KITSCH MONSTER THREATENS TO EAT MANHATTAN OR SUPERMAN DOES NOT UPLIFT FRANK LLOYD WRIGHT

"I'll take Manhattan" articulates the agenda of the commercial monoculture, the kitsch which pervades America. Manhattan, whose land is too expensive to turn into vast parking lots, stands (despite some inroads) as a fortress guarding against homodystopic suburban spread and epitomizes chaos and diversity. Part grid, part park, part narrow colonial street, part highway, bisected by grid-defying Broadway, bounded by flowing water and the sky's the limit, even Manhattan is not completely impervious to invading homodystopia. Corporate kitsch is ensconcing itself there. Although Manhattan will never resemble Levittown, Disney is on Broadway and Daffy Duck is on Fifth Avenue. Herbert Muschamp describes Daffy's residence, the Warner Brothers Store, in his *New York Times* piece "On West 57th, a Confederacy of Kitsch." He emphasizes the rivalry between New York and Los Angeles: "They [Porky Pig and the Ghostbusters' Ectomobile] belong, in short, in Los Angeles, or at least in a New York chauvinist's patronizing view of that capital of glitz. And Los Angeles, in fact, is the overarching theme to which 57th Street's theme establishments ultimately refer. . . . Urban rivalry is the subtext here: the fear that Los Angeles has overtaken New York as a cultural center, that Gotham is turning into little more than a trading post for Hollywood product. Who wants to see Manhattan . . . replaced with an extension of Sunset Strip? Now Manhattan is at risk of being L.A.'d" (Muschamp, 4). Manhattan resident Eileen Aubl responds to Muschamp in her *Times* letter about corporate misuse of public space and pervasive homogenization: "I wonder when we are going to appoint someone to really watch the store on builders who get tax abatements for including public spaces and who then use them commercially. . . . How are we New Yorkers going to hold on to what we consider sacred when the whole country, the world in fact, is living kitsch culture? I wish some social historian would look at the whole picture and educate the world to appreciate gracious being, and fast, before all that's left on the shelves is sliced white bread" (27). Here I look at a small part of the picture, the corporate kitsch profane invading sacred midtown Manhattan. Toward this end, I offer a reading of the Fifth Avenue Warner Brothers Store.

This store cross-dresses: the pervasive "WB" logo and characters are positioned to make customers feel as if they are somewhere other than within a store. The Warner Brothers Store presents itself as a museum, a home — or even a country. Reverential objects that no ordinary store contains generate a museum aura: an animation learning center, a pictorial time line called "Warner Bros. Animation History 1930–1993," and iconic pictures of directors (Tex Avery and Chuck Jones) and a voice characterization specialist (Mel Blanc). When the cartoon characters appear in famous paintings, they are positioned to transcend their popular culture status. Store walls exhibit Daffy Duck impersonating Mona Lisa (Mona Quack?) and the figure in *The Scream*, Wiley Coyote portraying Grandma Moses, and Daffy and Bugs Bunny appearing as Picasso creations. When these characters (playing themselves) are presented as framed high art works, usual distinctions between education and commercialism, and high and low culture, are eradicated. The store's huge film screens and oversized television which show the cartoons signal that its education center is really an exaggerated suburban TV room. Visitors intimidated by the store's pseudo-museum and educational aura can feel right at home sitting on a giant living room chair while watching the cartoon characters on an enormous television screen.

In the movies, the Muppets take Manhattan. In the Warner Brothers Store, Daffy and his fellows take the world. Pictures portray Bugs Bunny standing on London Bridge; Tweety, Sylvester, and Taz appear in front of the Kremlin. The store presents itself as a country. Store personnel (called "sales associates"), attired in black uniforms emblazoned with a WB crest, mimic bureaucrats. They are protected by the WB country's army — the security officers armed with walkie-talkies who circumnavigate the store's interior and street front. The cartoon characters are as pervasive in the store as Chairman Mao's visage once was in China. Their faces appear on all the merchandise; their voices resound. Like so many pyramids, their large plastic replicas loom above customers. All of this hype masks the expected distinction between the work of making money and the play of making fantasy. In the electric atmosphere that fantasy generates, electricity itself seems to be eradicated: a plastic Superman appears to raise and lower the store's elevator. The professional greeter standing at the door like the gatekeeper of Oz signals that the Warner Brothers Store is a fantasy world. Manhattan is not located within, thank you.

The same cannot be said for patriarchy. The enshrined animators and directors are all male. While Disney created Minnie Mouse and Daisy Duck, no females accompany Bugs and Daffy. Pepe Le Peu, the French skunk who — like *Star Trek*'s Captain Picard — is something Other than an all-American he-man, incessantly searches for a mate. The WB attitude seems to be that relationships with women stink. Further, in addition to female creators and characters, pigs are not welcome. While Bugs and Daffy appear everywhere, Porky Pig is noticeably absent within the store. Perhaps a fat, stuttering pig is not a kosher character. The WB male chauvinist pigs who exclude both their own pig and women allow no cognizance of political correctness and diversity to enter their world. The fact that Daffy is black is a ducked issue. Bugs the gray bunny (who is getting on in years) is not a member of the Gray Panthers. There is no indication that the Pink Panther could be gay.

Despite the emphasis upon demarcating the difference between the store's interior and Manhattan streets, violence is not excluded from within. Kunstler explains that a death theme is part of Disney's vision (219, 225–226). The same holds true for WB. Tweetie and Sylvester, Bugs and Elmer Fudd, and Coyote and Road Runner incessantly either hunt or are hunted. Since the quarry is never caught, WB as country engages in a forever war.

Like any sovereign state, WB casts itself as an imposing monumentality. Rather than a tawdry neon sign, the name "Warner Brothers Store" faces Fifth Avenue emblazoned in gold letters and encased within stone. Mimicking the dignity of the 42nd Street Library's lions, Daffy and Bugs stand at the store door like sentinels. The cartoon characters who grace the outside front and side street facades function as facades of importance. These characters are pictured playing parts which define the eight genres named and ensconced above the street etched in stone: sci-fi, action, suspense, musical, western, romance, mystery, drama. There is no genre fission here, no interaction between any of the stone squares, each alone representing one of the eight genres. However, genre fission does occur within each square, where, in Siebers' terms, things which are not expected to be placed together are placed together. The WB characters who scale walls separating high and low culture now move from animation to being positioned on a wall to represent popular culture itself — sci-fi: a gun-toting Marvin the Martian greets Daffy as he plants a flag on an alien planet; action: Road Runner chases the Coyote; suspense: onlookers wonder about Batman's adventure; musical: an operatic Elmer Fudd sports a Viking helmet; western: Bugs Bunny dressed as a cowboy encounters Yosemite Sam; romance: Pepe Le Peu kisses a cat; mystery: Porky Pig appears as Sherlock Holmes; drama: Sylvester threatens to ingest Tweety. The eight squares are signs signifying that — like world culture and high art — popular genres are synonymous with Warner Brothers. While Stalin and Hitler failed to take over the world, the same cannot be said for Bugs Bunny. Bugs has taken Manhattan — or, more specifically, Fifth Avenue at 57th Street.

Warner Brothers conquers by simultaneously presenting homogeneity and heterogeneity. In other words, WB at once is its own fantasy world and pervades the real world. WB characters are imprinted upon all things from evening attire to kitchen supplies. I heard one sales associate pose this question to his walkie-talkie: "Do we have any Daffy or Bugs body panties?" Hence, WB presents itself as a master narrative. By placing its characters on everything, WB pulls everything into itself and spreads out to everything. It is at once heterotopia (via its inclusion of art and merchandise objects which are not itself) and homodystopia (via its leveling of all things as itself). WB characters can become everyone both real and imaginary (Grandma Moses and Sherlock Holmes, for example). WB characters can go everywhere both real and imaginary (the Kremlin and a sci-fi planet, for example).

Although, as we all know, WB cartoons conclude with the phrase "That's all folks," WB does not accept the meaning of "that's all." There is no end to the genres, merchandise, and personages it can appropriate. Just as the sun never sets on the British Empire, there is no limit to what WB can pull into its sphere of influence. As the aforementioned *Times* letter writer Aubl says, "the whole country, the world in fact is living kitsch culture." This pervasive culture is suburban — and the less than welcoming Warner Brothers Store security army protects against the nonsuburban Others' intrusion. With very few exceptions, the Warner Brothers Store's customers are not black. Suburbia as imagined by a Los Angeles–based production studio appears on Fifth Avenue. And, as Muschamp stresses, Planet Hollywood and the Hard Rock Cafe are the Warner Brothers Store's neighbors. These West Coast enterprises position Los Angeles as a monster about to eat Manhattan. Since it has not yet succeeded, since something other than kitsch culture still exists in Manhattan, I turn to an example of what Aubl would "consider sacred": Frank Lloyd Wright's Guggenheim Museum. The Guggenheim is no Pizza Hut.

Siebers, when discussing postmodernism's utopian desire as "the romance of community," explains that "[m]y point, however, is that the new model of community is based on the romantic couple" (8–9). My point is that the circular Guggenheim and its new rectangular (almost phallic) wing are a romantic couple. Further, the new and old Guggenheim combined as a romantic couple represents juxtaposing the differences characterizing New York and Los Angeles. Understanding Siebers' romantic couple according to William Hamilton's "New Yang and Los Yingeles" further clarifies my point. Hamilton sexes Western art as male northern Europe and female Mediterranean region. He views the difference between New York and Los Angeles entertainment in terms of this geographical difference translated as gender difference. Los Angeles, the yin of the talk show and feelings, is analogous to the female Mediterranean region's "voluptuous domes, labyrinthine grottoes" (Hamilton, 120). New York, the yang of sports and news, is "[a]ll solitary towers" (120). Hamilton explains that men now appear in Julia Child's studio kitchens and women now anchor the business news. In other words, the yin and yang which once separately characterized New York and Los Angeles media styles have merged.

This merger is pictured by the Guggenheim as architectural romantic couple: the voluptuous round spiral newly attached to the tower annex. Wright's round spaceship building — so out of place in a residential neighborhood and on the island of skyscrapers — has a vertical tower of its own. In the form of the joined new and old Guggenheim, Los Angeles yin has become one with New York yang. Hamilton's following comment is an appropriate romantic narrative to describe the coupling of Wright's spiral with its adjoining tower: "Although the colorful, horizontal spread of Los Angeles yin may seem to be surrounding and sinking the stiff and vertical old New York yang, a yin can't exist without its yang" (120). The Guggenheim is now a happy romantic couple, the joining of the voluptuous and the vertical, a representation of merged New York yin and Los Angeles yang.[2] The Guggenheim spiral — the yin building as California girl (designed by a midwesterner) erected in Manhattan — is paired with a vertical tower, the kind of building which makes New York, New York a "helluva" town. Manhattan and its suburbs (Levittown, for example) form yet another romantic couple. This other romantic couple embraces Los Angeles — the metropolitan Levittown across the continent, which, in turn, embraces New York. (Bob and Carol and Ted and Alice would be very sympathetic toward this situation.)

Hamilton seems to address my version of postmodern urban desire when he indicates that architectural "high-rise erections" became boring and were followed by "malls, the same glittering labyrinthine grottoes" (120). As shopper / gawkers within Trump Tower indicate, high-rise erections are coupling with malls — and flirting with museums. The Warner Brothers Store places the stuff of the mall in a museum atmosphere situated among skyscrapers; Wright's spiral places the stuff of the museum in a mall atmosphere newly attached to a low-rise erection. (The Guggenheim annex, no Empire State Building, resembles a stunted version of the United Nations Secretariat Building.) In both the store and the museum, what is not usually placed together is placed together. (According to Wright's original plan, for example, his mall as house for art was supposed to contain go-carts.)

The film *1071 Fifth Avenue: Frank Lloyd Wright and the Story of the Guggenheim Museum* describes Wright's intention regarding the go-carts. Narrator Brendan Gill explains that Wright "was thinking of having go carts installed so that people would simply roll down the ramp past the pictures until they got to the ground." A go-cart located within a museum is as incongruous as Daffy Duck located within a Picasso. When I heard Richard Rodgers, another narrator of the film, comment that the Guggenheim spiral looks like a spaceship, it occurred to me that Wright's museum as mall potentially containing go-carts to place visitors in orbit around the pictures is an appropriate Disney World ride. There is little difference between Disney's Tomorrowland and Wright's spiraling futuristic design which upstages the art it exhibits. In addition, go-carts share commonalities with Kunstler's notion of the car as well as with Disney's notion of the people mover.[3]

Wright wished to place vehicles (i.e., people movers) within his museum which transcends the category "museum." The Guggenheim is itself an art object inhospitable to art. (Paintings, for example, must be hung at angles rather than flush against the walls.) Wright created a spiral which pulls people past the paintings to the spiral's top. The force that Wright's building exerts upon viewers indicates that he intended to blur the distinction between museum and painting. The film explains that Wright's desire to position his museum as art object involved making the museum "and the painting an uninterrupted beautiful symphony such as never existed in the world of art before." This intention does not coincide with the building's discordant relationship to the displayed art—the fact that the futuristic spiral overpowers the paintings. The building is heterogeneous: it is a voluptuous, mall-like, Disneyesque museum.

This heterogeneity contrasts sharply to the homogeneity Wright emphasized in the *Architectural Forum* when describing the spiral: "Here for the first time architecture appears plastic, one floor flowing into another instead of the usual superimposition of stratified layers cutting and butting into each other by post and beam construction. . . . The net result of such construction is a greater repose and an atmosphere of the unbroken wave — no meeting of the eye with angular or abrupt changes of form. . . . unity of design with purpose is everywhere present and naturally enough the over-all simplicity of form and construction ensure a longer life by centuries than could be sustained by the skyscraper construction usual in New York City" (144). Little could the writer imagine that, forty years later, the homogeneous repose would be backgrounded by an angular stunted version of the Secretariat Building — an unmanly something less than a skyscraper. Little could the writer imagine that the flowing spiral would form a romantic couple with a rectangle, that the spiral's round feminine layers — which absorb both viewers and paintings — are now attached to would-be vertical phallic Manhattan.

The rectangle which falls far short of skyscraper status — the annex which represents male genital inadequacy and plays second fiddle to the spiral in regard to architectural interest — seems to comment upon the masculine and the feminine (and seems to function as a literary feminist utopia in architectural form). Hamilton offers a similar comment when he emphasizes that the entertainment yin — the Los Angeles–style talk show — is more appealing than the New York yang — the male news show pundits. In other words, *Oprah* is more entertaining than *The News Hour with Jim Lehrer.*

And so too for the Los Angeles yin and New York yang forming the romantic couple that is the current Guggenheim Museum. The feminine flowing spiral is simply more eye-catching than the phallic rectangle inscribed with squares — and the rectangle itself is aware of this opinion: four openings reveal that the rectangle is supported by spirals, by circular pillars. These pillars are at once round and vertical, a heterogeneous integration of the differing spiral and rectangular annex, the disparity between yin and yang, woman and man. The pillars, structures which provide support, challenge Rockefeller Center's statue of Atlas holding up the world. Masculine-muscled Atlas stands erect and holds the round female world. Recasting this image, the Guggenheim annex reveals that at once vertical and round pillars support a rectangular masculine structure. Atlas's round world is on top; Wright's spiral is in front (of the rectangular annex). This positioning is accomplished without the assistance of the Superman (a contemporary Atlas) who seemingly moves the elevator in the Warner Brothers Store. Masculinity does not always dominate; Atlas shrugs.

SIX FLAGS OVER BROADWAY?

Hamilton's aforementioned sexing of New York and Los Angeles according to television entertainment indicates that applying Siebers' romantic couple story to the Guggenheim tells a tale of these two cities. I turn now to extending this tale to include other entertainment modes, Broadway theater and Hollywood movies. Members of the Hollywood movie industry are gravitating toward New York; Broadway theater is increasingly resembling a Disney theme park. This cross-fertilization (or romantic coupling) between New York and Los Angeles entertainment modes is revealed by discussing the New York events "Broadway on Broadway" and "Stars in the Alley" (in which theater is performed on the street on Broadway and in Schubert Alley) and the June 19, 1994, "A Day at the Movies Starring New York, N.Y." (in which 53rd and 54th Streets at Seventh Avenue were used to demonstrate New York's part in the film industry).

David Richards, in the *New York Times*, explains why Broadway theater has lately become analogous to a theme park: "It's long been known as the fabulous invalid and the Great White Way, but we may have to start calling it Six Flags Over Broadway. While there has always been a raffish, thrill-seeking side to theatergoing, the distinction between Broadway and a theme park grew decidedly narrower during the 1993–94 season. . . . You bought your ticket, took your seat and went on a ride. The seats just didn't move" (1). Perhaps a producer will decide to eradicate stationary theater seats by installing go-carts, following Wright's example, within Broadway theaters. Or perhaps the Disney Corporation, which is contributing to 42nd Street's refurbishment, will decide to build a real theme park there. Because Disney has already raised its flag over Broadway, this comment is not far-fetched. After all, according to Richards, Disney's Broadway production of *"Beauty and the Beast,* whatever its visual appeal, is very nearly content free . . . spectacle is very nearly everything. . . . the [1995] forthcoming season will see the big grow bigger, the stagecraft more amazing and the hype shriller" (32). *Beauty and the Beast* is no *The Crucible.* If one Disney flag already waves over Broadway, then it is reasonable to imagine that a theme park could appear on 42nd Street. Disneyland located in Manhattan is no less incongruous than Disneyland located outside Paris.

While Disneyland first appeared near Los Angeles and spread east to Florida and to France, the opposite is true of the movies. The movie industry, of course, began in New York and spread west to Los Angeles, which, in opposition to New York's extreme commercial heterogeneity, became a homogeneous film town. "A Day at the Movies Starring New York, N.Y." — a celebration made in, by, and about New York — is an attempt to pull film back to its roots. The event's title positions New York as a character — a star. (Did New York as star get her first break as a California girl who resembles Bo Derek in *10*?) The *Newsday* official event guide hints that "A Day" contains a love interest, that New York and Hollywood are positioned as a romantic couple: "New York is where it's at. . . . New York and Hollywood are joined at the hip" (Duggan, 3). Sydney Pollack indicates that a mythical energy force is a part of the romance: " 'New York has always had a mythical pull for people who have never lived in New York' " (Duggan, 3). Pollack continues: "New York is not right for everything, but the things it's right for, you can't get anywhere else" (3). New York is not right for "A Day at the Movies," an advertising gimmick disguised as an artistic event. A portion of Seventh Avenue was cast as a county fair arcade where people could win film posters — i.e., advertisements. The event's parade, which contains no movie star participants, consists of floats—i.e., advertisements for movies astride go-carts. "A Day at the Movies" is as vacuous and devoid of satisfaction as suburbia.

Although "Broadway on Broadway" and "Stars in the Alley" are also commercials, these events at least deliver what they promise. Broadway theater is performed on Broadway (on the street), and stars do appear in the alley. Seeing theater and stars is more satisfying than seeing advertisements for movies. By starring as itself, New York / Broadway pulls people into itself as real entertainment experience. *Times* letter writer Aubl would be happy to know that Broadway still remains sacred — despite the encroachment of the wicked glitz of the West. Broadway looks like New York.

And the *Playbill* cover for "Broadway on Broadway" looks like the Guggenheim Museum. The cover portrays a tall person, a linear structure,

holding a circular sign. Here, again, the vertical stands behind the spiral —
with a difference: the vertical image is a woman. Clad in high heels and a
man's tuxedo, she is simultaneoously feminine and masculine. Like the
new Guggenheim, she is a whole who incorporates both yin and yang. She
celebrates difference. And so does New York's most impressive show
(which does not occur in its theaters). This show is produced by the endless heterogeneity of New York's citizens and economy. To contrast with the
corporate *Beauty and the Beast,* consider a show I saw performed in the
subway: a black man playing a saxophone and sporting science fiction antennae on his head walked through the train saying, "I have come to Earth
from Mars for sex. If you don't give me money, I will not stop playing. I will
continue to hurt your ears." He is no suburbanite. He is a cast member of
New York's greatest show on Earth.

THE ANGELINOS ARE COMING,
THE ANGELINOS ARE COMING

Many of the Los Angeles film industry's chief players now choose to join
this cast, to move to New York. Because a large component of the industry
consists of transplanted New Yorkers, their decision is a move back. New
York, a destination of immigrants, often served as a place to emigrate from,
a jumping off point toward California. Such is the experience of one
George Papashvily, a Russian immigrant to New York — and later to Los
Angeles — who in 1940, together with his wife, Helen, authored an account
of their experiences called *Anything Can Happen.* For Papashvily, the
American dream consists of heading from New York to Los Angeles en-
sconced within a vehicular American dream machine. Here is his narrator's
lengthy description of Russians preparing to emigrate from New York to
Los Angeles:

> If I have to go any place I prefer California. . . . Besides from talking to
> Americans, I arrived at the conclusion California was a very highly val-
> ued place. . . .
>
> And now began preparations for our journey. I went in my scrap
> yard and put together a car from best parts I had on hand. . . . "But we
> need truck besides," Anna Feodorovna said immediately. . . .
>
> "But the truck. What's that for?"
>
> "My furniture naturally."
>
> "Anna Feodorovna," I said, "you surely don't mean we're gonna
> carry your furniture to California? . . ."

But she did mean.

So finally I found a truck for $150. . . . We started to load it.

Beds, tables, chairs, carpets. . . . the rubber tree's going in California, and a fifty pound bag of feathers, too. . . . Canary's house is all aboard for California, too. And finally after they loaded a harness with bells . . . and a hive of bees . . . I saw it was hopeless to say any more. . . .

"Now," I said starting up the truck, "follow me, everybody. Straight ahead. I'm on the right track and where the sun goes down we'll find California waiting." (Papashvily, 68–69, 70, 75)

When Papashvily and his troupe approached Los Angeles, they could appropriately announce, "The Russians are coming, the Russians are coming." As I read his description of less than glamorous aliens placing disparate objects in their eyesore truck to move to California, I hear the tune Los Angeles media once placed in my New York–based television set: "Come and listen to the story of a man named Jed. . . . The kinfolks said Jed move away from there. They said California is the place you oughta be. So they loaded up the truck and they moved to Beverly. Hills that is. Swimming pools. Movie stars." Papashvily's text charmingly retains a particular voice and grammar of difference. *The Beverly Hillbillies* continues to charm for the same reason. The sitcom (and the subsequent 1993 film) work by emphasizing the hillbillies' difference, the fact that they remain true to their community, the fact that they are forever alien in relation to Los Angeles suburbia. Like 1950s science fiction films, the alien hillbillies also address American suburbanization. When discussing these films, Rob Latham compares Lewis Mumford's *The City in History* to the *Invasion of the Body Snatchers*: if Mumford's "dire assessment conjures images of Kevin McCarthy running down the street screaming about the advent of the pod-people, it's not surprising, since many science fiction film critics have remarked on the dystopic allegory of suburban America conveyed by Don Siegel's classic *Invasion of the Body Snatchers* (1956)" (198). In the same vein, 1960s sitcoms which emanated from Los Angeles criticized suburbanization (I think of *Mr. Ed*, in which Wilbur Post carried on his most stimulating conversations with a horse). Los Angeles–based writers positioned Beverly Hills suburban conformity as an object of derision. They indicated that encapsulated Beverly Hills residents are the true Beverly Hillbillies.

Another sitcom song also echoes discontent with suburban uniformity: "New York is where I'd rather stay. I get allergic smelling hay. I just adore a penthouse view. . . You are my wife. Good-bye city life. Green acres we are

there." But where is *Green Acres*? *Green Acres*, which Kunstler could be expected to call the perfect name for a suburban development, is nowhere for
Lisa and Oliver Douglas. While residing in Hooterville, they are neither
urban nor akin to their neighbors. They are nowhere — sans New York
culture and sans the cultural ability to be farm folk. They are forever frus-
trated in Nowhere — the suburbia they construct in rural Hooterville.
When they say good-bye to city life, Lisa and Oliver move to a forever un-
satisfying limbo which is neither rural nor urban.

Hollywood sitcoms of the 1960s critique the lonely suburbanite surrounded by house, car, and television set. Although Wilbur Post has little
to say to his wife, Carol, he escapes from enclosing suburban accouterments via his horse (of course, of course). Mr. Ed the talking horse represents suburbanites' longing for connection to and communication with an
entity from real rural America. Ensconced in a stall in Wilbur's yard (like a
garaged car), Mr. Ed is a strange bedfellow of the machine in the garden.
For Wilbur, horsepower has nothing to do with cars. For Wilbur, horsepower means engaging conversational discourse.

Presently, some thirty years after California writers critiqued suburbia
· in a manner which will forever be a part of baby boomers' consciousness,
these writers (and many of their Los Angeles entertainment industry colleagues) are expressing their critique with their moving trucks. After Los
Angeles' earthquake and riots, many Los Angeles film people are moving
to New York. These people enact Lisa Douglas' exclamation, "New York
is where I'd rather stay." Their desire to avoid the vacuousness of Los Angeles' mono-economic emphasis upon film motivates their decision. They
now view Los Angeles as a homodystopia and New York as the heterotopian promised land.

New York Magazine writer Lisa Birnbach, in "Meet the New Neighbors," discusses this phenomenon when she describes the destination of
Los Angeles' fleeing film people: "Their destination — the promised
land — was New York" (40). These immigrants view New York as a utopian
alternative to the plagues of fire, riot, and earthquake. Plague, however, is
not the sole reason why people are leaving Los Angeles. Their move is white
flight from perceived vacuousness. Birnbach explains that it's "not just
earthquakes. It's the vast emptiness. Material things helped them [film industry people] forget the spiritual and intellectual emptiness" (40). Los Angeles film industry people — who have themselves become pod people —
now desire to escape from within their pod, the void of lack of intellectual
and spiritual stimulation. To move beyond the boundaries of this empti-

ness, they act in opposition to the Beverly Hillbillies: they are multi-millionaires who say that California is not the place they oughta be. So they loaded up their moving trucks and they moved from Beverly. Hills that is. Swimming pools. Movie stars.

They are pulled from a void toward what they perceive to be stimulating: New York as a place of depth. According to Birnbach, "And New York, meanwhile, has come to appear to Angelenos as it's looked to New Yorkers. A place with a past as well as a future, with depth. A place where individuality is valued and where creativity can flourish" (40). Like myself, Ruth Buzzi views the subway as a place where creativity and individuality manifests itself. Subways enthrall her: "'I love driving, but the most incredible creations are the subways. . . . I'm always under the ground. I'm addicted to subways'" (Birnbach, 41). Buzzi thinks New York is a "helluva" town because the people ride in a hole in the ground.

Kate Capshaw inadvertently describes her decision to move to New York in terms of homodystopia and heterotopia. She says that it "gets very oppressive living in a community that eats, sleeps, and drinks the entertainment industry. We [her husband Steven Spielberg and her children] feel that New York City will be a relief from it" (Birnbach, 42). She values New York precisely because it is not a suburb: "In New York City, you walk down the street and it's full of all the races and all languages and all of their arts and cultural influences. It's much more accessible" (Birnbach, 42). Creators of American popular culture have become cultural refugees who stage the convergence of Hollywood and New York: "And as Hollywood goes more New York, New York goes more Hollywood" (Birnbach, 44). Or, as Donald Trump explains, "a California person is a New York person" (Birnbach, 44).

Jerry Seinfeld epitomizes the New York person who has become a California person. He indicates that New York City is the force that strikes back against the evil empire of the car that Kunstler describes: "I always feel that cars in Manhattan are like germs and the city is like white corpuscles attacking them and trying to destroy them. The potholes, weather, and the other cars — every anti-automobile force is at work on the automobile" ("What's So Funny," 45). Seinfeld's New York as anti-automotive force is with Kunstler.

Seinfeld — when he alludes to Isaac Asimov's *Fantastic Voyage* — provides a happy ending to my story about cars and suburbs creating America as homodystopia: "they miniaturize these five scientists, put them in a submarine, and they go into this guy's body. And when you're in New York, it's like you're in the heart. You hear the pounding, you know" ("Funny," 45). New York, home of subway and pothole, is the pumping inner body cavity of America, the country's living heterotopian space. After parking their cars, people in New York can resemble submarines undergoing a fantastic voyage: they can become submerged in being walkers in the city.

New York's inner space is also subject to Seinfeld's applause. He describes New York as "a huge cocktail party. And you're glad that you're in that room, you know. That's what a good party's about. It's nice to be in the room" ("Funny," 45). New York as room, as inner heterotopian space, is a vibrant room of America's own. This vibrancy is threatened. There is now a computer in New York portrayed as a room that one is glad to be in. Robert Moses' impact upon New York takes a back seat to William Gibson's and Philip K. Dick's predictions about technology's impact. Science fiction writers have become more appropriate indicators of urban futures than urban planners. Kunstler's admonitions about car, suburbia, and theme parks are outmoded in relation to Brent Staples' description of a new threat: the information superhighway.

Staples predicts that this highway "could end up with infinitely more eyesores than its present-day, concrete cousin. Drive down your least favorite interstate in the riot of billboards, fast-food shops and muffler signs and you get the point. . . . Welcome to the information age" (A18). Concrete highways presently differentiate New York from Los Angeles. While New York is a walking city, one is hard-pressed to be a walker in Los Angeles. The information superhighway will level this distinction. It will cause New York and Los Angeles — and the world — to become a homodystopia in which the same advertising pervades every space. Encountering eyesores on the world's new highway has nothing to do with cars. In the future, it might be futile to load up the truck and drive to New York to escape spiritual and intellectual emptiness. In the future, computers in rooms located in both New York and Los Angeles — and throughout the world — might cause people to see the same view: the information superhighway's version of the interstate exit strip mall.

LOS ANGELES, A MANHATTAN-LIKE URBAN SUBURBIA, OR THE NEED FOR HOLES IN THE WALLS

Meanwhile, the car still reigns supreme in Los Angeles. This city is, of course, the quintessential example of an American landscape in which people move from home and office to car, where public space serves cars rather than pedestrians. Los Angeles is a car-dependent, self-created force. Failing to arise out of an existing natural asset (such as New York's harbor and Hudson River), Los Angeles, according to historian Kevin Starr, "envisioned itself, then materialized that vision through sheer force of will" (69). The force that is Los Angeles has imploded. Aaron Betsky describes the city as a utopia buried by the impossible demands of its own utopianism: "Los Angeles is utopia realized, lived, and buried by the impossibility of living in such an artificial state of (imagined) perfection" (Betsky, 99). Los Angeles, then, is a dystopian utopia. The burying of its utopia is quite literal: life in Los Angeles is lived inside. "Much of Los Angeles reproduces . . . interiorized utopia. The social life of the city takes place inside shopping malls. . . . The movies, made in walled-off compounds and shown in dark spaces or in the privacy of homes, may have created the model and the rationale for this development [of unusable public spaces]" (113–114). Los Angeles — the place of the sprawl, the interior, the car, and the wall — sharply contrasts with Manhattan's outside public interactions.

Los Angeles, however, does sometimes resemble New York. For example, the Plaza Vista development (a planned community built on land formerly owned by Howard Hughes), like Central Park West, integrates living space with controlled bits of nature. According to Betsky, this development derives "its imagery from a combination of Southern California traditions and New York urbanity" (101). New York–style urbanity, then, is a part of Los Angeles. The city's seemingly endless sprawl connected by freeways contains pockets of Manhattan-like culture and vistas.

Los Angeles is present on Manhattan's 57th Street; New York culinary culture is named and available throughout Los Angeles: Beverly Hills' Tribeca Restaurant advertises itself in *Buzz Magazine* by announcing, "[W]e've brought Manhattan to Beverly Hills"; a Venice Beach food concession stand proclaims via billboard that it sells "New York pizza"; Union Station houses Union Bagel; Fisherman's Village at Marina del Rey includes a restaurant named "Coney Island." New York's food is everywhere in Los Angeles.

Edward Soja says that "Los Angeles is everywhere" and "everywhere seems also to be in Los Angeles" (222). So too for New York. Fairfax, Los Angeles' original Jewish neighborhood — characterized by Hebrew lettering and Jewish names emblazoned on store fronts and the absence of wealthy Jews — resembles Manhattan's Lower East Side. Mike Davis calls the medium-rent townhouse and apartment development Park La Brea "a bit of Lower Manhattan *chutzpah* moored to Wilshire Blvd" (246); I call it a gated version of Manhattan's Stuyvesant Town. Davis' caption to a picture of Century City's tall apartment buildings foregrounded by a sculpture is "CATCHING UP WITH MANHATTAN" (77). It does seem as if Los Angeles is playing catch-up with New York. For example, Los Angeles now has a fledgling subway system (whose orderliness is more indicative of Germany's S-bahn than New York's subway). The Los Angeles skyline is a smaller version of its New York counterpart. Although burned-out sections of south-central Los Angeles are no part of a catch-up game to be proud of, these areas mirror the south Bronx.

More positively, Los Angeles is attempting to catch up to New York in terms of high culture. The city's arts funds are spent upon "imported culture (especially from New York)" (Davis, 78). Funds are being appropriated for the New York–style icon Los Angeles seeks to institute for itself: an investment company "has offered Mayor Bradley the initial contribution towards a 'Statue of Liberty' for Los Angeles (the favored proposal is actually a deconstructivist 'steel cloud' designed to be laid over the Hollywood Freeway next to the Civic Center)" (Davis, 76). Although the Statue of Liberty will never symbolize Los Angeles, and a steel cloud might say more about smog than about liberty, in Los Angeles, ethnic diversity rivals (or even exceeds) New York's (Davis 80).

With regard to financial interdependence, Los Angeles is becoming one with New York — and with Tokyo: "In a few years it may be more accurate to speak of a financial triangle of Los Angeles, New York and Tokyo" (Davis, 137). Los Angeles elites who are "tributary to the great financial centers in Shinjuku and Lower Manhattan" (Davis, 130) flow into Manhattan and Japan. While the upper echelon of the Los Angeles financial world comes together with counterparts in New York and Tokyo, togetherness is not the predominant experience of the diverse groups who inhabit the city. Los Angeles, which "has come to play the double role of utopia *and* dystopia for advanced capitalism" (Davis, 18), is a social homodystopia, a place where racial segregation eradicates heterotopia. Davis alludes to this when he discusses white 1960s Los Angeles teenage culture as monoculture: "The patented 'LA Look' of the 1960's ... was the avant-garde counterpart to ... the *Gidget* novels ... and the falsetto lyrics of *Beach Boys'* songs. It was the mesmerizing vision of a white kids' car-and-surf based Utopia" (65–66). The Beach Boys do not yet sing about the black experience; the wish that they could all be California girls does not yet include black girls. (Present-day Gidgets are not black.) Los Angeles is "the utopia of Aryan supremacism" (Davis, 30), a place where whites enclose themselves behind walls and gates.

This situation is counter to the Los Angeles official slogan "Brings it all together like Los Angeles" and the phrase repeated on Los Angeles television: "Together we are the best." The aforementioned proposed steel cloud symbol speaks to the fact that these proclamations are pipe dreams. Los Angeles, "the paradigmatic window through which to see the last half of the twentieth century" (Soja, 221), frames a view of racial segregation. People of color are absorbed within their neighborhoods; wealthy whites are absorbed within their walled condos or estates. Like the touted official and televised slogans, the Los Angeles city center fails to act as a force to bring together the wall-enclosed, car-enclosed, ghetto-enclosed diverse population.

Yet, despite this failure, Los Angeles does function as a city. This disparity of enclosed individuals and segregated areas converging to form a city — the togetherness of the separated, the joining of the unitary — is a contradiction communicated by the title of two of Soja's essays in *Postmodern Geographies: The Reassertion of Space in Critical Social Theory*: "Taking Los Angeles Apart: Towards a Postmodern Geography," and "It All Comes Together in Los Angeles." Los Angeles is an apart which at once comes together and remains a part, the simultaneous joining and separation of the disparate.

In other words, the opposite extremes epitomized by Bel Air and Watts are both a part of Los Angeles. As I stated at the start of this chapter, Soja describes the genre seepage which is Los Angeles' blending of the disparate when he states that "everything seems to come together in Los Angeles." He continues: "Its representations of spatiality and historicity are archetypes of vividness, simultaneity, and interconnections. They beckon inquiry at once into their telling uniqueness and, at the same time, into their assertive but cautionary generalizability" (Soja, 248). When everything seems to come together in the difference which is Los Angeles, anti–genre seepage (an insistence upon the different and the separate) at once loses and retains its separateness. Soja describes this process in terms of spinning and centripetal force: "Yet the centers hold. Even as some things fall apart, dissipate, new modalities form and old ones are reinforced. The specifying centrifuge is always spinning but the centripetal force of modality never disappears" (234). Los Angeles' reinforced space for movie stars is at once separate from and combined with the dissipated space for the ghetto vacant lot or burned out building. This is so because Los Angeles is a force which pulls its disparate modalities together in the manner of a spinning galaxy holding together its different stars and planets — and the empty spaces between them.

The force that is Los Angeles is rather analogous to a science fiction monster. While 1950s science fiction movies routinely depict monsters about to swallow cities (as my above subtitle about the threat of ingestion facing Manhattan indicates), Davis describes Los Angeles as an infinite sentient monster which ingests the desert: his Los Angeles is "a city without boundaries, which ate the desert, cut down the Joshua and May Pole, and dreamt of becoming infinite. . . . L.A. already was everywhere" (12). For Soja, Los Angeles, an infinite desert-devouring monster, defies the genre of city itself: "Los Angeles has been defying conventional categorical description of the urban, of what is a city and what is a suburb, of what can be identified as community or neighborhood, of what copresence means in the elastic urban context. It has in effect been deconstructing the urban into a confusing collage of signs which advertise what are often little more than imaginary communities and outlandish representations of urban locality" (245). Los Angeles seeps beyond the generic definition "city" and challenges this definition in terms of space: "its spatiality challenges Orthodox analysis and interpretation, for it too seems limitless and constantly in motion, never still enough to encompass, too filled with "other spaces" to be informatively described" (Soja, 22). Los Angeles, home of movie stars, is spatialized like a galaxy which defies the definition of galaxy.

Los Angeles, then, is the urban as something new under the sun, a new definition of city which unites the forever separate: exaggeratedly wealthy American suburbia and American ghetto. At the center of this impossible unity is a downtown which is a postmodern newness, a downtown which recreates the usual heterogeneity characteristic of "downtown" in a middle-class suburban homogeneity. Davis speaks of the "spatial apartheid" (230) and the "local Berlin Wall" (230) which is Los Angeles' "new 'postmodern' Downtown" (228), consisting of such structures as the Crocker Center, the Bonaventure Hotel and Shopping Mall, the Arco Center, Citicorp Plaza, and California Plaza (Davis, 229). "Photographs of the old Downtown in its prime show mixed crowds of Anglo, Black and Latino pedestrians of different ages and classes. The contemporary Downtown 'renaissance' is designed to make such heterogeneity virtually impossible. It is intended not just to 'kill the street' but to 'kill the crowd.' . . . The Downtown hyperstructure — like some Buckminster Fuller post-Holocaust fantasy — is programmed to ensure a seamless continuum of middle-class work, consumption and recreation, without unwonted exposure to Downtown's working-class street environments. . . . [T]his is the archisemiotics of class war" (Davis, 231). The city which defies the genre "city" has a new homogeneous downtown which defies the old generic heterogeneous downtown. This new Los Angeles downtown is a place where tall buildings, which form a Manhattan-like skyline, function as suburbia. Downtown's skyscrapers inhabited by middle-class workers— and its lack of streets and crowds — position it as a new newness within the postmodern downtown: an urban suburbia. Downtown is as much a homodystopia as the old-style suburbs Kunstler deplores. Or, in the opinion of Los Angeles Times urban critic Sam Hall Kaplan, downtown's juxtaposition of urban and suburban inhibits (or walls) the flow of human difference: "In his [Kaplan's] view the superimposition of 'hermetically sealed fortresses' and air-dropped 'pieces of suburbia' has 'dammed the rivers of life' Downtown" (Kaplan, 13, quoted in Davis, 229). Downtown, a Manhattan-like skyline which functions as suburbia, encloses the middle-class and dams the tide of difference to the outside. It too is an encapsulated space.

A dam is a wall; walls and fences are everywhere in Los Angeles. Fences around schools and schoolyards position students as so many animals locked inside cages. The opulent environments located beyond Bel Air and Beverly Hills estate walls might be stage sets for the zoo cage for humans that Kurt Vonnegut's Tralfamadorians construct in Slaughterhouse Five. Fenced schoolyards, walled estates, and gated communities absorb and imprison the people located behind them.[4] Many critics remark that Los Angeles already resembles the dystopian imagery pictured in the 1982 film Blade Runner (Betsky, 114). I add that Los Angeles already contains the walled enclaves and outside violence that Octavia Butler describes in her science fiction vision Parable of the Sower (discussed in chapter 8). Walls and fences epitomize Los Angeles' obsession with creating homogeneity.

The anecdote a UCLA humanities professor related to me reflects this obsessional anti–genre fission. Due to earthquake damage, some UCLA humanities departments were relocated to a Westwood corporate office building. Upon hearing of the professors' imminent arrival, the corporate types were far from welcoming. I imagine the original tenants shouting, "The professors are coming, the professors are coming" to express their fear that the professors (and their jeans-clad, backpack-carrying students) would spoil the ambiance of the building and ruin the neighborhood. To protect their homogeneous environment, the corporate tenants tried to make the newly ensconced professors adhere to a dress code. Since the professors were more jolted by the idea of a dress code than by the earthquake, the new tenants' attire remained heterogeneous. If the corporate types see professors and students as Other, what must they think of those who reside in ghettoes and barrios? No wonder those who might wish to fence in the UCLA campus itself enclose sameness and cast out difference.

Despite all efforts to perpetuate sameness, Los Angeles is a place of abrupt difference. The border between Beverly Hills and Hollywood — where a street fronted by estates is adjacent to one fronted by seedy bars — constitutes an immediate ambiance shift. This paradigmatic difference between adjacent streets is also present in Beverly Hills: one particular kind of tree lines a particular street. One Beverly Hills' street's palm trees differ from its neighboring street's magnolias. Diversity in regard to nature does not just result from human intervention: climate and temperatures vary in different sections of the city.

As I have indicated, in terms of the American landscape, Downtown Los Angeles positions the skyscraper as suburbia. Despite this aforementioned emphasis upon the homogeneous, there is an effort to make downtown function in a manner analogous to Manhattan's centrality vis-à-vis both the outer boroughs and the global capital: "after decades of public and private campaigns to defy the claims that Los Angeles was little more than a hundred suburbs in search of a city, there has developed in the past twenty years a visible and expansive downtown core to the giant regional metropolis. . . . Built into the new centrality of downtown Los Angeles has been a primary geographical locus for the accelerated centralization, concentration, and internationalization of individual and finance capital that has marked the contemporary restructuring of the world economy. Positioned increasingly as a 'capital of capital' in the Pacific Basin, Los Angeles has been surging toward the ranks of the three other capitals of global capital, New York, London, and Tokyo" (Soja, 209–210). Although Downtown Los Angeles is becoming Manhattan in terms of capital, its suburban skyscrapers are walls which enclose professionals. They are so many tombstones erected on the site of the death of community between people belonging to different classes.

While downtown "suburban" skyscrapers themselves function as walls, their less-imposing domestic counterparts situated outside Los Angeles resort to walls which are not metaphorical. Davis explains that "new luxury developments outside the city limits have often become fortress cities, complete with encompassing walls, restricted entry points with guard posts" (244). The skyscraper as wall and real walls turn Los Angeles and its surrounding areas into prison camps in which the rich cordon themselves off from "the third-world service proletariat," who experience "imprisonment" inside "increasingly repressive ghettoes and barrios" (Davis, 227). Los Angeles, exemplar of capitalism and worldwide financial interchange, is both within and outside its own borders a series of enclosed spaces analogous to the walled enclave that was the former East Germany. "Even as the walls have come down in Eastern Europe, they are being erected all over Los Angeles" (Davis, 227). The resident of a walled estate is analogous to a former East German who had travel privileges; the day laborer is analogous to Richard Wright's Big Boy (discussed in chapter 8).

Like Big Boy, these laborers are forced to place themselves within holes in the ground: "Since there is virtually no low-income housing between the Santa Ana barrio and East San Diego (a ninety-mile distance) thousands of day-laborers and their families . . . are forced to live furtively in hillside dugouts and impromptu brush camps, often within sight of million-dollar tract homes whose owners want the 'immigrant blight' removed" (Davis, 209). The million-dollar walled or gated homes are imprisoning holes, ultra-opulent versions of the hillside dugout. Los Angeles, whose separate and economically disparate areas come together to form a city, imprisons both rich and poor. Cars are the city's most liberated entities.

Money cannot buy a safe and leisurely stroll across a freeway. (Neither can power. Drivers would be outraged if President Clinton stopped traffic to indulge in such a stroll.) The most pervasive enclosed space in New York — the subway — brings difference together; the most pervasive Los Angeles enclosed spaces — the walled domiciles, the surrounding area's hillside dugouts, the cars on the freeways — perpetuate difference. Although New York and Los Angeles are coming together culturally and financially, disparities between the subway and the freeway represent the cities' different approaches to public encounters between members of separate economic classes. Despite all efforts to the contrary, the initial attempt to establish a popular new subway system in Los Angeles appears to be failing. To a New Yorker, an empty subway during rush hour is a contradiction in terms.

While midtown Manhattan streets are replete with throngs of diverse pedestrians, Downtown Los Angeles as suburb consists of "good citizens, off the streets, enclaved in their high-security private consumption spheres; bad citizens, on the streets . . . caught in the terrible, Jehovan scrutiny of the LAPD's space program" (Davis, 253). "Enclosed" epitomizes the sprawl that is Los Angeles. Within the limited space that is Manhattan, avenues reign supreme. Although Manhattan's skyline is reflected in Century City and Downtown Los Angeles—and although Warner Brothers is ensconced on Fifth Avenue and Third Avenue is replete with mall stores—New York is no East Germany. The ultimate class separating wall is located in California, not in New York. Writing in the *Los Angeles Times*, Miles Corwin describes this ultimate structure for separation—the Pelican Bay prison, whose "inmates are confined to their windowless cells, built of solid blocks of concrete and stainless steel" (Corwin quoted in Davis, 289). Ironically, Pelican Bay—according to the trend Betsky calls "theming" (112), in which original landscapes are ignored and random areas and modes are evoked—would be an appropriate name for a Los Angeles gated condo community. Southern California's wealthy condo dwellers and prison inmates are in a class by themselves. No Manhattan apartment building would call itself the Pelican Bay. The Dakota, yes; the Pelican Bay, never.

Pelican Bay is an enclosure which eradicates the human reality of its inmates by imprisoning their bodies in a controlled space. It is a homodystopia of no escape—and it has an effect which is the same in principle as that of Los Angeles, the utopia for escape that Manifest Destiny promises. Los Angeles is a place of enclosure in which human community—and the human body itself—disappears. Los Angeles interiorization, the city as walled hole, is "a point of closure in which any sense of community and any sense of corporeality are disappearing. This is indeed a utopia of escape, in which we abandon our very humanity and transform ourselves into something purely self-created" (Betsky, 114). A utopia of escape which eradicates humanity and the body is no place for people to live, an impossible space for people.

There is a potential hero waiting in the wings to save Los Angeles from being ground zero for the aforementioned nuclear explosion that Mumford predicted, a neutron bomb/social force (which destroys people and leaves buildings intact). The hero is the hole in the ground New Yorkers ride in or, more specifically, public transportation. This hero is "the dream of a 'connective tissue'" (Betsky, 116)—the subway. During the next fifteen years Southern California will spend two hundred billion dollars on a transportation infrastructure, on "a new subway system, light rail, commuter rail, improved and electrified buses, and highway enlargements or enhancements" (Betsky, 116–117). The subway as "utopian dream" positioned successfully to link Los Angeles' "diverse communities together" (Betsky, 117) is the hero which potentially could rescue the city of dreams.

Although I have expressed doubt that Los Angeles will embrace public transportation — that Los Angeles and its in-progress subway system will become a romantic couple — anything is possible. Angelinos could eventually learn to love public transportation. After all, who would have "thunk" we'd see Bugs Bunny ensconced on Fifth Avenue or Third Avenue functioning as a shopping mall.

Few New Yorkers would imagine a superhero's cape attached to the last car of a subway train. For New York commuters sweltering in urine-infused subway stations in August, the subway is no hero. The subway station in summer might be New York's version of the seasonal destruction that plagues Los Angeles: nature as dystopic entity, which, according to Betsky, "was always inherent in Los Angeles" due to "the searing heat, spring deluges, and wildfires" (115). On August 26, 1995, New Yorkers fought wildfires of their own, the flames which engulfed Hamptons communities as well as Brooklyn Heights' St. George Hotel. According to people interviewed by the *New York Times* in regard to the Brooklyn Heights fire, Brooklyn and Long Island seemed to merge: "Steve Schwartz found wry humor in the week's second major conflagration. 'It was our own little piece of the Hamptons,' he said. . . . It was surely a disastrous week for Norma Buckholtz, 68, and her husband, Sidney. The Buckholtzes fled their vacation home in Speonk, L.I., on Thursday afternoon, a day before wildfire that tore through thousands of acres in Suffolk County would have forced them out" (Hevesi, 33). In terms of wildfire, Brooklyn becomes Long Island — and New York becomes Los Angeles.

The St. George Hotel figures significantly in my discussion of convergences between New York and Los Angeles. Like Los Angeles, this Brooklyn hotel includes both movie star glamor and the ghettoized Other. As the *New York Times* explains:

In the eyes of many residents of the quiet neighborhood of brownstones and small stores, the hotel has devolved from a glamorous 2,800-room grande dame where movie stars once swam in the city's largest indoor swimming pool to a crumbling, cavernous eyesore housing a handful of the city's most downtrodden or forgotten residents [homeless AIDS patients]. . . . Betty Alford, 61, a social worker on disability who has lived at the St. George for 19 years, still relished memories of the hotel in its grander days. 'It was gorgeous, wonderful,' Ms. Alford said. The mirrored basement swimming pool where Johnny Weissmuller used to swim was still open, dances were still held in the grand ballroom, and she and her friends occasionally dined in the rooftop garden restaurant, Ms. Alford said. (Revkin, 33)

Johnny Weissmuller, of course, played Tarzan, namesake of Tarzana, California—which Edgar Rice Burroughs coined when he lived in Los Angeles. The Brooklyn pool Weissmuller and other movie stars once enjoyed exemplifies a seepage point between New York and Los Angeles culture. Like Hollywood, this pool is now much more tawdry than glamorous. For Fredric Jameson, the Bonaventure Hotel epitomizes postmodern Los Angeles.[5] For me, the St. George Hotel's dual position as representative of glamor and decreptitude epitomizes the extreme economic disparities which simultaneously characterize Los Angeles. The St. George is a faded Hollywood glamor space situated in New York.

The St. George is now passé. If security walls become passé, maybe utopia in Los Angeles will be realized. Los Angeles, Long Island, and Brooklyn have had their trial by fire, nature's way to renew landscape. Urban renewal for the New York and Los Angeles landscape could be realized as new versions of the "stories" that determine reality, "[a]ll of them . . . written by the white males who still control the [Los Angeles] region" (Betsky, 121). Urban renewal is more than a swapping of locality — more than a Warner Brothers store appearing on Fifth Avenue or Manhattan economic clout transplanted to Los Angeles. Urban renewal is a new story which offers an alternative to the totalizing power of economic stratification. America's Berlin Walls need to come down. At the very least, if some of the bricks are removed, vestiges of the Other might be able to permeate via the resulting holes in the walls.

LOS ANGELES' POTENTIAL JUMP TOWARD JOHANNESBURG

When Davis speaks of Los Angeles in terms of the aforementioned "spatial apartheid," "the local Berlin Wall," "Aryan supremacism," and "the archisemiotics of class war," it becomes clear to me that Johannesburg is a more extreme version of Los Angeles, that the present's most dangerous and most personally barricaded peace-time city portends Los Angeles' future.[6] In South Africa, Davis' aforementioned description of Los Angeles' architectural intention "to kill the crowd" manifests itself this way: the crowd is afraid of being killed. Almost every South African I met (during my 1995 sojourn as a visiting professor at the University of Cape Town) told me a personal narrative about encountering violence. (I even heard a radio commentator joke that after robbing Johannesburg banks, thieves are mugged on their way out.) Yet gentility — incessant tea drinking, for instance — predominates concomitantly with South Africa's prevailing fearful atmosphere. Although English-speaking South Africans who have lived there for generations still feel culturally bonded to Great Britain, they transformed part of Africa into America. Cape Town's new Victoria and Albert Waterfront development is more akin to Baltimore's urban renewal than to either Victoria or Albert. Sun City, the casino and resort located near Johannesburg, is artificial and exaggerated to the extent of parodying the American theme park. South Africa is the place of the highway and the shopping mall.

Johannesburg is the city where people who are afraid to walk on the street during the day — and who would never do so at night — live imprisoned within their cars and behind the walls and barbed wire surrounding their homes. This situation prevails throughout the city and its suburbs, not just within specific neighborhoods. Johannesburg is a sprawl of house / bunkers protected by barred windows and menacing barbed wire. Los Angeles is more ominously walled than New York; Johannesburg is more ominously walled than Los Angeles. An entertainment reporter for a Johannesburg newspaper told me that she felt afraid in Los Angeles because windows there do not have bars. In the manner of *Blade Runner*, Johannesburg portends Los Angeles' potential future. South Africa's former apartheid system is suburban America as homodystopia carried to an extreme, a manic method to turn the heterogeneous into the homogeneous. Although apartheid characterizes South Africa's past, it might be America's future. The South Africans, who have not taken down their walls, have deconstructed apartheid. The Americans, who are building more walls (especially in Los Angeles), are moving toward an apartheid system. Johannesburg is the Los Angeles American dream's worst nightmare — and the Republican Party's American dream.

Nadine Gordimer depicts this nightmare in "Once upon a Time" (collected in *Jump and Other Stories*), which confronts South African walls, the more extreme and secure versions of their Los Angeles counterparts. The wife and husband protagonists of "Once" author a fairy tale about how barricades will enable them (along with their son, trusted servants, and pets) to live happily ever after inside their house. In order to please his wife, the husband installs electronic security gates because "there were many burglaries in the suburb and somebody's trusted housemaid was tied up and shut in a cupboard by thieves while she was in charge of her employers' house" (Gordimer, 26). Although "Once" does not specifically say so, the trusted housemaid is obviously black. The family resorts to ever more stringent security in response to a black maid being forced into a cupboard — a contained space. The cupboard is a prison located within a home whose exterior resembles a concentration camp exterior. Its surrounding barbed wire suggests "pure concentration-camp style, no frills, all evident efficacy" (Gordimer, 29).

"Once" emphasizes that South Africa is not linguistically efficacious, that the country has twelve rather than eleven official languages. The twelfth language is "the electronic harpies' discourse" (Gordimer, 27), the burglar alarms that seemingly address each other in an electronic tribal tongue: "the alarm was often answered — it seemed — by other burglar alarms, in other houses. . . . the alarms called to one another across the gardens in shrills and bleats and wails that everyone soon became accustomed to" (26–27). The communicating burglar alarms speak a cyborg language heard and interpreted by security machines — and humans enclosed within domestic spaces that the security machines surround. This cyborg language is a new discourse practice.

The couple's young son acts according to genre fission when he rewrites a fairy tale in terms of the gates, walls, and barbed wire surrounding him. At Christmas, his grandmother gives his family extra bricks to build their security wall higher while "the little boy got a Space Man outfit and a book of fairy tales" (Gordimer, 28). After hearing a story read from this book, the child becomes an astronaut trapped in the enclosing space of his own tragic version of the fairy tale. He will be surrounded by "DRAGON'S TEETH" (29), "a continuous coil of stiff and shining metal serrated into jagged blades, so that there would be no way of climbing over it and no way through its tunnel without getting entangled in its fangs. There would be no way out" (29).

The boy's imagination casts him as a Space Man crawling within the inner space of this coil in a manner analogous to astronauts passing between the metal walls enclosing a space shuttle's inner spaces. Logically, the boy draws upon his familiarity with fairy tales to face the enclosing dragon's teeth, "the terrible thicket of thorns" (Gordimer, 30). Playing the prince in his own rewritten fairy tale, the boy places a ladder against the family's security wall and enters "the shining coiled tunnel [that] was just wide enough for his little body to creep in, and with the first fixing of its razor-teeth in his knees and hands and head he screamed and struggled deeper into its tangle" (30). The boy's new narrative, a fairy tale which is not about living happily ever after, propels him within the "tunnel," a place of false security, a fairy tale about safety which sucks households deeper into a space enclosed by ever more pervasive security devices. In the new South Africa, people are pulled deeper into the tangle of walls, fences, and bars. This country, which has suddenly decided to rewrite itself according to a new governmental story, needs a fairy tale prince (or princess) to rescue it from the social and economic disparities the old apartheid story left behind. The alarm "sent up wailing against the [boy's] screams" (Gordimer, 30) exemplifies the twelfth South African language communicating a warning to Los Angeles. As South Africa transforms itself into a new governmental and social entity, Los Angeles is also changing: enclosed by ever more pervasive walls, Los Angeles is on the brink of becoming Johannesburg — South Africa's extremely ethnically and religiously diverse city, which shares Los Angeles' sprawl and age.

Los Angeles is akin to the wife in "Once upon a Time." She "was afraid that some day such people ['people of another color'] might come up the street and tear off the plaque YOU HAVE BEEN WARNED and open the gates and stream in" (Gordimer, 25–26). "Once" is a warning sign which could appropriately be posted under the Hollywood sign. Los Angeles, the city which manufactures fairy tales, is ever more vulnerable to being mauled by the mechanistic security beast's "DRAGON'S TEETH." Los Angeles stands warned by Johannesburg's example not to cast itself as "the wise old witch, the husband's mother" who funds "the extra bricks" (Gordimer, 28) used to build higher walls.

Another fairy tale, "The Three Little Pigs," indicates that, in regard to extra bricks, moderation is wise. Although the pig residing in the brick house wins the day, the tale does not advocate surrounding the brick house with brick walls and barbed wire to keep out the Big Bad Wolf. If Los Angeles considers the sky to be the limit vis-à-vis security wall bricks, will Bel Air and Beverly Hills mansions be surrounded by walls high enough to rival the Empire State Building? I imagine a future in which a *King Kong* remake is shot in Los Angeles as cameras record the gorilla climbing up a security wall. This future scenario positions Gordimer's young protagonist caught within the razor-like dragon's teeth functioning as a literal Blade Runner inside an environment whose communicating alarms drown out the creative language of movie scripts. The boy is "hacked out of the security coil with saws, wire-cutters, choppers" (Gordimer, 30). These are useful tools for Los Angeles residents who require extra bricks to surround their brick houses with brick walls.

The boy's pet cat "effortlessly" jumps over "the seven foot wall" (Gordimer, 28) surrounding his house. Similarly, the menacing racial Other in the guise of King Kong (or the Big Bad Wolf) can effortlessly scale the Empire State Building–size walls I evoke as extrapolative examples of juxtaposed Manhattan, Los Angeles, and Johannesburg. Saws, wire cutters, and choppers are reasonable responses to the warning Johannesburg communicates to Los Angeles. Apartheid is a discourse which should not seep deeper within the story of the American dream.

The "house that surrounds" the unnamed teller of Gordimer's fairy tale is built upon the "undermined ground" of the gold mines in which "Chope and Tsonga migrant miners" (Gordimer, 24) sometimes lose their lives. As this teller describes, "the floor, the house's foundations, the slopes and passages of gold mines have hollowed the rock, and when some face trembles, detaches and falls, three thousand feet below, the whole house shifts slightly, bringing uneasy strain to the balance and counterbalance of brick, cement, wood and glass that hold it as a structure around me" (Gordimer, 24). The teller defines South African social inequality as an earthquake.

Higher walls offer no solution to the similar social earthquake which daily rocks Los Angeles. Instead, these walls form a fault line. Like Johannesburg gold mine disasters, Los Angeles walls inter people "in the most profound of tombs" (Gordimer, 24). Like the Chope and Tsonga migrant miners, Los Angeles citizens who barricade themselves in their houses risk being entombed. Hollywood, after all, is an economic gold mine. Walls potentially almost as high as skyscrapers built around gold mines do not rest on solid ground. They are social edifices which mask black faces and, by doing so, themselves face a social construction shift which — once upon a time — can tremble, detach, and fall.

6 AMERICAN MIDDLE-CLASS MALES MARK THE MOON

Retrospectively Reading the Apollo Program
or Lorena Bobbitt vs. the *Saturn 5*

It is certainly not an earth-shattering observation to note that Neil Armstrong's statement "That's one small step for a man; one giant leap for mankind" excludes women. The Apollo Program moon landings, of course, emphasize men, the Cold War, and patriotism — not women.[1] But the surprising point is that, since the Apollo era, little about moon forays has changed pictorially. I read imagery generated in the wake of the twenty-fifth anniversary of *Apollo 11* to show that American men still mark the moon—still treat the moon as a thing (like woman and nature) that men dominate. In the manner of dogs urinating on fire hydrants, men who landed on the moon established it as their own territory. This behavior continues.

I am not implying that the National Aeronautics and Space Administration remains the same. People other than American males fly in space shuttles. Here, for example, is the *New York Times* description of the crew of the space shuttle *Columbia* (launched July 8, 1994): "The international flavor of the mission is reflected in the crew, which includes six American men and Japan's first woman astronaut, Dr. Chiaki Naito-Mukai, a heart surgeon from Tokyo. Dr. Mukai . . . is the second Japanese astronaut to fly on a shuttle. . . . Dr. Mukai, already a celebrity in Japan for her role in the space program, said earlier that she hoped her flight 'encourages other Japanese to do things they might hesitate to do because they are women'" (Leary, 10). The six American male participants in the *Columbia* flight are described as "[o]ther crew members aboard the mission" (Leary, 10). Dr. Mukai is certainly the mission's star. I do not doubt that if Americans return to the moon NASA will send women and minority group members. My point is that despite this new inclusiveness, upon the occasion of the twenty-fifth anniversary of the first moon landing, what has not changed is the way pictures — and the words which accompany them — depict the

Apollo Program. The moon was represented as an extension of male middle-class suburban America. It still is.

In terms of this observation, I discuss past and present pictures and texts relating to Apollo flights. I include the following material both from the Apollo years (1969–1972) and from the 1990s: "Man on the Moon: The Apollo Adventure" (the Hayden Planetarium's summer 1994 exhibit commemorating the first moon landing), *The Flight of Apollo 11: Eagle Has Landed* (a 1969 NASA film shown as a part of the planetarium exhibit), postage stamps, book jackets, and newspaper photos. My conclusion goes back to the future to discuss pictures of the moon Georges Méliès created and Jules Verne inspired. Méliès would be sympathetic to my conclusion regarding the Apollo Program's male bravado.

THEN: THE APOLLO YEARS

The Hayden Planetarium exhibit includes Apollo Program pictures which portray men marking the moon. These pictures record men's footprints, American flags, and the designation "United States" appearing on the lunar module.[2] Armstrong's well-known photo of Edwin Aldrin's face masked by his spacesuit helmet visor is most striking. A commentator noting the tenth anniversary of *Apollo 11* observed that "we cannot see his face. Instead, in his visor, we see a reflection of the lunar module, the scientific equipment, and his fellow astronaut. We see in this one man, standing for the first time on a new world, a reflection of the ingenuity and teamwork of the people back on Earth that made this moment possible" (Littmann, 25). To my mind, Armstrong's camera records the eye of the patriarchal gaze viewing and reflecting itself. The visor, which resembles a computer or television screen, pictures patriarchy. Although Aldrin's visor makes him become an invisible man and although his visor / screen is gender free, observers of Armstrong's photograph construct the presence of a man's face. The visor functions as a psychoanalytic mirror stage in which patriarchy sees patriarchy. It is a television screen which hides women from view. Other moon-landing accouterments appearing in Armstrong's photo announce male power. The white spacesuit represents a white man. The flag sewn on the suit allows no one to forget that the white man is American. When Armstrong's image appears on Aldrin's visor, one individual mirrors his male colleague. The Armstrong and Aldrin team, standing for the first time on a new world, represents white men.

Ray Bradbury's *The Martian Chronicles* makes Mars as American as apple pie. The planetarium exhibit shows that the Apollo astronauts accomplish the same for the moon. They mark the lunar landscape as suburbia. On Earth, American male suburbanites rake leaves and drive cars; on the moon, these men pick up rocks and drive moon rovers. Astronaut Jim Irwin, pictured next to the lunar roving vehicle, looks like he came from central casting: a male suburbanite appearing with his car parked outside a split level. Underscoring this male suburban bravado, the planetarium's charted "Moon Facts" contains this comment: "Eugene Cernan to Jack Schmitt, the last two people to walk on the moon: 'Don't lock it . . . lose the key and we're in trouble.'" Like my understanding of the land rover, Cernan positions a lunar vehicle as a mundane car. Alan Shepard's version of the suburban moon is even more extreme than Cernan's. If he manages not to lose the key, he could appropriately drive his rover to a country club restricted to white men: "At the end of the *Apollo 14* mission," "Moon Facts" informs readers, "before Alan Shepard climbed into the LEM for the last time, he hit two golf balls." When I read the caption under another exhibition picture — "*Apollo 15* astronaut James Irwin is saluting the flag" — it became clear to me that the Apollo Program saluted the suburban America that white males built.

Astronauts flew a flag on the moon marked as Levittown: "The American flag that the astronauts flew was not made of fabric, but instead was made of foil," states "Moon Facts." Like Aldrin's visor, the foil is another mirror reflecting American patriarchy; it foils the national fabric — the aliens, the un-American Others, the women. The foil flag, like the astronauts' white spacesuits, unfurls the true colors of power. White American men ensure that the stars and stripes call the shots on Earth.

The foil flag remains on the moon to enshrine American manhood. Medals were also left on the moon — ostensibly to commemorate the American and Soviet astronauts who died in space tests. These medals result from pseudo-magnanimity, an example of one-upmanship to underscore that Americans reached the moon first. Americans left the mark of Soviet men for Soviet men. American pseudo-magnanimity also encompasses leaving messages of goodwill from seventy-three nations on the moon. I wonder what criteria were used to discern which nations would be included. To cite another example of what I call American pseudo-magnanimity, a plaque on the lunar module reads: "Here men from the planet Earth first set foot on the moon July 1969 AD. We came in peace for all mankind." In this message, which reiterates the Apollo Program's obsession with men and their footprints, the voice of male America establishes itself as the voice of humanity.

This voice resonates throughout the planetarium exhibit's NASA film, *The Flight of Apollo 11: Eagle Has Landed*. The film's narrator is a slow-speaking, deep-voiced male, who, at the start, pauses to let presidents have their say. John Kennedy: "I believe that this nation should commit itself to achieving a goal before this century is out to landing a man on the moon and returning him safely to the Earth." For Kennedy, sending a male American to the moon is a national imperative. He evokes no spirit of global cooperation. Lyndon Johnson adopts the American pseudo-magnanimous approach: "All that we have accomplished in space . . . we stand ready to share for the benefit of all mankind." Richard Nixon's "sharing" is more akin to *Star Trek: The Next Generation* than to the American male adventure called Apollo: "As we explore the reaches of space let us go to the new worlds together not as new worlds to be conquered but as new adventures to be shared."

The NASA film, like Armstrong's picture of Aldrin, obliterates the individual man and portrays Everyman, patriarchy: "July 16. The day had come. The moon awaited. The men rose early, ate breakfast, and dressed in their spacesuits," says the narrator. The moon, like the women patriarchal stories describe, has nothing better to do than await the arrival of men. The narrator casts the moon as Sleeping Beauty. But, according to the film, the moon is not waiting for her Prince Charming, one particular man. Viewers see no picture of individuals — Aldrin, Armstrong, and Michael Collins — eating breakfast and donning spacesuits. Instead, the camera, in the manner of a masturbatory hand, pans the length of the *Saturn 5* rocket. After the camera seemingly stimulates the rocket, smoking thrust lifts it off the launch pad.

According to the NASA film, the phallus — not individual men — contacts the round, complacently awaiting moon. The penis delivers sperm; the *Saturn 5* delivers the lunar module from its third stage. To comment further upon this rocket / penis analogy, just as Nixon's words are appropriate for a *Star Trek: TNG* script, *Eagle Has Landed* resembles Woody Allen's *Everything You Always Wanted to Know about Sex But Were Afraid to Ask*. In the film's section called "What Happens during Ejaculation," Allen, set against a background resembling a spaceship, plays a nervous sperm about to be shot from an erect penis. The NASA film reminds viewers that the astronauts / sperm are human: during the three-day journey astronauts "kept busy" with "check lists, navigation and observation, housekeeping." In *Eagle Has Landed* "housekeeping" in space is not feminine; housekeeping is represented by an astronaut shaving — not vacuuming the space capsule in the vacuum of space.

When the *Eagle* lands, "there is tension and caution" in the Sea of Tranquillity. In the film's view of the landing — accompanied by the joyous, tension-releasing announcement from the *Eagle*, "Tranquillity base here. The Eagle has landed" — NASA's foot obsession again steps forward. When Armstrong articulates his one small step for a man comment, viewers see a close-up of his footprint and hear the narrator state that "because there is no wind or rain on the moon, these footprints will remain for centuries." The film emphasizes that men's mark on the moon is most certainly enduring.[3]

During takeoff from the lunar surface, to establish that the moon is a homelike America when communicating with Houston during the countdown, *Eagle* comments, "We're number one on the runway." Here again, Apollo machinery is positioned as a mundane vehicle. When *Eagle* departs, the camera shows a close-up of the American flag the astronauts leave behind. The film asserts that, although American men vacate the suburban moon, an American presence remains there.

Despite all the film's attention to men, it does not completely exclude the feminine: "On July 21 the *Eagle* carrying Armstrong and Aldrin climbs slowly to rendezvous with the *mother* [italics added] ship *Columbia*." *Eagle* calls this meeting with the mothership "insertion." During insertion, the maternal *Columbia* is somehow inadequate: "While Armstrong and Aldrin explored the moon Astronaut Collins had kept a long and lonely vigil in the *Columbia*. The approaching *Eagle* was a welcome sight," declares the narrator. Collins, the *Apollo 11* astronaut who never set foot on the moon, is positioned as Woman — a housewife remaining behind in *Columbia* to await the return of "husbands" who venture out to do the work of transforming the moon into American suburbia. Although *Columbia* spawns the *Eagle* and her presence is necessary, like flesh-and-blood women, this "mother" machine does not touch the moon. "Mother" is one of the last words uttered on the moon, though. When *Apollo 17* left the moon, Eugene Cernan said, "Let's get this mother out of here" (Tierney, 15). Cernan's use of "mother" is decidedly not maternal. The moon is not the terrain of the mother.

But NASA's film is the terrain of black men. The camera focuses upon a black man participating in the recovery operation. The film, however, never depicts women working. Women appear only after the astronauts return and enter the mobile quarantine van. Viewers see women standing outside the van, uttering the adoring screams the Beatles elicited a few years earlier. Women, amidst a background of waving American flags, act as cheerleaders for the astronauts. All of the vehicles involved in shuttling men to the moon are so many mobile quarantine vans which separate the moon from women. The astronauts sitting in the real quarantine van bring these questions to my mind: Who are the most threatening polluters? Are the most threatening polluters male astronauts who don air-tight garments to "protect against any possible lunar contamination," in the words of the film's narrator, or the contaminating women cheering for them?

When the quarantine van (emblazoned with the American flag the camera makes sure to capture) moves, the film flashes back to the astronauts' presence on the moon, the place devoid of women and infused with American male heroism. In this instance, the narrator does deviate from using "man" and "mankind" to mean everyone. He states that the astronauts "see what no *human* [italics added] eyes have seen before" and that "a billion *people*" [italics added] watch the event. Although I am glad to hear these inclusive words, I must say that, at the time of Apollo, sexist language did appropriately represent NASA's attitude toward women. Using sexist language was at least honest. Nixon's language lacks such integrity. While aboard the aircraft carrier which recovered the *Apollo 11* crew, Nixon said, "Some way when those two Americans stepped on the moon the people of the world were brought closer together. That it is that spirit, the spirit of Apollo that America can now help to bring to our relationship with other nations. The spirit of Apollo transcends geographical barriers and political differences. It can bring the people of the world together in peace." Not so. The returning *Apollo 11* astronaut who called the moon landing "a technical triumph for the country" was more explicit than Nixon. The Apollo Program erected barriers between American men and the Others who did not reach the moon.

The film's narrator is also more precise than Nixon: "Wherever man journeys tomorrow across the ocean of our universe history will remind him that *Apollo 11* was mankind's first encounter with a new world." Despite the history of the last twenty-five years, our present world resembles the old world of 1969, when "mankind"—the people called "him" and "man"—went to the moon. The present, 1969's tomorrow, looks like our yesterday. It took the astronauts three days to reach the moon. In terms of the sexism I link with picturing and speaking about that journey, little has changed during the last quarter of a century. The sexism I associate with the Apollo Program seeps into the now.

NOW

Soon after the return of *Apollo 11*, a ten-cent air mail stamp was issued to commemorate the event. A father and son team (Paul and Chris Calle) drew and designed the *Apollo 11* twenty-fifth anniversary stamp. Since so little has changed regarding the event's pictorial imagery, it is appropriate for Paul Calle and his son to create the 1994 stamp. Their new design, re-plete with the flag imagery that pervaded the event during the sixties, is a patriarchal stamp of approval. Perhaps inadvertently reflecting our current lack of interest in men's moon walks (and in contrast to the footprint hoopla), the pictured astronaut's feet are not visible. His crotch, though, like a subliminal advertisement, suggests the presence of a penis. The Calles emphasize the spacesuit's codpiece.

They seem to think that bigger is better. Their $9.95 express mail depic-tion of *Apollo 11* shows two astronauts saluting a flag that is wider than the one appearing on the 29-cent version of the event. Perhaps, like the mythic Japanese soldier situated on a Pacific island who fights World War II in the 1950s, the Calles are unaware that the Cold War is over. On both of their twenty-fifth anniversary stamps, an astronaut's reflecting visor reflects nothing. This absence aptly communicates the fact that America has aban-doned Apollo, that new myths supplant the romance of the moon land-ings.[4] New myths are the forces which now pull in people's attention.

National Public Radio commentator Steven Stark says that Chappa-quiddick, not the moon landings, is the current prevailing American cul-tural myth. According to Stark, Chappaquiddick forms the basis for the notoriety Lorena Bobbitt, Tanya Harding / Nancy Kerrigan, and O. J. Simp-son generate. (Viewers of the O. J. trial verdict vastly exceed viewers of the moon landing.) A national obsession with the story of a woman as untainted hero, a narrative we still lack, would constitute a giant step for womankind. In 1971, the nation was in awe when Alan Shepard hit golf balls on the moon; in 1993, the nation was in awe when Lorena Bobbitt chopped off her husband's penis. Lorena Bobbitt's personal step to nullify one small penis became, in the hands of the media, Womankind's giant step to eradi-cate the phallus. Bobbitt instituted a new myth: woman with balls, woman as the literal castrating bitch. In 1993, it seemed as if a billion people watched a drama which could appropriately be described as Lorena Bobbitt vs. the *Saturn 5*. Stark would say that Lorena triumphed. The moon walks are old men's reminiscences. Their Soviet nemesis no longer exists. The *Saturn 5* rockets are rusting. Soap opera, not science, becomes headlines. With no media attention to heroic women in sight, Amy Fisher and Monica Lewinsky supplant Neil Armstrong.

The Calles' blank visor certainly makes an appropriate appearance during the present unreflective, "soap-operaesque" American national mood. When situating the Apollo Program in light of present reality, *Time* magazine senior editor Bruce Handy, writing for the *New York Times Magazine*, addresses the blank visor's relevance to a blank culture:

> An event that still seems so quintessentially futuristic — moon buggies — seems to have become, in the larger sweep of history, just one more thing that happened before Tori Spelling was born. And yet, contemplating the heroic, astonishing feats of Neil Armstrong and Buzz Aldrin and . . . was that his name? . . . and, well, the rest of those guys who went to the moon, aren't we in a situation not entirely unlike some band of Dark Age artisans who — scrofulous, proud if they can slap a hovel together — can only cower before the mighty glories of Antiquity. Sure, we have intimations of progress since 1969: ATMs, CDs, light beer, dry beer, ice beer. . . . [W]e were a better people 25 years ago. (62)

America has degenerated. We have forgotten the names of many of the men who went to the moon. Armstrong himself, who avoids public attention, might exemplify the timeliness of the blank visor. He did not attend the commemorative twenty-fifth anniversary parade held in his hometown (Wapakoneta, Ohio).

While many male moon explorers are forgotten, the media have not as yet related women and female images to moon exploration. In terms of respecting women, allowing women to comment on the moon, nothing has changed in more than twenty-five years. The *New York Times* front-page article, published on *Apollo 11*'s July 20, 1994, twenty-fifth anniversary, includes statements by intellectuals on the day *Eagle* landed. Here is a list of people the article cites: Isaac Asimov, Wernher von Braun, Pablo Picasso, Arthur Koestler, Lewis Mumford, René Dubos, Eugene Ionesco. Even if the *Times* did not query women intellectuals in 1969, it should certainly do so in 1994. Women were silenced then; women are silenced now.

The *Times*' present treatment of women exemplifies that they are not incorporated within discourse about Apollo's significance. Nor can we yet imagine picturing women in relation to the Apollo Program. Henrik

Drescher's illustration which accompanies the *New York Times Book Review* front-page (July 17, 1994) review of Andrew Chaikin's *A Man on the Moon: The Voyages of the Apollo Astronauts* and Alan Shepard and Deke Slayton's *Moon Shot: The Inside Story of America's Race to the Moon* pictures the idea of an astronaut walking on the moon emanating from a man's head. The man's skull is depicted as the Earth. Has no one informed Drescher that, on Earth, women also think — and that women thought about the Apollo Program?

The program now fares no better than women. Women are still silenced; Apollo is grounded. Perhaps present governmental indifference toward moon landings and the present lack of rockets capable of reaching the moon point to the lack of interest that phallic thrusters and white men presently evoke. In other words, the blank visor the Calles portray reveals that patriarchal stories are old hat, the literature of exhaustion. Most men, made uneasy by this new reality, try to cleave to patriarchal stories. In the same vein, the astronauts the Calles depict hold on to long, straight, erect flagpoles, present vestiges of the phallic *Saturn 5*. Significantly, the flag on the Calles' stamp is larger than the astronaut. Nationalism and phallocentrism tower over the individual man.

The planetarium exhibit, whose emphasis upon nationalism and the military seems to be created in a chronological vacuum, holds much in common with the Calle stamps. While, as I have mentioned, the NASA film uses the words "people" and "human," the same cannot be said for the 1994 Hayden Planetarium exhibit called "Man on the Moon: The Apollo Adventure." This title excludes the fact that women were certainly among the four hundred thousand people who contributed to the Apollo adventure. Female secretaries were NASA employees; women must have sewn the spacesuits. Women worked for contractors, as simulator instructors, and as astronomers. The ordeal of the astronauts' wives should also be respected and articulated. Yet the Hayden Apollo exhibit shows no awareness of the now old "new scholarship on women," which highlights women's contributions to history. Despite the quarter-century separating them, the Hayden exhibit is no more enlightened than the NASA film. The exhibit, like the film, is obsessive about footprints and flags. For example, this caption: "Astronaut Buzz Aldrin, Jr., poses for a photograph beside the deployed flag of the United States during the Apollo 11 EVA. The astronaut's footprints in the soil of the moon are clearly visible in the foreground." No explanatory caption retrospectively states that women did not stand on the moon and view Earth from a new perspective. Patriarchy, of course, does not emphasize that women have not gone to a new world — in terms of both the moon and Earth. The planetarium curator who writes that "in the photograph you can see that the fine-grained lunar soil is compacted by an astronaut's boot into a footprint which could stay preserved on the moon for thousands of years" does not imagine that, from a feminist perspective, this boot constitutes an Orwellian stomp on women's faces, that patriarchy preserves sexism for thousands of years and compacts women into limited spaces. The astronauts' footprints are sexist holes in the lunar soil.

In reference to Eugene Cernan's aforementioned comment about being in trouble if the lunar vehicle's key was lost, the Hayden exhibit never mentions that women who wanted to go to the moon were in trouble because they literally were never given the key. They were locked out of Apollo Program flights. While Shepard hit two golf balls on the moon, like present-day Saudi women who are forbidden to drive cars, American women who wanted to be astronauts lacked gender license — were locked in suburbia. Women were not welcome on the moon constructed as American suburbia, the place where aluminum foil depicted an American flag and did not serve as wrapping for green cheese sandwiches. Even though the notion that the moon is made for men is as fictitious as the origin myth about green cheese, Hayden curators, in the manner of the NASA film, would define "shaving" as housework.

Some present-day book-cover designers are no more enlightened than these curators — or the Calles. For example, the *Saturn 5* imprinted with "USA" flanks the entire left side of the book jacket of Shepard and Slayton's *Moon Shot*. Like the beginning of the NASA film, this jacket projects an adoring gaze at the rocket. And, like the film, the jacket pictures the rocket thrusting upward. Here, again, we see the rocket's smoke, and this time the rocket / penis covers half the background moon as it journeys toward it. The rocket is moving and active; the moon is motionless and passive. The moon appears to be smaller than the phallic, thrusting rocket.

The back jacket cover of *Moon Shot*, in the manner of the Calle stamps, shows an astronaut holding a flag which looms above him. His presence hides half the moon, insisting that the moon is subordinate to man and his rockets. The jacket also implies that the moon is subordinate to language. The *os* in the words "moon shot" are depicted as moons. Lovell and Kluger's book, *Lost Moon*, has a similarly designed jacket cover. The words "lost" and "moon," written vertically, appear parallel to the *Saturn 5*. The designers of these book jackets imprison the moon within language's symbolic order. In relation to language, graphics eclipse the moon.

The language of the title *Moon Shot: The Inside Story of America's Race to the Moon* reiterates the message the book jacket conveys. "Shot" denotes action — evokes ejaculation. "Race" communicates the frenzied objective to achieve a goal. Here, again, American men are active and the moon is passive—i.e., Woman. As for female participants in the events *Moon Shot* chronicles (the people the word "women," written with a lowercase *w*, describes), they are passive, lowercase persons — individuals listed under Shepard's and Slayton's dedication to "*The Wives*" (italics in original).

Andrew Chaikin's *A Man on the Moon* provides no linguistic or pictorial departures from my observations about the present's resemblance to 1969–1972 — no new, nonsexist descriptions of lunar exploration. He writes: "We touched the face of another world, and became a people without limits" (Chaikin, ix). Like the Hayden curators, Chaikin does not address the limitations patriarchy imposes upon women in relation to moon landings. He does not explain that the pervasive "unface" as male face that Aldrin's visor represents (which even appears on the Chaikin book's cover) communicates that women, NASA untouchables, were not permitted to touch the moon. Difference, in relation to *A Man on the Moon*, appears as Chaikin himself: a short, slightly built, charming and articulate Jewish man, he does not look like the Apollo Program astronauts. However, in regard to the program, it is Chaikin, not the macho astronauts, who is now the most relevant hero. He is the compiler of the astronauts' story — the narrative which is our most direct present means to share the Apollo experience. Chaikin, according to a new story of masculinity, is an American hero.

The moon appearing in David Goldin's illustration of Bruce Handy's humorous *New York Times Magazine* piece also reconfigures the macho male stereotype and aptly conveys how Americans currently regard moon landings. Goldin's male space traveler, who has more in common with Dagwood Bumstead than with a macho hero, is a cartoon presence who, in the manner of the *Dr. Strangelove* protagonist played by Slim Pickens, sits on a missile. However, even if the figure is a cartoon presence, he is still male. And he still actively thrusts toward the passively awaiting moon. Goldin's moon has eyes which look at an oncoming penile projectile rocket and a mouth which smiles with satisfaction reminiscent of Scarlett O'Hara's expression the morning after she spent the night with Rhett Butler. As Goldin's illustration indicates, even when NASA's verisimilitude gives way to new satiric rendition, a female moon traveler is not in the picture. Sexism is a black hole absorbing energy needed to re-represent women's relationship to lunar exploration. Sexism, in regard to the Apollo Program, causes the past to merge with the present.

BACK TO THE FUTURE: VERNE, MÉLIÈS, AND THE APOLLO PROGRAM

I start my journey back to the future by analyzing four untitled pen and ink sketches (exhibited in New York's Museum of Modern Art) Georges Méliès drew for his 1902 film *Le Voyage dans la Lune* (*A Trip to the Moon*). In sketches 1 and 2 (for clarity, I have arbitrarily assigned numbers to the untitled sketches), male explorers appear on the moon. The phallic objects they bring with them symbolize their masculine presence. In sketch 1, which shows a man holding an umbrella and pointing a telescope toward the sky, a rocket lies on the moon's surface. An umbrella again appears in sketch 2: located in a terrain of large mushrooms, the leader of a group of four male explorers uses his umbrella as a forward thrusting pointer. Sketch 3, which shows a personified moon face, seems to address sketches 1 and 2, implying that the moon might not be happy about being invaded by man and his phallic objects. This moon face is not akin to David Goldin's aforementioned smiling moon. Méliès imagines that a rocket hits the moon in the eye. Tears fall from the unhappy moon face. Unlike NASA and the artists who draw new depictions of the Apollo Program's achievement, Méliès does not portray the moon as gladly and complacently awaiting man's arrival.

In sketch 4, Méliès links women with the moon by depicting a gowned female sitting on a crescent moon. She hovers above bestial-looking men located on the moon's surface. Women who hold stars fly around her. These women appear to play Eloi to the men's Morlocks. They are privileged, beautiful women placed on pedestals who, in relation to men's space race, appear to be above it all. Méliès' vision of women touching the moon and stars implies that women perceive outer space differently from men. His women, like feminist science fiction characters, sans thrusters and phallus, grasp the moon and stars and fly.

Jules Verne is much more realistic than Méliès. His *From the Earth to the Moon* (1865, illustrated by Henri de Montaut) and its sequel *Around the Moon* (1870, illustrated by Emile Bayard) posit that Americans will undertake the first manned moon flight. Illustrations appearing in the 1872 editions of both books are replete with American flags and smoke surrounding a thrusting rocket. These pictures are precursors to all the nationalistic and male-centered images I discuss.

Just as importantly, Méliès' flying women are precursors to an alternate category of existing space exploration pictography. In addition to the Calles' Apollo Program twenty-fifth anniversary stamps, the post office issued a book of "Space Fantasy" stamps. With not a flag, footprint, "USA" logo, or rocket in sight, these stamps portray two women flying together sans *Saturn 5*. (Small engines are attached to their backs.) The space travel vehicles appearing on the stamps are decidedly nonphallic. "Space Fantasy" is a vision of nonmacho, nonmilitaristic space exploration. These stamps indicate that when the moon is absent, in regard to space exploration, women fare better pictorially. The two female space adventurers flying in "Space Fantasy" would never think of hitting Méliès' moon in the eye. They would cause his crying moon to smile.

Méliès' moon would also enjoy the cover (designed by Debora Greger) of my *Lost in Space: Probing Feminist Science Fiction and Beyond*. Greger's lunar surface, backgrounded by a small and distant Earth, dominates her picture. Woman (in the form of a female hand) and nature (in the form of a bird) authoritatively point the way. Greger emphasizes the moon's own craters, not men's footprints. She replaces the flag placed atop a phallic pole with a bird perched on a woman's finger.

Méliès' moon women, the cover of *Lost in Space*, and the "Space Fantasy" stamps challenge patriarchal views of space exploration. And so does, in one instance, unbeknownst to itself, the Hayden Planetarium exhibit. One "Moon Fact" states that "pre-Apollo hypotheses about lunar origins were shown to be inadequate." In other words, patriarchal science is a story, a narrative (subject to revision) which can eventually be defined as a myth. The moon, in the presence of Apollo Program science and technology, was positioned as Woman in a male-authored myth: the moon was seen as subservient, passive, complacent — something to be conquered and subsequently controlled. Scientists later learned that the moon and Earth are made from the same original material. This does not have to mean that, like Eve, the moon is made from Adam's rib, that the moon must be an appendage to man—an American suburbia. Although the moon revolves around the Earth, it is no woman revolving around American men. If science itself can become a myth, then the moon can be understood as something other than a feminine character in a male story. We need a new story about the moon. We should, in the wake of more than twenty-five years, free the moon from a sexist enclosure.

Vera Charles provides one such new story of the moon. Vera, a character in *Mame*, Patrick Dennis' tale about his world-traveling aunt, portrayed in the original Broadway cast production by none other than Beatrice Arthur (star of *Maude* and *The Golden Girls*), sings "The Man in the Moon." Just before doing so, she informs Mame "that well, on the night of the rising of the moon, I, a mere woman, made a universe-shaking discovery." This is her discovery:

> The man in the moon is a lady,
> A lady in lipstick and curls,
> The cow that jumped ovah
> Cried, 'Jumpin' Jehovah,
> I think it's just one of the girls!' . . .
> Oh, her friends are the stars and the planets,
> She sends the Big Dipper a kiss,
> So don't ever offend 'er,
> Remember her gender,
> The man in the moon is a miss. (Herman)

The *man* in the moon is amiss. "The Man in the Moon" contrasts sharply with another song which is newly relevant to the moon: "My Darling Clementine." Project Clementine, an unmanned probe America sent to the moon in the mid-1990s, is a cooperative program between the Ballistic Missile Defense Organization, the Naval Research Laboratory, and NASA to develop a new generation of lightweight advanced-technology satellites. And, yes, the project does derive its name from the song. Project Clementine, which will never return to Earth, is lost and gone forever. The same holds true for the contribution of women who never set foot on the moon. "Dreadful sorry, Clementine" applies to them — and to us all. "Dreadful sorry" can be said to all women deprived of playing key roles in the Apollo Program. But, although the possibility of an Apollo Program female astronaut's one small step for humankind is lost and gone forever, we do not have to be dreadful sorry. Regardless of the fact that representations of the Apollo Program have remained virtually unchanged for more than twenty-five years, Americans are currently bored by white male astronauts — the exhausted patriarchal story of white male heroes. We need a new genre. Male heroes no longer have the right stuff. Even though most pictures do not yet portray a new story of moon landings, people can now accept the possibility that the man in the moon is a Ms.

And she has the last laugh. Despite Cernan's aforementioned comment about getting "this mother out of here," a maternal mother does figure in Apollo. Current discourse positions the male herioc astronauts as infants.

Erik Davis, writing in the *Village Voice*, states, "Despite their bravery, space still infantilized our heroes. During space walks, the astronauts floated in an amniotic void, their puffy thermal ware tethered by an umbilical cord to the mama-machine" (24). Davis reveals that Cernan's reference to "mother" did, after all, have a literal maternal connotation. The late Carl Sagan would have agreed with this statement: "The Apollo experience reminds Dr. Carl Sagan . . . of a 'toddler who takes a few tentative steps outward and then, breathless, retreats to the safety of his mother's skirts'" (Wilford, 20). Although the daring Apollo astronauts would not have welcomed these descriptions, the crew of *Apollo 13*, whose flight was aborted because of an oxygen tank explosion, did redefine heroism in terms of nurturing. When *Apollo 13* LEM pilot Fred Haise contracted a kidney infection while journeying back to Earth within the cold confines of the lunar module, Mission Commander Jim Lovell used the proximity of his own body to keep Haise warm (Lovell and Kluger, 325). *Apollo 13* also showed that science and machinery do not always save the day. Using cardboard and duct tape, the astronauts solved the problem of removing carbon dioxide from air-scrubbing cartridges.[5]

International cooperation now replaces competition as a means to make space exploration possible: "A major civilian space program has now been identified with an important foreign policy objective . . . and the paradox is that this time it involves cooperation with the Russians . . . trying through cooperation in space to help insure the success of Russian democracy" (Wilford, 20). The paradox is also that the best science could have been accomplished by jettisoning the astronauts from the Apollo Program: "Had we elected to explore the moon with automated vehicles and invested just a fraction of the cost of Apollo, we could have produced more and better science" (Roland, 25). The male astronauts, then, were extraneous — hindrances within encapsulated space. On the occasion of the *Apollo 11* twenty-fifth anniversary, none other than Mother Nature herself made this point. She seemed to rail against men marking the moon with their footprints and flag.

I refer to the fact that Americans simultaneously looked back at the moon walks and looked up at comet Shoemaker-Levy 9 assaulting Jupiter. Erik Davis comments upon the juxtaposition of these two events: "What can we say about the conjunction of the moon landing anniversary and an exploding Jove? . . . So following the grainy, melancholic footage of Michelin Men planting an American flag on a world without wind, the news broadcast a cosmic image of errancy, fragmentation, and cataclysmic frenzy. The universe now seems less a place to take giant steps than a place to get squashed. The patriarchal planet will weather the storm, of course" (25).

Earth is a patriarchal planet too. The Apollo Program reveals that Earth shares more in common with Jupiter than with Venus. The Apollo Program also reveals the fragility of swashbuckling men — and of Earth itself. The most enduring picture space exploration has yielded is the image of Earth set against the blackness of space. This famous picture portrays Earth as a round blue hole in that blackness. We can see that Earth is a spaceship, that our patriarchal planet is a nurturing mother. Jupiter, the war planet, is rightfully challenged by what I like to think of as feminist kamikaze comet Shoemaker-Levy 9. Unlike Jupiter weathering the comet, earthly patriarchal bravado can get squashed. The *Saturn 5* is now flaccid — and, hence, poses no threat to Lorena Bobbitt. The Ms. in the moon smiles while looking down at America's current moon-travel impotence. Presently (Viagra's advent notwithstanding), American men cannot use their boots and flagpoles to poke holes in the lunar surface.

III premier discourses
first times

Gert H. Wollheim, The Victor, *1924. Kunstmuseum, Düsseldorf.*

WOMEN "CHURTENING" VIA THE CHA CHA

Ursula K. Le Guin and Hispanic-American Authors Write to the Same Rhythm

In *A Fisherman of the Inland Sea* Ursula K. Le Guin introduces two terms: "churten," which refers to discourse cohesion, and "transilience," which refers to shared perceptions. Churten and transilience are names for forces which pull all things together toward Italo Calvino's "All at One Point" (discussed in the introduction). These new words also denote "spaceship fuel": if a crew fails to reach churten and transilience, the ship fails to fly properly. The disparate individuals who form crews cohere in regard to the stories they tell. Hispanic-American women writers' protagonists act analogously to Le Guin's crews. Julia Alvarez's *How the Garcia Girls Lost Their Accents*, Ana Castillo's *So Far from God*, and Cristina Garcia's *Dreaming in Cuban* involve women who move their narratives by telling tales together, by forming discourse community — by churtening.

This chapter bridges Le Guin's science fiction and the Hispanic-American novels — and Edvard Munch seems to represent this bridge in *The Scream* (see p. 2). I emphasize the point that Castillo's protagonist Fe screams in response to a patriarchal culture with which she cannot churten (and a cat present in *Garcia Girls* echoes Fe's scream). Munch's screaming figure fleeing from men resembles the screaming Fe fleeing from patriarchy via churtening with her sisters. Contrary to Fe's flying sister La Loca and Le Guin's flying ships, the ships that Munch draws floating in contained, demarcated water remain earthbound. Contrary to Le Guin's churtening crews and the churtening sisters that Alvarez, Castillo, and Garcia depict, the crews in Munch's ships are communicatively mundane. What I describe as Munch's Fe figure flees patriarchy's contained seepage and grounded ships and moves across a bridge toward Le Guin's vision of churten and transilience.

In other words, Alvarez, Castillo, and Garcia blur distinctions between the real and the fantastic to generate magic realism, which, I think, re-

sembles Le Guin's *Fisherman*. Here I discuss their Hispanic-American protagonists in terms of how women — defined as wives, mothers, sisters,
daughters, and aunts — achieve churten. The household that Indian author Indrani Aikath-Gyaltsen creates in *Daughters of the House* serves as
my introduction to understanding "alien" Hispanic-American women by
viewing them through a science fiction lens. This chapter flouts usual categories — brings together for the first time that which does not belong together — by positioning Le Guin's science fiction, an Indian author, and
Hispanic-American authors as mutual illuminators of a shared context.
In other words, I place expected differences in churten sameness. Before
turning to Aikath-Gyaltsen's Indian women and to Alvarez's, Castillo's, and
Garcia's women who are alien in relation to hegemonic United States culture (their Hispanic-Americans who discover and rediscover mainland
America), I explore Le Guin's merger between discourse and fuel.[1]

WHAT WRITERS AND WIZARDS KNOW OR LE GUIN'S "CHURTEN" AS FUEL FOR REAL LITERATURE AND FAKE SCIENCE: *A FISHERMAN OF THE INLAND SEA*

Fisherman retells fictional and critical tales. A section in its introduction, called "On Not Reading Science Fiction," recasts Le Guin's essay
"Why Are Americans Afraid of Dragons?" by reiterating that science fiction deserves respect. What Le Guin's introduction does not say, however,
is that *Fisherman* particularly calls for respecting feminist science fiction.
The work, in addition, positions churten as a fuel applicable to both literature and imaginary science. Churten is fake technology which propels
spaceships; it is also, I think, a means to move feminist science fiction from
point *A* (the old separatist stories) to point *B* (versions of these stories
which do not demonize men). Churten and its corollary transilience are efforts to synchronize discourse (*Fisherman*, 115; unless otherwise indicated,
all following Le Guin citations refer to *Fisherman*). The manner in which
the first four stories in *Fisherman* (I call them part 1) have an impact upon
the last three "churten stories" (I call them part 2) shows why *Fisherman*
can be read as metafiction about widening perception and revitalizing feminist science fiction. I discuss how *Fisherman* defines churten as a limitless
propellant which broadens feminist science fiction and addresses literature's separation from science.

The four stories in part 1 churten toward the last three. "The First Contact with the Gorgonids," the first story, resembles a 1970s feminist dystopia which eradicates men. Snake-haired aliens turn protagonist Jerry

Debree into stone, evoking Donald Barthelme's description of fathers who "are like blocks of marble" (129). In Le Guin's humorous take on Cixous' "The Laugh of the Medusa," Jerry Debree becomes debris and his maligned wife, Annie Laurie, becomes "the heroine" (21). Softly humming aliens turn Jerry the prick into a "stiff" (20), a phallic symbol. Le Guin's science fiction revenge tale version of Cixous' essay — which I want to call "The Hum of the Medusa"— is exhausted literature. Why does Le Guin now create the type of story which thrived twenty years ago? The answer, I believe, is that *Fisherman* is a churten progression toward a new version of feminist science fiction. *Fisherman* eventually retells what Joanna Russ calls "The Clichés from Outer Space."

Successful churten travel — which, to my mind, makes a spaceship analogous to an instantaneously arriving e-mail message — is not mastered automatically. The crew in "The Shobies' Story" must practice achieving the transilience necessary to churten. In this vein, the stories comprising part 1 of *Fisherman* also constitute practice sessions, exercises in perception enhancement needed fully to appreciate part 2's churten stories. The Shobies crew "have to believe in it [churten] to make it work" (101), and they achieve transilience by telling stories. In order to understand the churten stories as moves beyond feminist science fiction's clichés from outer space, readers also must practice and believe in expanded perceptions. The stories in part 1, then — like the Shobies crew's exercises in shared narration — are efforts to expose readers to diversified viewpoints. Catharine R. Stimpson and Le Guin express similar views about shared narration. When discussing the interchange between female subordination and insubordination as an imaginative failure to evoke multiple versions of liberation, Stimpson merges rocket and text: "Like a great rocket that resistance inadequately fuels, the text goes up — to explode and then fall back" ("Female," 158). She seems to describe imaginative stagnation as a failed churten experiment.

"Newton's Sleep," part 1's second story, is also a failed churten experiment. The protagonists are the Rose family, Jews placed in Earth orbit who inhabit a sterile colony consisting of professionals. The colonists see hallucinatory visions of unsterile hordes — the "debris people" left behind on Earth. The story, like the introduction to *Fisherman*, rephrases Le Guin's question "Why Are Americans Afraid of Dragons?": "Newton's Sleep" seems to ask this question: "Why are suburban professionals afraid of the underprivileged?" Le Guin's story responds by stressing that, like fantasy, social and cultural diversity are necessities. The antiseptic orbiting ghetto for professionals that the Roses inhabit, like Stimpson's rocket, turns out not to fly. "Newton's Sleep" concludes as visions of dust, debris people, and nature permeate the colony's pristine environment. Le Guin emphasizes that placing professionals in an orbiting antiseptic "hospital" does not cure social ills, that economic segregation is no lofty human height.

This commentary upon supposed social heights has a humorous counterpart, "The Ascent of North Face." "Ascent," another version of Le Guin's "Sur," challenges the myth of the male hero conquering nature. What else can be said about explorers who treat an apartment building like a Himalayan peak?

"The Rock That Changed Things," a story containing more complex humor than "Ascent," further emphasizes metafiction. "Rock" retells Suzy McKee Charnas' *Walk to the End of the World*. Charnas' Holdfast, in Le Guin's hands, echoes the culture wars: Le Guin imagines a class-stratified collegiate environment in which Others challenge a personified "Canon." Charnas depicts privileged men and denigrated "fems"; Le Guin depicts privileged "obl" and denigrated "nurobl." Like fems, nurobl are routinely raped and forced to live in subhuman dwellings, the "nests" that nurobl children called blits inhabit (the blits and nests respectively evoke the "kits" and "kit pits" that Charnas describes). One word signals that Le Guin parts company with Charnas: readers eventually learn that one of the nurobl is a "he" (61). All fems are female; nurobl are socially constructed as Woman. Nurobl attain freedom by inventing churten literary theory of their own: they position themselves as professors of nurobl transilience, a new method to interpret the stone patterns that obl venerate.

Because a nurobl named Bee courageously says that she sees one rock differently, she rocks her world. She deciphers a Rosetta Stone that provides the key to nurobl interpretations. Empowered by the new ability to interpret, a nurobl passionately tells the Canon to "[l]ook for the freedom!" (67). The Canon, as is to be expected, refuses to accept marginalized interpretations of rock patterns. He responds to the singing nurobl (who, perhaps, echo the fems' "self-songs") and to the rock the nurobl throw at his window. "What is the meaning of this?" (67) he asks. Hence, the Canon himself asserts that meaning is open to question (rather than etched in stone) and that nurobl can supply answers. The Canon faces a potential revolution fueled by the power to interpret — to throw rocks. "The Rock That Changed Things" recasts "Sticks and stones can break my bones but words will never harm me." When words are equated with rocks, the usual weapon of the disempowered, revolutionary theory becomes praxis. Nurobl, who articulate the theory of speaking difference and follow their new discourse with praxis in the form of rock throwing, act according to Stimpson's notion of the "feminist switching point." According to Stimpson, "[E]ventually, though, our conversations must end in action, our remonstrations . . . in demonstrations. . . . Finally, we need a feminist switching point when we must move from cultural explorations to explicit political practice" ("Hat," 196). Nurobl, who literally deconstruct repressive rock texts by throwing rocks, function according to Stimpson's feminist switching point when they realize that actions of rock throwing speak louder than hegemonic rock words. Their remonstrations (articulating the need to reinterpret rock) are the same as and different from their demonstrations (throwing rocks). Both are at once conversations and actions which result in canon reformulation.

Freedom to interpret forms the crux of "The Kerastion." Le Guin's friend Roussel Sargent, who invents the Kerastion, describes it as "a musical instrument that cannot be heard" (10). Le Guin calls Sargent's definition a "Borges story" (10). A forever silent apparatus designated as a musical instrument exemplifies the Borgesian contradiction about the same being different described in Borges' "Pierre Menard, Author of *Don Quixote*." This Borgesian contradiction, the assertion that Menard's *Quixote* is at once identical to and different from Cervantes' original, prevents churten and transilience from becoming fixed definitions — i.e., cast-in-stone mental caste systems analogous to the stringent social caste system characterizing the fictional world which claims the kerastion as its own.

In the manner of John Barth's evocation of Borges in "The Literature of Exhaustion," Le Guin uses her churten stories to claim Borges — and the recognition that the postmodern guys who descend from Borges enjoy — for herself. This claim is not new. Odo, protagonist of Le Guin's "The Day before the Revolution" and "mother" of planet Anarres, exemplifies juxtaposing the same and the different. Although Odo invents concepts of freedom, her responses to them differ from those of younger citizens: "Besides, they had grown up in the principle of freedom of dress and sex and all the rest, and she hadn't. All she had done was invent it. It's not the same" ("Day," 861). "Day" describes how the aged Odo is not the same as her younger self who authored a revolution. "Indeed she had been the tireless worker and thinker, but a blood clot in her vein had taken that woman away from her. . . . There was nothing left, really, but the foundation" (868). This is another example of how *Fisherman* recasts Le Guin.

Further, when positioned with Borges, the churten stories can be read as postmodern fictions which involve rewriting and retelling. Le Guin's direct reference to Borges, and the particular way Gveter (a member of the churten test crew in "The Shobies' Story") pronounces certain words, signals her intention to open postmodern canons to women authors. Gveter's hard *k* sounds are idiosyncratic: his "why" becomes "khwy" and his "what" becomes "khwat" (93–94). Gveter's linguistic fabulation evokes postmodern canons which are different from the ones we know. In other words, Le Guin rocks the canon by questioning khwy males (Barth, for example) are predominantly designated as postmodernists, and she confronts the issue of khwat texts enter postmodern canons. Gveter might specifically evoke Barth; the character's particular *k* brings to mind the alternative hard and soft manner of pronouncing Barth's title *Chimera*. (The fact that *Chimera* can be characterized as fantasy—and even as science fiction time travel—has not retarded its inclusion within postmodern canons.) Gveter also points to a second potential pronunciation of "churten." The word's *ch* can be a hard sound—churten can be curtain. *Fisherman* might be read as Le Guin's effort to raise curtains which shroud feminist science fiction as something separated from postmodern canons. Churten is a force which propels feminist science fiction from denigrated generic paradigms to postmodernism. Churten reveals that forming postmodern canons is a guise which enables guys to bask in literary limelight. Churten positions Le Guin as a nurobl who throws rocks at the Canon.

The Borgesian notion that the same is different figures in "The Shobies' Story." The crew consists of Le Guin's usual Gethenians and Anarresti—and unexpected humanoid categories: older women and children. The crew's mission is to practice achieving "relational coherence in terms of transiliential experientiality" (83)—the narrative accord which enables them to e-mail their ship through space. Telling stories near the ship's big library fireplace forms the crew's raison d'être. When the crew members need more in-flight practice, they tell "another story" (83). Another story propels readers to "Another Story," the last piece in *Fisherman*. Telling stories enables the crew to ascertain the narrative "thread" of "crewness," to curtail the hallucinations, reminiscent of "Newton's Sleep," which signal churten malfunction. Churten does not work unless the crew believes in this thread (101).

Churten, then, shares much in common with *Peter Pan*. Failure to believe causes the death of Tinkerbell as well as churten malfunction. The Shobies crew's diverse narrative voice is space flight fuel; their literature is science. The crew's assertion "more freedom" (104) is a more forceful articulation of the "freedom" (67) that diverse interpretation yields in "The Rock That Changed Things." *Fisherman* self-referentially indicates that feminist fabulation, the category which encompasses churten narrative, is story-made fuel for social propulsion. When the Shobies crew is asked "what happened" in regard to the churten testing, they respond by explaining, "'Well, it's quite a story" (105). Their successful churten flight is a story about their stories — i.e., metafiction. However, instead of retelling patriarchal stories (in other words, instead of behaving according to the definition of my term "feminist fabulation"), the crew members retell their own stories. "The Shobies' Story" transforms feminist fabulation into a same which is different.

"Dancing to Ganam" also includes a same which is different. "Dancing" is at once the same as and different from "The First Contact with the Gorgonids." The former simultaneously exemplifies and moves beyond the separatist feminist science fiction "males are the enemy" motif. In "Dancing," Commander Dalzul, called from central casting as a Captain James T. Kirk he-man clone, dies when he grasps a phallic symbol: "He smiled, and put out his hand, and seized the scepter" (145). The "scepter" is an electric rod (an appropriately shaped technological means to confront phallic power); Dalzul expires due to failed interpretation. He is a faulty fabulator who incorrectly rewrites the story that Ganam inhabitants attribute to the rod. While Dalzul defines the rod as a symbol of male power, Ganam natives are more literal than symbolic. Their rod *is* imbued with power: electric current (135). Because he is a bad literary critic, Dalzul suffers a fate worse than loss of tenure. He dies because his story about the rod violates Ganam's interpretive community's understanding of the rod's meaning and function.

Dalzul fails to see that the people of Ganam are far from primitive, that he is the has-been — the macho male hero about to be sacrificed on the altar of narrative progress. A character named Forest describes Ganam as "a non-gender-dominant society" (131). Dalzul, who in regard to the Earth Priestess Ket acts as a male character in the usual story of patriarchal domination, would look askance at Ganam marriages. These marriages are certainly diverse: "polyandry may be the most common, two or three husbands. A good many women are out of heterosexual circulation because they have homosexual group marriages, the iyeha, three or four or more women" (131). There is no place for Dalzul within the configurations Forest describes; he cannot even imagine such a place. Le Guin once announced that the word for world is forest. Dalzul fails to author the proper words to place himself within a story appropriate for Ganam. Although he can travel via churten, he does not share Ganam narrative perception. Ganam (which exemplifies Earth's feminist literature of replenishment) lacks a context for Dalzul's story of the macho commander who sexually appropriates the native Earth Priestess. Dalzul is male debris, discarded because he is a macho cliché from outer space. The author of a story about male bravado which is now as inappropriate on Earth as on Ganam, Dazul is erased from the social text. Placing himself as Brian McHale's "text under erasure," he dies *due* to "perceptual dissonances" (111).

Despite Dalzul's fate, "Dancing" is humorous and evokes the comedic aspects of "The Ascent of North Face" and "The Rock That Changed Things." Dalzul is the stereotypical male who refuses to ask for directions. A character named Shan notices what "Dalzul's unexpected male-heterosexual defensiveness prevented him from doing: go ask for advice and help of Forest and Riel" (127–128). No wonder he misinterprets Ganam culture. He views Ganam culture as "a factional and sexual competition among intelligent barbarians who keep their pruning hooks and their swords extremely sharp" (127). (This description is applicable to many American university English departments.) The landing party described in "Dancing," like revisionary professors, are nurobl confronting interpretation as a fixed definition appearing on a stone terrace: "Shan rubbed one hand against the rough stone of the terrace, puzzled at his own sense of confusion" (127). Shan is confused because he has not yet become a competent reader of the Ganam social story. The electrified rod is the Rosetta Stone in "Dancing," the key to decoding the Ganam social text. Dalzul hears the Ganam social story with a "stone ear" ("For Hélène Cixous"); he grasps the rod whose meaning he cannot grasp. Never understanding the Ganam story of Ganam life, he is the prick who dies when he grasps the phallus. He doesn't get it — and he never will.

In some separatist feminist utopias, women kill male invaders without trying to generate mutual understanding. In "Dancing," Le Guin's retold version of these stories, the obtuse macho male dies simply because he is obtuse, insensitive to the Other's story. Dalzul cannot move beyond the familiar; he cannot see that another version of his story of reality exists. He does not act according to Forest's description of churten.

Forest explains that "[f]aced with chaos we seek or make the familiar, and build up the world with it. . . . In churten, the universe dissolves. As we come out, we reconstruct it — frantically" (132). Churten is metafiction —

and feminist fabulation can be understood in terms of churten. Imagining that the patriarchal universe dissolves, feminist writers reconstruct it in other than patriarchal terms. Dalzul, no feminist fabulator, does not discern that, on Ganam, the patriarchal story is absent and the Ganam social story is present. He cannot fathom that something other than the patriarchal story determines social order. Because he fails to reconstruct the story of patriarchal power, Ganam power (electricity) deconstructs him. Dalzul ignores the fact that people "have their own story, and *they're* telling it! How we'll figure in it I don't know — maybe as some idiots that fell out of the sky once!" (141). Here "Dancing" alludes to the film *The Gods Must Be Crazy* (in which Kalahari Bushpeople believe that a Coca-Cola bottle which falls from a plane is a religious object). From the perspective of Ganam citizens, the gods — Dalzul, who wants to be a god, and his landing party colleagues — *are* crazy. The spaceship's crew does not immediately understand Ganam social codes — i.e., how to act as characters within Ganam's social story.

According to the Ganam viewpoint, Dalzul's death via electrified phallus, the electrocution of a "fatherly" (142) alien, "was deliberate, intentional, arranged" (145). On Ganam, having sex with the Earth Priestess logically leads to death: "If you lie with the Earth, you die by the Lightning" (145). "Dancing," then, is a fable whose moral involves advocating an astute cultural studies approach to one's surroundings. The story insists that the world is a text which must be read insightfully. By emphasizing the importance of interpretation, Le Guin extends the parameters of separatist feminist science fiction. When she defines interpretation as a necessary survival skill for space travelers, Le Guin melds science, fiction, theory, text, and critic. She uses alien worlds to reiterate the expansive spirit of Edward Said's title *The World, the Text, and the Critic.*

Text is emphasized at the start of "Another Story Or, A Fisherman of the Inland Sea": "I shall make my report as if I told a story, this having been the tradition for some time now" (147). These words recall Genly Ai's statement at the start of *The Left Hand of Darkness.* The Borgesian notion of the same being different appears again: "Another Story" is not *The Left Hand of Darkness* — hence, the same words Genly articulates are subsequently different. Le Guin becomes one with Pierre Menard when she rewrites her own words. Barth evokes Borges; Le Guin goes one better when she herself mirrors a Borges character. And she acts in the manner of a fellow science fiction writer who enters postmodern canons. When Genly's words appear in "Another Story," Le Guin liberates her text in the same way that Kurt Vonnegut liberates his protagonist Kilgore Trout. Trout flouts the boundaries of textual endings. So do Le Guin's words. Her text becomes a force. Her text can time travel.

Genly's words travel to "Another Story," protagonist Hideo's story of O, his home world. O is another version of Le Guin's Gethen. Gethenian sexuality, the possibility of one individual becoming either female or male, has become more complicated: on O "each of four people must be sexually compatible with two of the others while never having sex with the fourth — clearly this takes some arranging" (151–152). As "Dancing" is more complex than "Gorgonid," sexuality on O is more complex than sexuality on Gethen. "Another Story" revises Le Guin's Gethenian version of a sexual scenario in which it takes two to tango. On O it takes four who must be three. Le Guin once asked, "Is Gender Necessary?" Not on O, she now answers. O is a round enclosure which pulls people into complex sexuality.

In addition to Barth and Vonnegut, "Another Story" alludes to another of Le Guin's colleagues: Joanna Russ. When Hideo says that "[e]verything now was for a while" (160), his "'for a while'" echoes the concluding words of Russ' "When It Changed." Again, the same is different. "When It Changed," however, is a very appropriate title for "Another Story." Paraphrasing the Italian mother who describes the universe as a point in Italo Calvino's "All at One Point" (discussed in the introduction), Hideo's mother says, "'[Y]ou will shrink the galaxy — the universe? — to . . .' and she held up her left hand, thumb and fingers all drawn together to a point" (170). His mother's left hand (no left hand of darkness) illuminates how "Another Story" becomes "When It Changed" at one specific point: the place in the narrative where Hideo's self divides and he returns to his past life on O. "O is a good world to time-travel in. Things don't change" (182). Not so. Things absolutely do change for Hideo when he goes back to his past from the standpoint of his present. His same becomes different. After a while, Hideo reappears. After a while, Genly Ai's words and Joanna Russ' words reappear in "Another Story."

Patriarchal stories, unlike the structure of "Dancing," do not reappear in "Another Story." While "Dancing," in the end, eradicates the patriarchal hero, "Another" presents this hero and his story as an absence. Hence, when Russ' words figure in "Another Story," instead of rewriting patriarchal stories, feminist fabulation rewrites itself; feminist fabulation becomes a metafictional textual closed system, an O — a hole. "Another Story" is another story in which feminist fabulation comments upon itself within a fiction. Le Guin's and Russ' stories told in tandem exemplify churten; churten propels feminist fabulation forward. Imaginative and theoretical discourse, then, both figure within the circle/hole of Le Guin's churten story of O. Critic and writer are both fishermen in Le Guin's inland sea, the place of story, a corollary to Salman Rushdie's ocean of story.

Like Le Guin's blurring of distinctions between art and science, and fiction and theory, the inland sea is also indeterminate. Hideo tells the story "of a poor fisherman, Urashima, who went out daily in his boat alone on the quiet sea that lay between his home island and the mainland" (148). Is a sea which lies between an island and the mainland an inland sea? This question is open to interpretation. It is possible to achieve transilience in regard to the boat's function, though: "Story is our only boat for sailing on the river of time" (147). An example of postmodern contradiction, *Fisherman* functions in terms of fixed definition and lack of fixed definition. Le Guin's inland sea differs from the one Munch portrays in *The Scream*. No contained body of water, Le Guin's inland sea is all about genre seepage. It pulls different stories, and fiction and science, together.

"Another Story" is certainly a feisty text. Hideo contradicts one famous male critic's story of American literature as well as the demeaning and pervasive social story about women's intuition. As we all know, Leslie Fiedler reads American literature as the story of male heroes lighting out to the territories to escape civilization, defined as the mother's influence. Hideo retells Fiedler's story, told in *Love and Death in the American Novel*, of American literature. He returns to his mother: "I came back to the day I left, but I didn't leave, I came back, I came back to you [his mother]" (185). He also describes his mother in a manner which respects the range and power of female cognition: "'Hideo,' said my mother, in the terrifying way women have of passing without interval from one subject to another because they have them all present in their mind at once, 'you haven't found any kind of relationship?'" (170). Hideo describes the female mind in terms of churten force, the simultaneous presence of many narrative threads. His serious insight is also infused with humor: when she *nudges* him about finding a relationship, Hideo's Japanese-ish mother seems to be quite Jewish. (Would Portnoy complain about his mother's response to the complex sexual relationships on O?) Like Stanislaw Lem's Ijon Tichy, Hideo encounters different versions of himself: "It was possible, that another I was living on Hain, and would come to Udan in eighteen years and meet myself" (186–187). Perhaps, within his milieu of genre fission of the self, Hideo meets his mother's Jewish counterpart. (I imagine another story in which Le Guin's story of O becomes a story of Oy. After all, as I have mentioned, sex on O "takes some arranging"[152]. On O, Yenta the Matchmaker would have her work cut out for her.)

The only evidence of Hideo's divided experience is his "word, and . . . [his] otherwise almost inexplicable knowledge of churten theory" (191). Hideo's word speaks in the voice of science fiction's past, of stories Barth, Le Guin, Lem, Russ, and Vonnegut authored. His word time travels. It allows text and reader and character to remain in Russ' "for a while" during the future. This locational stasis occurs because churten fuels the word — and, hence, real change which is based upon accepting new paradigms (or new stories). Change, fiction, and science are all merely another story. Le Guin, in her introduction, emphasizes this point by blurring the distinction between reality and fantasy, literature and science: "physics and religion are aspects of one science. As writers and wizards know, the name's the thing" (9). Churten, a new name for a new imaginative science, has an impact upon both real literature and fake science — and, hence, positions both on equal footing as texts, stories. Feminist fabulation, my new name for a new understanding of postmodern canons, has an impact upon women's noncanonical texts and men's canonical texts and, hence, positions both on equal footing as canonical texts — i.e., postmodern stories. Difference appears in the face of this sameness. To provide one example, churten (which includes feminist science fiction rewriting itself) is simultaneously a part of and not identical to feminist fabulation (the literature I define as feminist fiction which rewrites patriarchal stories). To provide another example, Le Guin's "for a while" differs from Russ' "for a while." This will be true not once — not for a while — but for all time.

The female Bengali family that Aikath-Gyaltsen describes could appropriately inhabit Russ' Whileaway. *Daughters* and the Hispanic-American novels — Alvarez's *How the Garcia Girls Lost Their Accents*, Castillo's *So Far from God*, and Garcia's *Dreaming in Cuban* — form a textual community which functions via churten theory. These works portray women experiencing different environments. Aikath-Gyaltsen's Chchanda temporarily travels from her home to the outside world. The Hispanic-American protagonists who reside in the United States engage both their own and dominant U.S. culture and, hence, do not abandon their heritage. These women are aliens who, as a group, achieve churten transilience which enables them to travel forward.

"NAGGED BY TYRANTS WITH PENISES":
DAUGHTERS OF THE HOUSE

Daughters is a realistic feminist utopia, another story of the generic science fiction feminist utopia. Eighteen-year-old Chchanda (the protagonist), her younger sister Mala, and their servant Parvati inhabit a house which is a perfectly functioning women's world, a real world Whileaway located in India. Chchanda shares Whileaway denizens' notions that men are extraneous: "The matriarchy of Panditji's House was a universe of nuns, young and old. It was an oasis. Mala and I had no reason to envy the normal family lives of the few children we knew, nagged by tyrants with penises. . . . [W]e considered men of about as much use as the . . . rooster who laid no eggs, the bull who gave no milk" (Aikath-Gyaltsen, 15). Men come to Whileaway; a tyrant with a penis enters Chchanda's house when her aunt Madhulika returns with a husband, lawyer Pratap Singh. Harkening back to 1970s feminist science fiction, Aikath-Gyaltsen positions a man as an invading enemy who must be removed from an all-female society. Chchanda, in the manner of a Whileaway resident, explains, "I loved each stone and leaf of Panditji's House and all of a sudden the entrance of a stranger threatened me" (45). Viewing Pratap as an "interloper" (70), Chchanda embarks upon a war to nullify his domestic presence. He is the patriarchy, "the Man-of-Law" (50) violating Chchanda's woman's world, which is akin to feminist outer space.

Daughters signals the simultaneous appearance of two new stories: (1) a non-Western rewriting, in realistic terms, of feminist science fiction and (2) a non-Western retelling of personal events which dominated American tabloids. Simply stated, Aikath-Gyaltsen at once brings the feminist utopia down to earth and echoes the doings of Woody Allen, Mia Farrow, and Sun Yi Previn. When Madhulika becomes ill, happenings within a fictional Indian house resemble events within the Allen and Farrow apartments, which face each other across Manhattan's Central Park. When Chchanda describes her affair with a man who is practically her guardian, she seems to echo Sun Yi: "That Pratap was practically my guardian, or that I was practically his ward, was only a detail and though a village jury might choose to emphasize this detail, it was still just an accident that he saw Madhulika across the river while I was still growing up" (Aikath-Gyaltsen, 122). While sexually engaging with Pratap, Aikath-Gyaltsen's daughter of the Indian feminist utopia plays Sun Yi, the daughter of another house, Central Park West's Dakota apartment building. The Dakota — home of Farrow and the setting of her role in *Rosemary's Baby* — could serve as an appropriate abode for Madhumita, the daughter Chchanda and Pratap engender. Madhumita is, after all, the product of a union between a woman and an invading devil, Pratap the male intruder.

Because Madhulika and Chchanda embrace the male intruder, *Daughters* shares much in common with texts I call postseparatist feminist utopias. Like Spinel, who journeys to Shora in Joan Slonczewski's *A Door into Ocean*, Pratap is a lone male who enters and functions within a woman's world. Chchanda, in the manner of Lystra's response to Spinel, eventually rethinks her hostile attitude toward the male invader: "What a fool that girl back at Panditji's House seemed now, carrying on guerrilla warfare, needling this man who was strong enough even to permit himself a certain affection for her, the weakness of opposing me and Paro with the light armor of sympathy and consideration" (83). Chchanda leaves her house / feminist utopia to experience a new "world that spread so infinitely beyond our own" (76). Her engagement with this new world occurs because Pratap functions as a force who moves Chchanda from her seemingly confined women's world to involvement with sexuality and the business world. The house and the women within it ultimately exert the strongest pull upon Chchanda, however. This house, no limited space, functions as a spaceship which provides an enclosed, life-giving environment to protect women from the outside hostile patriarchal atmosphere. Like the Shobies crew located within their homey ship, these women ensconced at home move forward via churten transilience.

Their house / ship becomes personified when Chchanda converses with it and gives it "a face" (133). This anthropomorphized feminist utopian abode becomes Pratap's rival and emerges as the love of Chchanda's life. Choosing the house rather than the man, she cleaves to separatist feminist utopia and rejects postseparatist feminist utopia: "I will never, never forgive anyone who makes me give up this house. It means more to me than anyone or anything in the world" (152). She expels Pratap from her house, from the women's world which is "his enemy" (153). The house exemplifies the dominating male sexual role that Le Guin's Dalzul fails to achieve. Pratap is Le Guin's Jerry Debree, the male debris cast out of the text. Pratap, like men in Pamela Sargent's *The Shore of Women*, is expelled from women's civilization immediately after completing his procreative role — after he fathers Madhumita.

Chchanda keeps her daughter and her property — retains Whileaway; the personified house vanquishes Pratap. The house is an enduring fort which can repel Pratap if "he comes back to attack. . . . Already conquered by Panditji's House, how could he overcome it now, in the name of the daughter of the house who had become its very future?" (197). Chchanda's relationship with her house will last longer than "for a while." Chchanda is a hero who prevails against a male antagonist: the house is her personified space, her vehicle / spaceship which enables her to live within a world of feminist churten transilience.

"SIMULTANEOUSLY TWO (OR MORE) SELVES IN CONFLICT": CHURTENING HISPANIC-AMERICAN PROTAGONISTS

Home is also at the heart of *Dreaming in Cuban, How the Garcia Girls Lost Their Accents,* and *So Far from God.* Chchanda, like experimental churten users in "The Shobies' Story" (and like the first NASA astronauts), ventures out before returning almost immediately. The Hispanic-American protagonists I discuss, in contrast, experience more complex journeys. Roberto González Echevarría speaks about these journeys when describing Hispanic writers' depictions of growing up in mainstream U.S. culture's alien environment. Echevarría also addresses a real-world version of "Another Story," Le Guin's tale of a divided self. His view of Hispanic-American protagonists applies to Hideo: Echevarría explains that a "person can emerge not a harmonious blend, but simultaneously two (or more) selves in conflict. This predicament is much more dramatic when people speak two or more languages, for the inner life can be like a United Nations debate, complete with simultaneous translations and awkward compromises. All this, of course, is the stuff of literature, which is why it has become the central concern of Hispanic writers in this country" (18). I am concerned with the stuff of literature which forms the Hispanic-American women writers' central emphasis.

Alvarez's, Castillo's, and Garcia's female protagonists — who, unlike Hideo, cannot literally live two lives — are split in terms of family. The sisters these authors create experience culturally disparate lives from their respective standpoints of difference between hegemonic United States and Hispanic North American societies. Aikath-Gyaltsen's women are analogues of these Hispanic women. The Hispanic grandmothers are, like Paro, female elders who lovingly nurture young women. Some sisters, in the manner of Mala, never move beyond the family domicile. Others — reflecting Chchanda's and Madhulika's experiences — leave home, return, and have an impact upon the domestic environment after encountering the Pratap figure, the male invader. All the Hispanic-American women I discuss engage in communicative and experiential flow between old and new environments. Echevarría describes these flows: "Hispanic Americans today have 'old countries' that are neither old nor remote. Even those born here often travel to their parents' homeland, and constantly face a flow of friends and relatives from home who keep the culture current. This constant cross-fertilization makes assimilation a more complicated process for them than for other minority groups. This 'living origin' is a determining factor for Hispanic writers in the United States" (18). The Hispanic-American protagonists face flows in the form of genre seepage pulling them toward being surrounded by their new old countries.

Like Hideo, then, the Hispanic-American protagonists are divided selves negotiating two versions of reality. They travel between cultures as routinely as Le Guin's spaceship crews churten between planets. Like these crews, the female communities in *Dreaming in Cuban*, *Garcia Girls*, and *So Far from God* function as cohesive groups which share and narrate their experiences. Differences between individuals enhance group solidarity. Alvarez, Castillo, and Garcia are engineers, scientific designers who use words to build churten-fueled female communities. Churten propulsion mode enables authors, characters, and readers to travel to different homes — different worlds. Usual distinctions between artist and scientist, narrative boundaries, and individual authorial voice are blurred. The protagonists, for instance, are akin to Vonnegut's aforementioned Kilgore Trout, appearing as a real world Hideo. Like the Trout / Hideo I imagine, they are split in relation to different cultures and could travel with ease between their respective novels (Garcia's Pilar blends with Alvarez's Garcia girls, for example). Hence, indistinct boundaries and kinship with feminist science fiction characterize United States–based Hispanic-American women writers' use of magic realism.

"PLANET CUBA": DREAMING IN CUBAN

Cristina Garcia's *Dreaming in Cuban* presents the divided self as Lourdes and Felicia, Celia and Jorge del Pino's daughters. Lourdes emigrates to the United States; Felicia remains in "Cuba. Planet Cuba" (134). Both sisters are linked to the fantastic. Lourdes is named for "the miracle-working shrine of France" (42); Felicia, who "had a true vocation to the supernatural" (186), practices Afro-Cuban cult rituals. She turns "Planet Cuba" into a real world of woman's revenge.

No resident of a separatist feminist science fiction utopia is more adept at terminating men than Felicia. After she sets fire to her husband, her daughter Luz matter-of-factly remarks, when "Mamá set him on fire, we knew Papi wouldn't return" (120). Luz rightly assumes that Papi's absence is not "for a while." Felicia's third husband's fate is communicated as a story: "I don't know if this part is true, but Felicia said that she'd pushed this man . . . from the top of a roller coaster and watched him die on a bed of high-voltage wires" (185–186). This husband, a Dalzul figure appearing in Hispanic-American fiction, like Dalzul, learns that sexuality can be electrifying. Felicia, in the manner of the Earth Priestess of Ganam, writes her own story about how a man lights up her life. For Felicia, cult rituals — not marriage vows — are enduring ceremonies. These rituals function as "a kind of poetry that connected her to larger worlds, worlds alive and infinite. . . . My father used to say that there are forces in the universe that can transform our lives if only we surrender ourselves" (186). Rituals are Felicia's churten force, texts that propel her to other spheres. She surrenders to stories and vanquishes husbands. She is a gender battle warrior, Russ' Jael who dreams in Cuban.

Lourdes and her father are connected to the supernatural by earth and shadows. Le Guin mentions that "[w]e are Earth" ("Introduction," 11). When Lourdes is born, she has "no shadow . . . the earth in its hunger had consumed it" (Garcia, 43). Instead of remaining buried in the earth, Lourdes' dead father returns as a ghost / shadow: " 'Lourdes, I'm back,' Jorge del Pino greets his daughter forty days after she buried him with his Panama hat, his cigars, and a bouquet of violets in a cemetery on the border of Brooklyn and Queens" (64). In *Dreaming*, the dead father fares better than Felicia's (temporarily) living husbands. Despite Felicia's less than harmonious relationships with her husbands, *Dreaming* is not totally adverse to men. Jorge is a harmless soul.

At first, it seems as if Garcia does not resurrect the dead mother. Celia's decision to drown herself appears to be quite final: "Celia steps into the ocean and imagines she's a soldier on a mission — for the moon, or the palms, or El Lider. The water rises quickly around her. . . . *Sing, Celia, sing*" (243). Celia, who drowns herself in the manner of Virginia Woolf, reappears as an art form that her granddaughter Pilar (Lourdes' daughter) creates. Celia's artistic convergence with the ocean is, then, a form of generational genre fission. Her death positions art as women's most effective revolutionary tool. When Celia dies, she at once evokes Woolf and bonds with an artistic granddaughter residing overseas in New York. Pilar, a painter, looks toward her grandmother to act as her catalyst for imagining an alternative life.

Pilar mentally reconfigures herself as another Hideo, a second self who could live in Cuba with her grandmother: "I wonder how different my life would have been if I'd stayed with my grandmother. . . . I ask Abuela if I can paint whatever I want in Cuba and she says yes, as long as I don't attack the state. . . . Then she quotes me something El Lider said in the early years, before they started arresting poets. 'Within the revolution, everything; against the revolution nothing.' I wonder what El Lider would think of my paintings. Art, I'd tell him, is the ultimate revolution" (235). To address Celia's revolutionary fervor, Pilar formulates a definitive, woman-centered view of art. She believes that art transcends Castro's revolution and that art is the most effective weapon for a woman's personal revolution.

Pilar is confused, pulled between two cultures. Even though she loves both her grandmother and Cuba, she knows that she belongs in New York (235–236). Yet, despite years of separation, she feels closer to her grand-mother than to her mother: "I feel much more connected to Abuela Celia than to Mom, even though I haven't seen my grandmother in seventeen years . . . she's left me her legacy . . . a love for the sea and the smoothness of pearls, an appreciation of music and words . . . and a disregard for boundaries" (176). When Celia dies after evoking song and giving "her drop pearl earring to the sea" (244), she becomes a female artist who, with her own body, authors a connection to her granddaughter's love of the sea, music, and pearls. The sea enables Celia to erase the geographical bound-aries and cultural differences which separate her from Pilar. Celia, in other words, shares narrative with Pilar, churtens toward her via another version of Le Guin's inland sea.

Celia and Pilar — and Le Guin and Woolf — are female artists whose approach to boundaries and fixed definitions is revolutionary. Pilar, flout-ing biological law, wonders how her mother "could be Abuela Celia's daughter. And what I am doing as my mother's daughter. Something got horribly scrambled along the way" (178). Because Celia's death forms a transcendent link which propels Pilar toward her own psychologically sat-isfying story of female familial continuity, Pilar can unscramble the gener-ational dissonance she describes. Pilar's story, a tale about a granddaughter wishing that her grandmother could be her mother, is biologically aber-rant. Her peculiar version of biology connects her to Celia, making Cuba something other than an "island prison" (173). Sisters Felicia and Lourdes are forever divided selves separated by differing experiences in Cuba and New York. In contrast, magic realism — Pilar's science fiction fantastic version of biology mixed with Celia's artistic response to the sea — enables grandmother and granddaughter to merge.

While thinking about Celia's letters, Pilar "started dreaming in Spanish" (235). This textual link between grandmother and granddaughter occurring at Celia's death coincides with Pilar's ability to dream in Cuban, a nonexistent language, which, I believe, relates to the nonexistent science Le Guin imagines. Le Guin's *Searoad*, like *Dreaming in Cuban*, is about coastal highways, the sea, generational continuity, and (as I have explained elsewhere) Virginia Woolf.[2] Young Pilar seems to echo *Searoad* protagonist Virginia Herne when she says, "We take the coastal highway to my grandmother's house. I look at the sea" (Garcia, 216). The daughters of the houses in Garcia's Cuba and New York — and in Le Guin's Pacific Coast — like Woolf's Orlando, march forward through time and leave female creativity in their wake. Garcia, Le Guin, and Woolf engage each other in churten transilience. Celia's drowning alludes to a Woolf who could appropriately dream in Cuban. Woolf, in turn, has previously seeped within women's noncanonical literature: Jody Scott's *I, Vampire* describes a dolphin-like alien who becomes Woolf. *Searoad* and *Dreaming* speak to each other — and address Woolf. Woolf, the writer who drowns herself, shares an artistic affinity with the Cuban grandmother who makes drowning an art form. Women's art transcends national and generic boundaries. Women's art enables Woolf to dream in Cuban.

TIME'S ARROW POINTS BACKWARD
TOWARD THE DOMINICAN REPUBLIC:
HOW THE GARCIA GIRLS LOST THEIR ACCENTS

In *Garcia Girls*, the daughters of the Garcia house — Carla, Sondra, Yolanda, and Sofia — dream in both English and Spanish to negotiate between United States and Dominican culture. In the manner of Martin Amis' *Time's Arrow* (discussed in chapter 9), *Garcia Girls* concerns time shooting backward. Amis' protagonists move backward to the Holocaust; the Garcia girls move from the United States back to their Dominican past. The girls describe, through various "petites histoires" (Hassan, 169), the personal indignities that two cultures' slings and arrows of outrageous sexism inflict upon them. In the Dominican Republic, machismo positions the girls as second-class citizens. In the United States, they face Chchanda's nemesis, the tyrant with the penis, who this time appears as flasher and penis / pistol. While women in *Dreaming* contend with Fidel Castro's revolution, the Garcia girls coin their own definition of revolution. For them, revolution means women rebelling against sexism and subverting cultural demarcations. Here, as in Le Guin's *Fisherman*, stories act as propellants, fueling the girls' revolutionary zeal. The sisters' diverse narratives, individual differences, and shared experiences move them backward to their childhood. When speaking their experiences through shared stories, they alone venture back to their future and forward toward understanding how sexism is rooted in their lives.

Orality — the mouth, words, stories — functions as the girls' revolutionary apparatus. Their mother, Laura, however, does not immediately define the mouth as an orifice open to violating rules: "[t]he dreaded and illegal marijuana that was lately so much in the news! Mami was sure of it. And here she'd been, worried sick about protecting our virginity since we'd hit puberty in this land of wild and loose Americans, and vice had entered through an unguarded orifice at the other end" (Alvarez, 114). The unguarded mouth is an orifice from which the girls' art — their seemingly limitless stories — emerges. Sight as well as speech pertains to their narratives. In the United States, the girls at once lose their accents and their blindness toward institutionalized sexism. The United States, a location of cognitive estrangement for the girls, distances them from their homeworld's sexism. Exposed to new mainland American cultural manifestations of sexism, their tongues are sharpened in regard to articulating their experiences. Revolution is born when the Garcia girls lose their accents — when they feel free to speak their lives.

The girls' revolution is as systematic as their father's fight against dictatorship in the Dominican Republic: "we had devised as sophisticated and complicated a code and underground system as Papi had when he and his group plotted against the dictator. . . . We sisters gave each other the V for victory sign. It's still a guerrilla revolution after all!" (110, 118). Their insurrection, however, consists of their own story about Fifi smoking in the bathroom, Carla using hair removal cream, and Yolanda reading *Our Bodies, Ourselves*. Winning the right not to return to the island, where they could be forced into "marriage to homeland boys" (109), is their most important victory. The girls win their revolution: "It was a regular revolution: constant skirmishes. Until the time we took open aim and won, and our summers — if not our lives — became our own" (111). Their victory depends upon solidarity.

Mainland America gives the girls a space for freedom, a new world which yields a new perspective. They go to the United States, read Simone de Beauvoir, and plan "lives of . . . [their] own" (119). Newly adept at using words as weapons, they talk back to their cousin Manuel, insisting that women have rights in the Dominican Republic as well as in the United States (122). When Manuel declares that "men wear the pants,"[3] they reply that the "revolution is on" (122). Their version of churten emphasizes that pants are a curtain which hides the truth about the phallic power that tyrants who possess penises wield. Donald Barthelme echoes the girls when he describes penises as vulnerable, less than awe-inspiring entities that cloth conceals: "The penises of fathers are traditionally hidden from the inspection of those who are not 'clubbable,' as the expression runs. . . . Most of the time they [penises] are 'at rest.' In the 'at rest' position they are small, almost shriveled, and easily concealed in carpenter's aprons, chaps, bathing suits, or ordinary trousers. Actually they are not anything that you would want to show anyone" (140). The loss of the Garcia girls' accents involves attributing the same pronunciation to "churten" and the concealing "curtain." Their discourse yields a churten / curtain material more durable than "the pants" (or the cloth Barthelme mentions): a mutually articulated language flag. They routinely flash their flag.

For Carla, liberation means articulating a trauma which involves pants: describing her response to a flasher. The sight of the flasher's penis temporarily silences her, however: "Not one word, English or Spanish, occurred to her" (157). The flasher shows his penis; so too, metaphorically, do the police, who have belts which "were slung around both their hips, guns poking out of holsters. Their very masculinity offended and threatened. They were so big, so strong, so male, so American" (160). When police resemble flashers, guns become indistinguishable from (or metaphorically seep into) penises. Penises are the girls' tyrants; violence is juxtaposed with sex. Their mother contends with this juxtaposition when Dominican thugs confront her: "The two men turn and, almost reflexively, their hands travel to their holsters. Their gesture reminds her of a man fondling his genitals. It might be this vague sexuality behind the violence around her that has turned Laura off lovemaking all these months" (210–211).

The Garcia girls are daughters of the house who, like Lourdes del Pino, flee Caribbean dictatorship and revolution. Their own story of revolution is most important to them, however. Daughters joined in solidarity, they rewrite usual governmental revolution stories as tales of women's fight against tyrants with penises. Tales told in an accent uniquely the girls' own nullify threatening penises. In other words, their mouths confront rather than engulf penises: storytelling is more crucial than performing marital fellatio upon island homeboys. Instead of taking in penises, their mouths expel narratives. The sisters are not pulled into the patriarchal story about women's sexual work.

Alvarez positions the United States and the Dominican Republic as separate texts. Her characters behave differently in each locational story. For example, Cousin Manuel: "When he's in the States, where he went to prep school and is now in college, he's one of us, our buddy. But back on the Island, he struts and turns macho, needling us with the unfair advantage being male here gives him" (127). When the girls travel to the island, their experiences are analogous to Hideo's alternate self returning to his past. This comparison holds especially true for Yolanda (who returns to the island after successfully moving forward as a revolutionary woman).

Garcia Girls begins when 39-year-old Yolanda visits her homeland. A grown woman armed with a firsthand account of mainland America, she is a critic rereading the Dominican macho story. She is an experienced translator who can interpret the usual discourse of men's war stories as a vocabulary particularly useful to her. For example, she authors her own version of the Cuban missile crisis: "I heard new vocabulary: *nuclear bomb, radioactive fallout, bomb shelter*" (167). She defines these words as "phallic power"; her bomb shelter manifests itself in the form of the interconnected stories she authors with her sisters. Words become bombs in the sisters' war to control their own space. When Fifi spends clandestine time with Manuel at a family gathering, one of her male relatives "hurries over to the men's side, knowing the first bomb will explode among the women" (129). Island gender roles are also bombs — and they explode women's freedom. The girls' solidarity deters the nuclear fallout which emerges after they blow up myths about sex roles and rules. Translation of war rhetoric enables the Garcia girls — daughters of Dominican and United States houses — to become "a household of independent women" (146).

To achieve their independence, they transcend obstacles. For example, Yolanda describes an impediment placed in her aunt Mimi's educational path: "Mimi was known as 'the genius in the family' because she read books and knew Latin and had attended an American college for two years before my grandparents pulled her out because too much education might spoil her for marriage" (228). The young Garcia girls author a story about Mimi. "'The day Tia Mimi marries, cows will fly.' We cousins teased. I [Yolanda] did not think any less of my aunt for being single" (229). Mimi does marry — and the cows remain earthbound. The girls' one-sentence story, immediately followed by Yolanda's response, exemplifies a patriarchal narrative that feminist revision counters. Simultaneously acting as author of patriarchal myth and feminist fabulator who critiques that myth, Yolanda is poised to repel the phallic bombs that tyrants with penises aim at her.

The tyrants' incessant assault — and women's continual revolution against sexism — positions *Garcia Girls* as a recast version of Joe Haldeman's *The Forever War*. Alvarez presents *The Forever War* as woman's story about unceasing war between the sexes waged across barriers of time and differing cultures. The Garcia girls band together to survive the forever war between women and men. Their fallout shelter is a cognitive space derived from churtening between two cultures. They never arrive at the fixed definition of particular destination. Neither Dominican nor mainland American, they are forever positioned between two countries and seek shelter from gender war's fallout.

When Yolanda sees a vision of a female black cat (289), she — in the manner of the Shobies crew — describes hallucinating. Yolanda distorts time within a novel which portrays time moving backward: "You understand I am collapsing all time now so that it fits in what's left in the hollow of my story?" (289). Like Pilar, Yolanda at once defies time, writes her grandmother's story, and discusses her art (290). While doing so, she looks at darkness and hears a black cat: "I wake up at three o'clock in the morning and peer into the darkness. . . . I hear her, a black furred thing lurking in the corners of my life, her magenta mouth opening, wailing over some violation that lies at the center of my art" (290). She looks into the dark, into the female cat's mouth — into a magenta source of the female "beast's" cry generating stories counter to patriarchal stories. Alvarez portrays this beast as Dominican women who at once lose their accent and flout the island's sexist behavioral codes. The cat's wail, a Munchian scream, functions as an air-raid siren resounding in response to phallic bombs aimed at women. Yolanda takes cover within her recast version of Cuban missile crisis fallout shelters. Her version of these shelters is the mouth as origin of her art: her newly unaccented voice which, functioning in tandem with her sisters, speaks her story.

Garcia Girls describes a Dominican missile crisis. The girls recast John F. Kennedy[4] — they become individuals who keep penises / bombs at bay within silos / pants. During Kennedy's Cuban missile crisis, Soviet missiles threaten the United States' western hemisphere space; during the girls' Dominican missile crisis, patriarchal missiles threaten to enclose them within stereotypically appropriate female spaces — confining spaces out of which they cannot seep. When words shield the girls from the impact of patriarchal stories (or, metaphorically speaking, when the black cat wails and when the curtain is pulled back) the girls see that man is a mouse, that the phallus — as Barthelme emphasizes — is a bombastic patriarchal story about vulnerable penises. The girls' words and stories about lives sometimes experienced in tandem enable them to survive their revolution against the tyrant with a penis. Penile missiles, for a while, retract; the girls are free to declare more space as their own. Instead of acting as characters in the island's patriarchal stories, they tell tales in their own voices. The most important story of revolution in *Garcia Girls* is not the father's struggle against the dictator. It is, instead, how the Garcia girls band together and win their freedom from patriarchal repression, the story of girls' revolutionary acts.

SO FAR FROM PATRIARCHY: *SO FAR FROM GOD*

While *Garcia Girls* focuses upon women's revolution won via stories, Ana Castillo's *So Far from God* involves a war of words fought to institute a paradigm shift pertinent to religion and the workplace. *So Far* combines the revolutionary fervor portrayed in *Dreaming*, the sex war portrayed in *Garcia Girls*, and women's attachment to their home portrayed in *Daughters*. These juxtaposed plots describe how religious and corporate master narratives are rewritten in a New Mexico town called Tome. Protagonists Sofia and her four rather supernatural daughters (Caridad, Esperanza, Fe, and Loca), when they author fictions which eventually become reality, reconfigure religious and secular tomes. These women, in other words, create churten fuel to propel society in new directions.

Sofia accomplishes nothing less than relegating the Jesus myth to the literature of exhaustion. By using her four miraculous daughters' deaths to generate religious fervor regarding revering mothers, she makes god the father obsolete. Sofia's newly established organization called MOMAS — Mothers of Martyrs and Saints — poses a worldwide challenge to usual Catholic dogma. Her impact upon corporate paradigms is no less revolutionary: as Tome's new mayor, she creates alternative workplace cooperatives for Tome's citizens who are poisoned while working for the chemical industry. Sofia's imagination and her ability to implement the new ideas she mentally conjures alter Tome — and the world. *So Far* is about how feminist utopian notions — changes a marginal mother envisions — can become real.

This emphasis upon real change begins when Castillo's first chapter frenetically plunges readers into the fantastic. Baby Loca dies, is resurrected, and flies to a church rooftop during the novel's first three pages. Castillo calls upon the hyperbolic fantastic to challenge Catholicism. Although Jesus himself does not fly, flying is routine in Sofia's family: "I had to produce the kind of species that flies" (84), Sofia exclaims when she describes Caridad flying (sans plane) in the mountains as well as Esperanza's jet flight to her job as a Middle East reporter (84–85).[5] The sisters' real and fantastic relation to flying indicates that the feminist fantastic potentially can become real. Fe, the only sister who remains earthbound, begins to scream incessantly, enacting Munch's *The Scream*. When doing so, she echoes the cry of Yolanda Garcia's imagined black cat, articulating the need for paradigm shift. The flying sisters also call for such a shift. Their call is answered when their churten transilience provides Sofia with the impetus to change the world.

The sisters do not permanently focus upon the public world. Like Chchanda, they decide there is no place like home: Loca's sisters "had each gone out into the world and had all eventually returned to their mother's home" (25). Loca, who "had grown up in a world of women" (151), would feel comfortable in Chchanda's house. But, while Chchanda engages the larger world in the manner of Loca's sisters, Loca's own attachment to home is more extreme: "Loca had never left home and her mother was the sole person whom she ever let get near her. . . . She had never been to school. She had never been to a dance. . . . Loca had never had a social life" (221). Neither part of society nor socialized in terms of patriarchal imperatives, Loca inspires her mother to construct alternatives to patriarchy. Venturing into the world causes the death of Loca's three sisters. Loca, the woman who never experiences sexual intercourse, dies of AIDS. No wonder Sofia is motivated to establish new religious and secular master narratives.

The women's world in which Loca grows up resembles a 1970s separatist feminist utopia. Supernatural daughters live perfectly satisfactory lives without men. Caridad, for example, enjoys a close relationship with her horse, Corazon. When having a vision in which Corazon leads a herd, she feels "like . . . [she] was one with them" (49). Here Caridad is quite akin to Suzy McKee Charnas' Riding Women. Sofia's feminist utopia is, for the most part, separatist. Domingo, Sofia's husband, who is absent during the girls' childhood, is cast out by her after he returns. He is this novel's intrusive male driven from a women's world. None of the sisters enjoys permanent relationships with men; men desert them. Sofia deserts the myths about family, religion, government, and work that men author. Little else can be expected from a woman who receives messages from a feminist utopia stock character: the "loving mother goddess" that Castillo calls "La Llorona, Chicana international astral-traveler" (163).

So Far positions New Mexico, "The Land of Enchantment," as the "Land of Entrapment" (172). Enchantment and entrapment both figure in Castillo's New Mexico. She makes the state's nickname real by imbuing Tome with enchantment and depicts the town's entrapping lack of economic opportunity. Sofia uses enchantment mixed with reality to assuage entrapment — to make Tome something other than an enclosure for people's life force. She herself becomes a loving Chicana mother goddess who creates a new position (the mayor of Tome) and ensconces herself within it. Ditto for her religious MOMAS organization. Mayor Sofia, with a realistic abracadabra, creates a new economic space: a sheep grazing and wool-weaving enterprise which provides its two dozen female employees with child care (146–147). Her enchantment becomes part of the real world, assuaging economic entrapment. Sofia successfully uses her own voice to create alternative social structures: "Since becoming La Mayor of the village council, even if it wasn't official (nor was the village council, for that matter, since Tome was not incorporated), there was no stopping Fe's mom from ever speaking her mind no more" (157). Sofia uses two methods to generate feminist magic realism: she appropriates formerly non-existent institutional space and authors alternative social stories which have an impact upon other individuals. In other words, when Sofia turns to feminist enchantment to change the world, she churtens toward paradigm shift.

Sofia's self-resurrection stems from her efforts to foster community improvement. Instead of silently grieving for her dead daughters, Sofia uses her maternal voice to revitalize society. Some of her daughters are resurrected via the fantastic. Sofia, in contrast, is reborn in terms of religious, political, and economic realism. Fe remains dead. She is killed by patriarchal stories, by those who expose factory workers to carcinogens. Esperanza, who returns from the dead "ectoplasmically" (186), dies in the Middle East while reporting men's story of war. Esperanza and Fe, deeply ensconced within reality, die because they act as characters in patriarchal stories. Despite their miraculous doings, Loca and Caridad also die. They are too tied to the fantastic. Sofia thrives because she successfully balances the real and the fantastic. She is a feminist fabulator who changes the world by critiquing and rewriting patriarchal stories.

Sofia juxtaposes the personal and the political. When she addresses a crowd to discuss the fact that Esperanza will not return from the Gulf War (241–243), it is apparent that there is no difference between Esperanza's disappearance (after a jet flight) and Caridad's disappearance after flying (again sans plane) over the mountains. The point is that, like enchantment, war is a story. Castillo challenges — and, within her novel, changes — the patriarchal myths which comprise reality. For example, the section of *So Far* called the "Way of the Cross Procession" connects religious myth to the problematic (poverty, toxic exposure, nuclear power plants, AIDS, and pesticides). In Castillo's alternative reality novel, boundaries between the fictitious and the real are blurred. By questioning the fixed definitions of real and fantastic — for example, by having women who fly with and without planes meet the same end — Castillo subverts patriarchal myths and the symbolic order these myths perpetuate. The title *So Far from God* underscores that the resurrection of women, and the social rebirth that feminist enchantment inspires, is so far from male-imbued religion and social stagnation. This distance does not make change impossible. Many people live so far from irrelevant religious myths.

Castillo's version of enchantment brings readers so far from patriarchy's penchant to mask (or to curtain) detrimental science by attributing faultiness to women's bodies. For example, women dying from chemical poisoning at Acme International, the company responsible for Fe's death, are given "ibuprofen tablets, advice about pre-menopause and the dropping of estrogen levels in women over thirty, and pretty much that it [their medical problems] was just about being a woman and had nothing to do with working with chemicals" (178). The false stories that often characterize patriarchal science — for instance, the lies that Acme International (a name which smacks of a Warner Brothers cartoon) perpetrate — are appropriately categorized as enchantment. Many people, however, believe the Acme Internationals of the world as surely as they believe religion. *So Far from God* insists that dangerous patriarchal myths — misogynistic religion and life-threatening science — must be countered. Le Guin positions stories as propellants; Castillo positions stories as feminist Patriot Missiles which shoot down SCUDs representing the myths that exploit the poor and hamper women. SCUDs as symbols of religious and corporate dogma are patriarchy's most sacred tomes. Revolutionaries like Sofia, Pilar, and the Garcia girls shoot these metaphorical SCUDs down.

Not stopping short at reconfiguring corporations, politics, and religion, Castillo challenges the definition of death itself. As I have mentioned, Esperanza, after dying, is "still around" (204); Fe "was really dead" (205). So too for the metaphorical SCUDs. In Castillo's novel of combined oppositions, patriarchal master narratives (religion, science, corporations) resemble Fe and Esperanza's combined experiences. They are at once existent and (due to Sofia's efforts) replaced, still around as well as really dead: Sofia's cooperative confronts Acme International, Mayor Sofia confronts politics as usual, and MOMAS confronts Catholicism. Sofia's world-changing institutions are so far from the fantastic.

So Far from God acts as a vortex which pulls the real and fantastic together. Castillo's novel celebrates the mother and the possibility that mothers can make change. Like Gerd Brantenberg's *Egalia's Daughters*, *So Far* is a feminist gender-role reversal utopia: the Holy Mother replaces the Holy Father. At the novel's conclusion, MOMAS — the pervasive cult of the mother — is successfully fueled by churten force emanating from those who no longer wish to demean mothers. As a New Yorker, I offer another interpretation of MOMAS: alternative museums of modern art. Aikath-Gyaltsen, Alvarez, Castillo, and Garcia create women's art which can inspire change.

These authors' combined artistic creations form a real-world version of Le Guin's "United Nations" of planets (called the Ekumen). Like Ekumen representative Genly Ai, the authors make their report on potential social changes in the form of a story. They imply that the possibility for change to last longer than "for a while" is not fantastic. Churten fuels paradigm shift.

The alien female authorial voices I explore in this chapter speak in tandem with a female science fiction author's protagonist — they echo Genly Ai. "Truth is a matter of the imagination" (Le Guin, *Left*, 1), say these authors' texts in ways which are at once the same and different. Joined in churten, the authors scream out from Yolanda's imagined black cat's mouth, the space (which resembles Le Guin's planet O) that Munch draws in the form of his screaming figure's rounded mouth. Their combined message: feminist imagination must alter patriarchal "truth"; it is necessary for women to remake their homeworld.

8

WRAPPING THE REICHSTAG VS. RAPPING RACISM OR "A COLORED KIND OF WHITE PEOPLE"

Black / White / Jew / Gentile

Race and religion are customarily viewed as rigid categories in which such supposedly distinct groups as Jews, gentiles, blacks, and whites are positioned separately. These enforced differences disappear on the Internet, where self-presentation and identity are individual choices. A Jewish man, for instance, can easily appear on-line as a black woman. In this chapter, I argue that religious and racial genre fission is part of the real as well as the virtual world. For example: current discourse includes the idea that Jews are not white;[1] Jews routinely pass as gentiles; blacks routinely pass as whites. Furthermore: in England, the Irish are not considered to be white; in the former West Germany, the former East Germans are not considered to be white; Austrians residing in South Tyrol, a part of Austria annexed to Italy after World War I, are defined as Italians. The real world presents race as a fiction. The point is that, when considering race and religion, it is possible for the different to be the same. Self-presentation on the Internet can resemble self-presentation in reality. Here I explore texts which challenge the supposed lack of differentiation between blacks and whites, Jews and gentiles.

Popular culture and reality are replete with counterversions of the supposition that racial and religious differences are fixed definitions. For example, *The Jeffersons* is funny because, although their skin color matches that of their black maid Florence Johnston, George and Louise Jefferson are economically white. This sitcom's theme song makes this color sameness as difference clear: "Beans don't burn on the grill. Took a whole lot of trying just to get up that hill. . . . We're movin' on up." While "movin' on up," George and Louise leave black culture behind. They move above and beyond their former neighbor Archie Bunker, who, in relation to the economically privileged Jeffersons, is financially black. Fran Drescher, when she plays the lead in *The Nanny*, is a new version of the color sameness as difference that the Jeffersons' maid epitomizes. Nanny Fran, the Jew employed in a WASP household — unlike her colleague Niles, the butler — is not white. In the manner of these sitcoms, Spike Lee's *Jungle Fever* implies that blacks and whites are the same. When commenting upon the female leads (dark-skinned Italian actress Annabella Sciorra and light-skinned African-American actress Lonette McKee) in this film which confronts the women's racial difference, Michelle Wallace states that "visually, the racial difference between Sciorra and McKee is nil" (*"Jungle Fever,"* 130).

During the apartheid era, the South African government, for monetary reasons, decided that the racial difference between Japanese and Chinese people is not nil. Because the Japanese are rich tourists, the South African government declared that Japanese are white and Chinese are black. Distinctions between Jews and Germans in today's Germany are similarly capricious. Sander Gilman points to this arbitrary categorization when he describes the deaths of Heinz Galinski (a Jew) and Karl-Hans Rohn (a gentile German), who respectively passed away on July 19, 1992, and November 12, 1992. Galinski, the most visible head of the Jewish community in Germany, was represented in death as a gentile: "Galinski, the survivor, the exemplary Jew, whose Jewishness defined him in the public sphere, memorialized as a Jew, was represented in death as a German, that is, as a Christian. However unconscious this act may have been in the German context, it signified the inability to see him as a Jew and as a German simultaneously" (*German Culture*, 32). The *Berliner Zeitung* marked his death with a cross. Rohn, a 53-year-old disabled retiree, died because he was mistakenly marked, because two skinheads defined him as a Jew: "Rohn was not Jewish but was evidently attacked because a bartender identified him as a Jew. After beating him to death, the skinheads burned his body with the cry 'Jews must burn!' His death was reported in the Israeli, American, and German media as that of a Jew" (*German Culture*, 34). These deaths mark the death of clearly demarcated racial distinctions.

My discussion of racial categorical blurring centers upon Richard Wright's *Uncle Tom's Children* and Alan Gurganus' *White People*. Michael Lerner's term "politics of meaning," Octavia Butler's *Parable of the Sower*, Erica Jong's *Fear of Fifty*, John Updike's *Bech: A Book* and *Bech Is Back*, Aharon Appelfeld's *Katerina*, and Walter Abish's *How German Is It* inform my ideas about Jews and gentiles. Shirlee Taylor Haizlip's insights about "passing," Salomo Friedlaender (Mynona)'s "The Operated Goy," Oskar Panizza's "The Operated Jew," Jack Zipes' term "operated Jew," and Christo's artistic wrapped Reichstag figure in my response to the imaginative texts. I begin to consider the meaning of the racial and religious "alien" by first turning to Stanislaw Lem's and Pamela Zoline's science fiction aliens.

"ME PALEFACE!": PAMELA ZOLINE AND STANISLAW LEM

Zoline's "Instructions for Exiting This Building in Case of Fire" underscores that attitudes which, in the past, resulted in decisions to burn Jews and blacks could, in the future, cause nuclear conflagration. The story exemplifies an effort within science fiction to eradicate the alien. Zoline imagines that secret agents kidnap children and relocate them in foreign countries. The agents hope to eradicate nationalistic differences and avert the nuclear holocaust that differences might generate. They create a situation in which "Russian, American and Chinese children have been scattered over the planet like grains of rice; in Northern Ireland such is the nature of the horrid conflict that Catholic and Protestant babies have been exchanged and re-worked so that they are often living down the street from their biological parents. And so throughout the world, every barrier of nation, race, class and religion has been crossed and recrossed with our tender future citizens.... If a nuclear missile aimed at my 'enemy' is now, also, by definition, aimed at my children, will it stay my hand?" (Zoline, 109). Chapter 7 views United States cultural aliens in terms of feminist utopian scenarios. I now discuss racial and religious difference in terms of Zoline's science fiction leveling of such distinctions. Before approaching texts which question the categories blacks, whites, Jews, and gentiles, I briefly turn to Stanislaw Lem's "Prince Ferrix and the Princess Crystal," a science fiction story whose protagonists, in the manner of Zoline's secret agents, subvert cultural classifications.

In Lem's once upon a time the prince and princess are machines whose transportational mode, "the royal spaceship" (873), is no horse-drawn coach. Lem merges science fiction and fairy tale — and distinctions between sentient entities (humans and machines). All is not well between the technological and human life forms. Ferrix's father, King Armoric, retells the tale about Capulets and Montagues when he explains that "there can be no agreement nor traffic between them and ourselves, for we go in changor, sparks and radiation, they in slushes, splashes and contamination" (871). Crystal, questioning this story of racism, is a Juliet who will marry any Montague. She desires any Other, any white male human husband. Refusing to bet upon the prince who is a machine, she instead insists upon her own story: "Every suitor who seeks her radioactive hand is denied audience, unless he claim to be a paleface" (871). This princess desires a consort from a despised racial group, the "paleface" we designate as a white male human.

Not to be outdone by Crystal's new version of *Romeo and Juliet*, Ferrix counters her tale when he authors a parodic retelling of Oskar Panizza's "The Operated Jew" and Salomo Friedlaender's "The Operated Goy" (which retells "The Operated Jew"). In Lem's science fiction fairy tale, which helps adults cope with racism and aims a phaser at racist fixed definitions, Ferrix the machine disguises himself as the maligned paleface. When doing so, he becomes analogous to the transformed (or reconceptualized) Jew, to Jack Zipes' "operated Jew." Zipes explains this term: "What I want to suggest by this image is that there is a fusion of the social engineering of modernism, the reification process of late capitalism, and traditional forms of anti-Semitism that sets the context for the way outsiders define Jews and the way Jews define themselves. . . . The operated Jew is always active, changing, trying on new bodies, if you will, new parts, to fit into the scheme of perfecting the world and to become part of the world's operations" (36).

The operated Jew trying on new parts (or new mechanisms for new mechanizations / schemes) is the cyborg as Jew. Zipes' image also applies to the Jewish woman who, to appear more acceptably gentile, undergoes rhinoplasty and dyes her hair blonde. The operated Jew is analogous to Fay Weldon's "she-devil" — as well as to Poe's M. Valdemar (discussed in chapter 1). Valdemar is the experimental subject of "postponed operations" (Poe, 197) who ultimately — like Panizza's odoriferous "crumpled and quivering . . . counterfeit of human flesh" (Panizza, 74), Itzig Faitel Stern — becomes a "mass of loathsome — of detestable putridity" (Poe, 203). Gilman's description of Stern links him to Valdemar: "On his wedding night, Stern becomes intoxicated and in his drunkenness all his newly acquired qualities of body, tongue, and mind disintegrate. . . . The Jew unravels under the influence of drink. . . . Jews become their true selves when the constraints of civilization are removed" (*Body*, 204). Stern and Valdemar are things that fall apart.

When Ferrix decides to win the princess by casting himself as an operated paleface, like Stern and Valdemar, he does not present a pretty sight. He quite resembles a separatist feminist science fiction description of men: when looking at a mirror image of his transformed self, he sees "a hideous monster, the very spit and image of a paleface, with an aspect as moist as an old spider-web soaked in the rain, flaccid, drooping, doughy — altogether nauseating" (Lem, 872). The mirror reflects a Nazi propaganda film, the "monstrous" (Panizza, 50) Stern who is moist Woman rather than Friedlaender's rigid Aryan Count von Rehsok. The transformed Ferrix is another version of the Nazi's untransformed Jew and the patriarchy's untransformed woman (the she-devil who has not been operated upon). In Lem's fairy tale oozing with science fiction, before returning to his original form, the prince / machine decides to become a frog / white male human. When a "real paleface" (Lem, 876) is presented to the princess, Ferrix's true identity becomes apparent: "Ferrix, though he was smeared with mud, dust and chalk . . . could hardly conceal his electroknightly stature, his magnificent posture, the breadth of those steel shoulders, that thunderous stride" (876). Ferrix is flaccid no more. He, in fact, is akin to Friedlaender's Count von Rehsok, whose "legs . . . took strides as though descending from Mount Olympus" (76). The real paleface (like Panizza's description of Stern, the "real" Jew) remains a putrid monster. Friedlaender defends the Jew as well as the paleface when he asserts that the Aryan can imitate them successfully. In other words, Gilman explains that Rehsok is "passing": "Count Reschock-Moshe retains his Jewish image at the conclusion of the tale. This is Mynona's point: the Aryan can become a Jew and live happily ever after. The Aryan can reshape his body and mind into that of a Jew by means of a Jewish science and learning. But is he a *real* Jew, or just a disguised Aryan? The story leaves this point unsettled. Isn't Reschock 'passing' after all?" (*Body*, 207).

Ferrix addresses this ambiguity. The human monster he imitates is both black and white. Ferrix's disguise, which resembles the merger of black and white that Allan Gurganus portrays in *White People* and Richard Wright portrays in *Uncle Tom's Children*, is constructed from two materials: black mud and white chalk. Lem also brings stereotypes attributed to Native Americans to bear upon his conflation of black and white to denote "monstrous human." When the real paleface appears, he announces himself by saying "Me Paleface!" (Lem, 876). Here Hollywood linguistic racism is called from central casting to confront fixed definitions of usual racist stories. The word "paleface" is Hollywood's articulation of difference uttered from the despised Other's point of view. In Lem's story, all human men are the paleface, the monster, the species that captures its fellow human and "sell[s] it to the highest bidder" (873).

According to Lem's version of the operated human, juxtaposing Africans, Caucasians, and Native Americans evokes a familiar text: What's black and white and red all over? The answer, of course, is another text: the newspaper, the chronicle of racist atrocity. In Lem's story, which speaks against racism by flouting the generic boundaries between science fiction and fairy tale, the human is positioned as joke. When Ferrix and the paleface battle, the human becomes the punch line, the literally deconstructed Other who meets the same amorphous end as Stern and Valdemar: the "paleface fell against the prince . . . and it smashed and broke, and splashed apart, and was no more" (876). The human paleface is erased; the princess, who changes her mind about her own kind, rewrites her story of racism. The human does not live; the prince and princess, who are machines, live happily ever after. Lem's science fiction fairy tale communicates a happy ending in regard to racist stereotyping: the paleface is perhaps "just another empty invention — there are certainly fables enough in this world" (877). Lem suggests that stereotyping is itself merely fairy tale.

"I'M WHITE, I THINK" OR NOT AS SIMPLE AS BLACK AND WHITE: SHIRLEE TAYLOR HAIZLIP

Our world certainly contains enough fairy tales / racist myths. Distinctions between blacks and whites constitute one such myth. Writers indicate that these distinctions are not simply black and white—i.e., iron clad. As Lem juxtaposes science fiction, reality, and fairy tale, Shirlee Taylor Haizlip (an African-American whose *The Sweeter the Juice* recounts her search for her mother's missing white family) argues that rigid racial categorization is a fairy tale. Before turning to Haizlip, I want briefly to mention that John Guare's *Six Degrees of Separation*, a work which juxtaposes reality and fiction by appropriating the biography of David Hampton, reflects Haizlip's argument. Paul, Guare's protagonist, eradicates class distinctions when he claims to be, and in the eyes of beholders becomes, Sidney Poitier's son. When Paul ensconces himself within a white upper-class household, he is something other than a black ghetto youth: he operates upon himself — dons linguistic and cultural drag — and emerges as a black Ivy League–educated white.

Hampton shares much in common with O. J. Simpson. Simpson also emerges from the ghetto, becomes something Other than despised racial minority, and is ultimately presented as an exaggerated version of the black ghetto inhabitant: the black male murderer of a white woman. He is at once treated as white *and* as Willie Horton. Bell hooks' comment about the many scenes in black literature "where black people, most often males, fight one another publicly, to entertain white folks, making of themselves a dehumanized spectacle" (92) leads me to conclude that hooks would characterize both Hampton and Simpson as "dehumanized spectacle." America, fascinated by the idea of black men as something other than men (monsters or spectacles outside the category "human"), turned Hampton's and Simpson's real stories into respective spectacles: play / Hollywood movie and media circus.

Haizlip argues that blacks and whites are often connected by even less than six degrees of separation — that blacks and whites are often the same. Writing in *American Heritage*, she states that members of her black mother's family "looked like white people" ("Passing," 46). Haizlip seemingly applies Zoline's science fiction scenario about nullifying differences to science when she mentions anthropologist Ashley Montagu's wish to abolish the concept of race, geneticist Luigi Cavalli-Sforza's confirmation that DNA consists of genes emanating from many ethnic sources, and microbiologist Jonathan Beckwith's assertion that scientists cannot measure genetic differences between races (47). These scientists author instructions for exiting Zoline's burning building; they theorize about rewriting stories of human difference which, for example, result in American urban conflagrations. When Haizlip stresses that blacks and whites can pass for each other, she describes, in terms of the science fiction alien encounter, a convergence between Zoline's imagery and scientific theory: "Population experts tell us that large numbers of black people are 'missing.' I doubt that they were abducted by aliens" (48). Zoline's agents, who kidnap children and place them within an alien social context, could have abducted the missing blacks.

According to Haizlip, rather than being a fixed definition, racial categorization is in the eye of the beholder: "In different periods the same people in my family were listed as mulatto, black, or white. The designation could depend on the eye of the beholder or the neighborhood where they lived" ("Passing," 48). In addition not to being as simple as black and white, differences between blacks and whites often do not exist. "Some geneticists claim that as many as 80 percent of black Americans have white bloodlines and that a surprising 95 percent of white Americans have some black ancestry" (48). Haizlip's description of Cavalli-Sforza's findings in *The History and Geography of Human Genes* indicates the appropriateness of comparing his view of biological reality to Zoline's science fiction story: "all ethnic groups hold an array of overlapping sets and subsets of mixed gene pools. He notes that modern Europeans (the ancestors of America's immigrants) have long been a mixed population whose genetic ancestry is 65 percent Asian and 35 percent African. There never has been any such thing as a 'Caucasoid' gene. Nor is there such a creature as a 'pure' white or black American" ("Passing," 48).

The pure white or black, then, is as fictitious as the science fiction alien. In light of this fact, racism is obsolete. When participating in the hearings of the Senate Committee on Government Affairs on the Human Genome Diversity Project, Cavalli-Sforza and Mary-Claire King described racism's obsolescence more vehemently: Haizlip explains that these geneticists "called racism 'an ancient scourge of humanity' and expressed the hope that further extensive study of world populations would help 'undercut conventional notions of race and underscore the common bonds between all humans'" ("Passing," 48).

UNCLE TOM'S CHILDREN AS WHITE PEOPLE:
RICHARD WRIGHT AND ALLAN GURGANUS

Gurganus and Wright respectively express the same hope in *White People* and *Uncle Tom's Children*. Although it might, at first, appear that Gurganus and Wright depict rigid race classifications, close examination reveals that these authors could serve as Zoline's secret agents. Gurganus and Wright, who articulate the lack of distinction between blacks and whites, echo the science and science fiction I discuss. *White People*, the collection whose title announces racial categorization, questions such categorization. Helen Larkin Grafton, the protagonist of Gurganus' "Nativity, Caucasian," is "unmistakenly a white girl" (56). Bryan, the protagonist of "Breathing Room: Something about My Brother," however, might take issue with this statement. Bryan, a self-described controller of white paper, decides to eradicate color when depicting people: "Here at the big kitchen table, my favorite artist's studio, I control a piece of vast white paper; in easy reach enough peeled crayons to map a war. I am ready to commit myself to the drawing of those persons I know best, I know too well. Today each will get not a color — because white people are not, colored, or are they? — but, one shape apiece" (75).

Like the scientists Haizlip mentions, Bryan questions distinctions between blacks and whites. And, like Zoline's agents, Bryan nullifies color and reconfigures the map of human genres. He applies his shape classification method to Ardelia, his family's domestic worker. This black woman becomes a brown shape: "She is a brown (colored) triangle, she is a sweet dark tent" ("Breathing Room," 76). Bryan's family is nurtured within the space of Ardelia's sheltering tent. From the white family's perspective, the sweet dark tent associated with Ardelia, a "lifelong helper, cook, and company" (76), is a positive enclosure.

Ardelia as "tent" does not belong on a battlefield. Hence, "sweet" domestic workers play no role in *Uncle Tom's Children*, Wright's mapping of the American racial war, the burning of black men's flesh. Jim Crow once provided the only instructions for how blacks might exit the social building (or construction), which result in their own burning. Wright describes his experiences regarding learning these instructions, acting as a character in the story of Jim Crow. When Wright's white employers fire him for allegedly violating this story, he reports to his family that they "told me that I must never again attempt to exceed my boundaries. When you are working for white folks, they said, you got to 'stay in' your place if you want to keep working" (8). Jim Crow, the cultural imperative that blacks remain in their place, is analogous to Isaac Asimov's robots' relation to the Three Laws of Robotics. Asimov's robots must adhere to the laws of robotics; Wright's blacks must act as merged humans and robots who adhere to Jim Crow laws.

Within the white world Gurganus describes, another entity emanating from outer space and science fiction, the black hole, is an unspecified dangerous space: Bryan, who reappears in "A Hog Loves Life: Something about My Grandfather," explains that "[d]uring breakfast I can't help noticing — this milk carton is coated with Wanted posters. Posters no longer seek the hurters. The hurt ones are now shown. Missing kids. Lost to what? To maniacs, or black holes, or a new child-slave trade?" (215). In contrast, for Wright's Big Boy, a member of a race that an old child-slave trade victimizes, the threatening hole is literal and specific. During his escape from white pursuers, Big Boy flees to a hillside, where "he got to his knees and backed slowly into the hole" (42). Racism brings this black man to his knees and places him within a hole. When Big Boy peers out from his hole, he witnesses the burning of a black man, his friend Bobo (48–49). He sees the black man tarred, the black man made blacker, the black man recreated as the operated black. "He knew the tar was on Bobo. . . . He saw a tar-drenched body glistening and turning" (49). He sees the body of the operated black being torn apart by whites who classify Bobo's ear and finger as "SOURVINEERS" (49).

Wright's operated black is both black and white: Bobo is feathered as well as tarred. In addition, Big Boy regards his burning friend in terms of black and white: "the wind carried, like a flurry of snow, a widening spiral of white feathers into the night. . . . Then he saw a writhing white mass cradled in yellow flame. . . . the writhing white mass gradually glowing black, growing black in a cradle of yellow flame" (49). The burning black mass depicted as a writhing white mass points to contemporary notions of eradicating racial difference—to the fact that the crowd, the white mass, is burning one of its own. The white mass—the humans—behaves according to the manner in which Ferrix, the operated human, describes humans exploiting animals as a food source. Ferrix, when imitating the human paleface, presents an unusual description of human eating habits: "we perforate until they expire, and we steam and bake their remains, and chop and slice" (Lem, 874). The whites who murder Bobo perforate and steam and bake and chop a member of their own species. Their behavior underscores that the operated black is an animal, meat prepared at a barbecue. While witnessing the burning of his friend Bobo, Big Boy hears an order to "'PO ON MO GAS!'" and retreats "back into the hole" (Wright, 49). Subhuman language reconstructs Bobo as a subhuman, cows him. Subhuman whites perform a real version of Lem's parodic view of carnivore paleface eating habits.

Uncle Tom's Children deviates from presenting the hole as a completely negative space in "Long Black Song," the story of Sarah, a black woman who commits adultery with a white man. Sarah's lover Tom's "leaving had left an empty black hole in her heart, a black hole that Silas [her husband] had come in and filled. But not quite. Silas had not quite filled that hole" (106). Snakes fill the hole Big Boy inhabits; Silas creates the hole of Sarah's longing which results in her attraction to Tom. During Sarah's lovemaking with Tom — before the empty black hole appears — his color is inconsequential to her. She does not care that "hes [*sic*] a WHITE man! A WHITE man! (112). When Sarah and Tom make love, black is blended with white to form red, silver, and blue — colors which are not racially tinged: "she rode on the curve of white bright days and dark black nights . . . till a high red wave of hotness drowned her in a deluge of silver and blue" (113).

Wright underscores that men's race war, not women's heartfelt interracial love, pervades society: "killing of white men by black men and killing of black men by white men went on in spite of the hope of white bright days and the desire of dark black nights" (126). Murder is described via blurred color imagery and descriptions of nonblurred days and nights. Silas' response to Tom negates distinctions that Jim Crow perpetrates. Instead of playing the subservient black male, Silas insists upon his manhood: he protects his wife, his property which another man appropriates. When Silas asserts himself and shoots a white man (126), he defends his masculinity—becomes a white man. The white man, in response, becomes Lem's pale-face articulating disgusting gastronomic inclinations: "'Cook the coon!' 'Smoke im out'" (127). One of the white men tries to justify gastronomic word usage which connotes cannibalism: "'Yuh think yuhre white now, nigger?'" (127). The white men eradicate the transgressor of race roles, quashing black manhood.

Responding by insisting upon the slippage of racial categories, Wright, in "Fire and Cloud," defines racism as a white engulfment. Taylor, the protagonist, explains that "black folks is jus los in one big white fog" (130). The black folks, in other words, are lost in a white space which clouds black subjectivity. Bruden, white racist protagonist of "Fire and Cloud," states that a "niggers a nigger! I was against coming here talking to this nigger like he was a white man in the first place" (152). How would Bruden respond if he encountered a member of Haizlip's family — a "nigger" who is white? He would insist upon clinging to racism. He would place those he defines as Other within Big Boy's hole. He would perpetuate Taylor's fate. After Taylor is whipped, he finds himself located within his own version of Big Boy's hole: "In him was a feeling that some power had sucked him deep down into the black earth, had drained all strength from him" (164). The force of racism is in him, draining his strength by sucking him into a hole. There is, however, a positive aspect to Taylor's experiences. White light shines within Taylor's hole. His lacerated back "seemed to glow white hot" (165). This glow sheds light on the fact that black and white are not separate categories.

Gurganus' "Blessed Assurance: A Moral Tale" also counters the assurance that black and white remain within specific boundaries. At the start of the story, Jerry, the young protagonist who sells funeral insurance to blacks, asserts that "I myself am not black" (232). Within Jerry's world, racial categories are rigid to the extent that dogs are "trained to attack Whitie" (237); interracial interactions are encounters between faceless black or white blurs rather than meetings of individual minds. This situation changes for Jerry when he grows especially close to one of his customers, the elderly Vesta Lotte Battle. During his initial interaction with Vesta, Jerry acts as a real-world Prince Ferrix. While trying to change a tire in the rain in front of Vesta's house, he becomes disguised, an operated white. He "turned the color of the mud, then the color of the tires and was standing here considering sobbing" (243). When Vesta rescues him, she is something other than a black blur: "her whole head gleamed with the same flat blue-gray color. Like a concord grape's — that beautiful powdery blue you find only on the freshest ones" (245). Vesta, a gleaming blue-gray presence, appears as an operated alien radiating the color purple.

When Jerry finally learns to recognize blacks' individuality, his new knowledge acts as a force which nullifies his own individuality: "the more vivid each dark person became, the blanker, blander, and whiter I felt" (254). A part of white anonymity, Jerry regards himself as a blank white page. "Blessed Assurance" is about nullifying the recognitional blur with which blacks and whites regard each other. The story insists that blacks and whites need to reconstruct each other's faces in a manner analogous to Vesta's expert approach to repairing broken china. Gurganus optimistically compares broken china to the broken interracial connections. Vesta's sign, placed outside her house as an advertisement, communicates his uplifting message: "Can Fix" (256).

This repair depends upon racial convergence, stressing racial commonality. Jerry experiences this commonality when he realizes that, like blacks, his parents have been economically exploited: "Vesta Lotte Battle's former owners still mostly owned my own broken-down wheezing parents" (268). Racial convergence occurs when Jerry learns that his parents have a literal colored body part — Brown Lung: "Cotton starts out white but if you breathe white cotton for years enough, it gives you something called Brown Lung. You figure it" (272). An important insight for Jerry emerges from recognizing cause and effect regarding white cotton and Brown Lung: whites own, harm, and change other whites — his parents are both one with black experience and operated whites. Their operation is permanent. Ferrix can remove his paleface disguise; Jerry can remove the mud which covers him; Jerry's parents cannot color their lungs something other than brown. His white parents acquire a forever brown body part and are forever economically positioned as blacks.

Economics ultimately defies color lines for Jerry. In later life, he could appropriately echo Johnny-Boy, protagonist of Wright's "Bright and Morning Star": "'Ah cant see white n Ah cant see black. . . . Ah sees rich men n Ah sees po men'" (192). Like Johnny Boy, "Blessed Assurance" insists upon transcending color lines in relation to economics. The multimillionaire heir to the funeral insurance fortune is a "coffee-and-cream-toned gent" (269). Gurganus evokes the doings of Zoline's secret agents when he presents "coffee-and-cream"— combined white and black— as a means to assuage racial social dysfunction. He alludes to a potential biological occurrence which could result in blurred racial characteristics:

"Our baby girl lives in St. Louis with a black airlines mechanic who plays jazz on weekends" (302). It is not necessary for Zoline's agents to kidnap this couple's child. If the black airline mechanic impregnated the white daughter, the couple would perform a mechanical biological operation which caused racial categories to fly away.

Gurganus and Wright question categories which separate black and white. Taylor, the aforementioned protagonist of Wright's "Fire and Cloud," articulates this questioning when he expects whites to join blacks during a protest march: "'Ah think the white folksll be there. . . . Theys hongry, too'" (156). Because blacks and whites are both human, it is necessary for both to eat. In Lem's science fiction / fairy tale world, this paleface necessity would become a means to generate racial antipathy. Like Gurganus and Wright, Lem insists that racism is grounded in vacuousness. Like Lem, Gurganus and Wright insist that racism is a fairy tale which prevents people from living happily ever after. In other words, racism is an at once black and white hole which drains human energy. Racism evokes science fiction writer Jody Scott's title *Passing for Human*: people who burn people are something Other than human.

PASSING FOR JEWISH / "PASSING FOR GENTILE" OR SOWING A PARABLE OF MEANING: OCTAVIA BUTLER AND MICHAEL LERNER

In the context of the ambiguity which characterizes Haizlip's family, upon the occasion of her thirty-fifth Wellesley College class reunion, one of her classmates says, "'You'll never guess what my husband just asked me. . . . He wanted to know if you were Jewish. Boy, is he going to be embarrassed when he hears your talk'" ("Passing," 49). Although it is safe to assume that most blacks are not Jewish, I want to focus upon an example of shared Jewish and black discourse. More specifically (even though Michael Lerner and Octavia Butler have both told me that they have never heard of each other), I argue that Lerner's "politics of meaning" and Butler's *Parable of the Sower* belong within the same genre. Butler and Lerner, responding to and disheartened by the real world, fuse political discourse with religion to generate social change. Lerner equates liberal politics with Judaism to stress community; *Sower* concerns Lauren Olamina, a young empath and prophet who forms a community and starts a new religion. Both Lerner and Lauren juxtapose community, religion, and politics to generate paradigm shift.

Lerner's "politics of meaning" is a strategy for change, a new way of thinking. Not merely a means to garner political clout, the politics of meaning is the antagonist of selfishness. According to Lerner, "The politics of meaning is an attempt to shift the dominant discourse of our society from an ethos of selfishness and cynicism to an ethos of caring and idealism. . . . Let every social policy, economic and political institution, movement, or way of life be judged as productive to the degree to which it tends to produce human beings who are idealistic not cynical, caring and not selfish, demonstrably capable of sustaining loving and committed relationships, and who are ethically, spiritually, and ecologically sensitive and alive . . . our goal is . . . healing, repair, and transformation from a system based on selfishness to a system based on love and caring" ("Jews," 1). Lerner's ideas are rooted in his experience as a mental health practitioner for the working class. While listening to his clients, he notes the dearth of meaning in their lives.

Listening also inspires Butler to write *Sower*. Five items garnered from news reports particularly inspire her: (1) the effects of drugs on the children of addicts, (2) the widening gap between rich and poor, (3) the throw-away labor resulting after factories move to low-wage countries, (4) the fact that forty-six percent of Americans are semiliterate, and (5) global warming (Butler reading). These conditions stem from the unimpeded selfishness Lerner describes. He explains that "the dynamics of unimpeded selfishness have led to a monumental . . . social crisis (manifested in rising alcoholism, drug abuse, family breakdown, and societal violence) so intense that most people will eventually come to see that their long-term self-interest is being destroyed by a society that validates every individual and corporation seeking their own narrow material short-term self-interest" (Lerner pamphlet). Both Lerner and Butler wish to assuage the commercial and professional selfishness that destroys the quality of individual lives.

Sower depicts a near future in which social breakdown is carried to an extreme: people live in walled enclaves to protect themselves from cannibalism and random fires. The enclaves, the ghettos, are desirable locations in a world analogous to a pervasive concentration camp which victimizes everyone. Butler creates this future because she believes that "we need not make this future" (Butler reading). Both Butler and Lerner want to engender a future which improves upon the present. To accomplish this objective, Lerner, former analyst and present charismatic guru, speaks and writes about religious commitment, community, and caring. When she creates a new community and religion, Butler's Lauren accomplishes a fictional version of Lerner's efforts. Lerner is a psychotherapist; Lauren suffers from hyperempathy syndrome. The Jewish man and the black female protagonist are both attuned to the pain of others.

Lauren uses her new religion, called Earthseed (the name of Pamela Sargent's 1983 novel), as a tool to repair broken social structures and broken people. She is a power seeker who learns by using the power she attains. Like Lauren, Lerner also wishes to use spirituality as a tool. He describes a new form of relevant Judaism which combines religion, social awareness, and intellectual discourse. He is a power seeker who has influenced Hillary Rodham Clinton and appeared on the *New York Times* editorial page. People feel uplifted and form community when they flock to Lerner's home and conferences.

Butler's science fiction emanates from reality; Lerner's reality can be understood in science fiction terms. Lerner and Lauren both function in a manner analogous to Ursula Le Guin's notion of churten (discussed in chapter 7): they move people by establishing a common point of view. Lerner's *Tikkun* magazine and politics of meaning are hyperempathetic churten vehicles which transport people toward generating social change.

Lauren at once generates change and transcends categories. "Lauren," a strange name for a black prophet, evokes juxtaposed blacks and Jews. "Lauren" is the stage name of the Jewish girl from Manhattan's Upper West Side who went to Hollywood and married Humphrey Bogart. Lauren Bacall journeyed west and impersonated a glamorous *shiksa*. Lauren Olamina journeys north and changes from walled neighborhood inhabitant to androgynous leader of an interracial community. Her community bands together to repel marauders with painted faces who themselves are multicolored questioners of racial categories. In the manner of the Wicked Witch of the West attacking the Scarecrow, the marauders hurl fire at Lauren's group, which walks north on California highways. Unlike Dorothy, Lauren can never return home; the California highway is no yellow brick road.

Lauren must build her own Oz. Zahra Moss, Lauren's second convert, responds to Lauren's construction plans: "if you want to put together some kind of community where people look out for each other and don't have to take being pushed around, I'm with you" (Butler, *Parable*, 200). Lauren hopes that she and her followers will "grow our own food, grow ourselves and our neighbors into something brand new. Into Earthseed" (201). Earthseed, a mixture of politics and spirituality, is a science fiction analogue to a *Tikkun* community. When describing the essentials of Earthseed, Lauren could be paraphrasing Lerner. She says that she wants "to learn to shape God with forethought, care, and work; to educate and benefit their community, their families, and themselves" (234). Lerner and Lauren both combine religion with education, community, family, and individual satisfaction. According to Lauren, the "world is full of painful stories" (235). Lerner and Lauren wish to restructure society, to rewrite the stories of people's pain. Butler and Lerner address present-day slavery: people enslaved by degenerating social structures. Butler and Lerner would concur with Haizlip's opinion that in "America I believe there is now a profound need, a deep preternatural yearning to connect — to feel related, to be part of that special group we call family" ("Passing," 54). *Tikkun* and Earthseed are about connecting with nonbiological family members.

JEWS / GENRES / GENTILES: ERICA JONG

I have so far explored how texts communicate racial uncertainty: how blacks can be white and whites can be black. To underscore this point, in the previous section I have described how, unbeknownst to themselves, a black woman and a Jewish man reflect each other's discourse. Writing counter to this fluidity, Erica Jong (in the section of her *Fear of Fifty* called "How I Got to Be Jewish") situates Jewishness in terms of fixed definitions and lack of fixed definitions. Ambiguity characterizes her discussion: on the one hand, she argues that Jews can never escape Jewishness; on the other hand, she states that Jews turn to writing to "reinvent" themselves (Jong, 67). Her point reiterates Zipes' notion of the operated Jew: Jews are made.

According to Jong, writing enables Jews to make themselves, to define themselves as something other than the Other. As Jong explains, Jewish children are excluded from the private schools which create the George Bushes who run the world (62). Jews are "defined, designed" (62); Jews are social constructions. Writing enables Jews to be something other than Jews — the fixed definition Jong describes: "A Jew may wander from Egypt to Germany to America to Israel . . . but nevertheless remains a Jew. And what is a Jew? A Jew is a person who is safe *nowhere* (i.e., always in danger of growing *payess* at inopportune times). A Jew is a person who can convert to Christianity from now to Doomsday, and still be killed by Hitler if his or her mother was Jewish. This explains why Jews are likely to be obsessed with matters of identity. Our survival depends upon it" (68). Gilman's version of Jong's point that Jews are forever Jewish: "All of the changes which the Jew acquires are useless" (*Body*, 204). Jong and Gilman reiterate Panizza's "The Operated Jew."

Jong (along with Gilman and Panizza) implies, then, that Jews are the constantly shifting people forbidden genre fission, the people forever vulnerable to being swallowed by Nazis' ovens. Since Jews are invented, they turn to writing to reinvent themselves, to rewrite their given identities. However, the ultimate goal of the reinventions is for Jews to remain Jewish, to enter the heaven that is the "Hebrew Home for the Aged" (Jong, 60). Jews, who cannot escape being Jews, use texts to transform themselves into a re-created same which is different: Jews. For example, Jong — who could never be anything other than Jewish — calls her section "How I Got to Be Jewish." Jews write "to be repeatedly self-created," to give themselves "a class" (70), to reclassify themselves as Jews, to reclaim Jewishness in terms of genre fission which seeks to absorb itself. This Jewish self-absorption, the need to create the same as a difference from gentile exclusion (or extermination), manifests itself when Jews seek other Jews during old age and death.

This need is also applicable to the Jewish woman writer's working life. Jong rightfully explains that Jews are always in danger of growing *payess* — or, in Zipes' terms, Jews are always in danger of becoming operated Jews. In this respect, Jews and women merge. Jews are always subject to anti-Semitism; women are always subject to sexism. Jews offend gentile decorum by supposedly sprouting *payess*; women offend patriarchal decorum by the ever present possibility of the public menstrual bloodstain. Jong's response: Jewish woman writers should become more Jewish. Since Jewish women writers can never pass as Jane Austen, they should "reclaim Emma Goldman and Muriel Rukeyser" (Jong, 296). Jewish women, who are discouraged from claiming the identity of both woman *and* Jew, need to stake this claim by acting in the manner of other minority women: African-American women who are celebrated for exploring their ethnicity, for example. While black woman writers are free to articulate their cultural differences, "Jewish women writers have mostly hidden our ethnicity as if it were unimportant" (295). In other words, if Michael Lerner can achieve commonality with Octavia Butler, so can Jewish women writers. If Jewish women writers treat ethnicity in the manner of black women writers, they will be free not to assimilate, to rewrite themselves as themselves.

According to Jong, when all women writers claim the power of the black woman, color and gender will no longer be important: "The black woman is *allowed* to be our seer, our poet laureate, our oracle. I would like to see all women writers — whatever their ethnicity — claim this power, so that eventually both color and gender can become insignificant" (295). Color and gender become insignificant in Arthur C. Clarke's *Childhood's End* (when humans merge with an Overmind), in Butler's Xenogenesis series (when humans merge with aliens called Oankali), and in Jong's vision of all women writers claiming black women's communicative power. When articulating ethnicity involves making color and gender irrelevant, humanity becomes the science fiction unitary entity. For Jong, then, Jewish women can establish Jewish writerly identity by entering black women's authorial space (in which articulating racial difference is generated and admired). In terms of postmodern contradiction, when Jewish women writers speak their difference in the manner of examples that black women set, difference will lack importance. Jewish writers re-create themselves as Jews; Jewish women writers would do well to express difference in the manner of black women's freedom to do so. Speaking difference in a different voice leads to insignificant difference.

Jong, then, provides a method to place such supposedly disparate voices as Michael Lerner, Octavia Butler, and Letty Cottin Pogrebin (a Jewish woman writer who asserts her Jewishness) within the same genre. Lerner's and Pogrebin's color and gender become insignificant when they, in the manner of black women, speak their difference. In fact, according to Jong's argument, Lerner and Pogrebin could write a chapter called "How I Became Black." (This imaginary chapter would be quite congruent with Lerner's "Jews Are Not White.")

UPDIKE'S JEW AS OPERATED GOY; APPELFELD'S GOY AS OPERATED JEW: *BECH* AND *KATERINA*

John Updike's *Bech: A Book* and *Bech Is Back* and Aharon Appelfeld's *Katerina* pertain to Jong's notions about how Jewish women writers can use (black) difference to create the same (the Jew as Jew). Appelfeld describes the Holocaust — describes his own identity — by creating that which differs from and is the same as himself: Katerina, the gentile woman who is a Jewish woman who is Aharon Appelfeld. Updike describes the male writer's life, describes his own identity, by creating that which differs from and is the same as himself: Henry Bech, the male Jewish writer who is the male gentile writer who is John Updike.

Bech is more gentile than Jewish. (Little else can be said about a Jewish protagonist who does not say *goyim* until page 173.) It is Jong's black woman, the woman free to articulate difference, who insists upon describing Bech's ethnic identity. A black student who attends the Virginia college Bech visits informs him that "[c]alling me a Negress is as insulting as calling you a kike" (*Book*, 113). She uses language to pin ethnic identity upon him, transforming him into Jong's Jew sprouting *payess*. It is this black student — not her Jewish teacher — who makes Bech confront his Jewishness. When Bech meets Professor Ruth Eisenbraun, he categorizes her in terms of negative physical stereotypes: she is a *zoftig* woman whose nose is too long (121). Although Bech thinks that he "should have more to do with Jewish women" (123), he has sex with Ruth and then leaves Ruth.

In light of Jong's points about solidarity between Jewish women, I must become a resisting reader in response to Ruth. Instead of establishing "a false solidarity with Jewish men who would never accept . . . [Jewish women writers'] prayerful presence at the Wailing Wall of literature" (Jong, 296), I turn to Ruth in sisterhood. I make the same turn toward Bech's mother. No nice Jewish boy, Bech deserts her: "he had stuck his mother into a Riverdale nursing home. . . . His father . . . would have become his mother's nurse. His grandfather would have become her slave. Six thousand years of clan loyalty were overturned in Bech" (*Book*, 118). Bech the overturner rewrites the potential actions of his father and grandfather, nullifying thousands of years of Jewish custom. Bech is a gentile male writer's Jewish male fantasy of a Jewish male. He is the Jewish male who can dump his mother, screw Jewish women, be lauded by *goyim*, and marry a *shiksa*.

Updike is a translator, the articulator of a Jewish male power fantasy. Bech, during his stay in the Soviet Union, is escorted by translator Ekaterina Alexandrovna — and Updike is her colleague. Bech defines the triumph of American Jewry as Hollywood filmmakers whose "Jewish brains projected Gentile stars upon a Gentile nation" (*Book*, 5). Updike's gentile brain projects a Jewish male fantasy upon a screen which reflects Philip Roth. Updike eradicates the nemesis of Roth's Portnoy, the Jewish mother. He turns the Jewish mother into the dead father, the parent who dies and remains present (discussed in chapter 1). Although Bech tells his mother not to be "fantastic" (175), fantastic is exactly what she becomes. Bech's mother, who "had died four years ago" (187), appears in the audience when he wins a literary award. Updike portrays the solution to Portnoy's complaint: he removes the Jewish mother's reality, changing the Jewish mother into the powerful and present dead father. When Bech receives his award in the presence of his dead mother, he "had made it, he was here, in Heaven. Now what?" (187). This heaven has nothing to do with Judaism.

This heaven is a Jewish male fantasy involving attaining power and removing the Jewish mother's maternity and female identity. Updike, in relation to male Jewish readers, becomes a science fiction writer. He places the Jewish man within a male power utopia — turns the Jewish man into a Superman who, while flying from one *goyische* culture to another, relegates his Jewish mother to the Phantom Zone.

Bech's question "Now what?"— articulated from the "Heaven" of male power — is answered by the aforementioned black woman student who has the courage to call Bech "somewhat racist" (*Book*, 113). She inquires, "'How do you feel then about "Jewess"?'" (114). This black woman speaks in the place of Jong's Jewish woman and confronts Updike's Jewish male power fantasy text. Now what? This black student — or a feminist critic — might relate Bech's *Brother Pig* and *The Chosen* to the men who, as a result of being the chosen people, become male chauvinist pigs. She could position *Think Big*— Bech's novel which "had died" (*Book*, 159)— as canon fodder for the books that eventual dead white men write. She could read Bech's description of women "as pulpy stalks of bundled nerves . . . holding some pounds of jelly in which a trillion circuits, mostly dead, kept records . . . and generated an excess of electricity that pressed into the hairless side of the head and leaked through orifices" (*Book*, 115) and insist that cyborg imagery is no fertile ground for planting sexism, that Woman is not Lem's Princess Crystal. Bech is not a Jew. Bech *is* a book, an obsolete fantasy text of male power.

Bech comes back. And when this novel does so, it asserts that Jewishness is a story: "Jewishness too became a kind of marvel — a threadbare fable still being spun, an energy and irony vengefully animating the ruins of Christendom" (*Back*, 118). Bech now resembles an astronomer who views the story of his Jewish New York childhood "through the precious wrong end of the telescope" (119). Bech's writing is a force which propels him from limited Jewish New York space to the vast gentile American universe. Countering Jong's point that Jews write to create Jewish identity, Bech writes to erase Jewish identity: "I've spent my whole life trying to get away from them [Jews], trying to think bigger" (88). *Think Big* concerns escaping from enclosed Jewish space — from New York and from Israel (which Bech views as "just a ghetto with farms" [*Back*, 88]).

Bea Latchett, Bech's "plump Wasp wife" (*Back*, 89), no thin *shiksa* who would excite Portnoy, enjoys Israel and would choose to remain there (88 – 89). In contrast, Bech appreciates Scotland and appropriates Scotland from

Bea. Expressing locational genre seepage, Bea tells her Jewish husband, "[Y]ou're more of a Scot now than I am" (102). The couple enacts a reversal in which the Jew wishes to settle in Scotland and the WASP wishes to settle in Israel.

Moving neither to Israel nor to Scotland, Bea and Bech experience a marriage analogous to outer space antimatter: Bea "rattled at her night table. . . . The very space of the room had changed, as if their marriage had passed through a black hole and come out as anti-matter. . . . She had a toughness, Bea" (130). Bea is no rattling ghost, a present absence analogous to Bech's mother. She refuses to be pulled into the space constituting Jewish men's stories of Jewish women. She will not enter Bech's "mind, being digested, becoming a character" (103). Bea, in other words, will not become Ruth Eisenbraun. Bea Latchett, WASP incarnate, is a strong and *zoftig* Jewish woman who, instead of being rejected by Bech, rejects him. Bea and Bech, exemplars of cultural role reversal / antimatter, cannot share the same space.

As opposed to Bea and Bech, Jong and Updike (like Butler and Lerner) speak in tandem. Both position the black voice as the voice of truth and redemption. Bech explains that "America at heart is black. . . . Snuggling into the jazz that sings to our bones, we feel that the Negro lives deprived and naked among us as the embodiment of truth, and that when the castle of credit cards collapses a black god will redeem us" (*Back*, 192). The heart of America is an organ quite analogous to the white Brown Lung Gurganus describes. According to Bech, all of American culture passes for white. If America at heart is black, then the doings of whites are not the crux of America. If America at heart is black, then white American hegemony is a fiction. If America at heart is black, then white Americans' fiction is not at the heart of America.

Jews are aliens in Katerina's Polish world: "With their appearance, their way of sitting and bargaining, they weren't like creatures of this world but like dark spirits scuttling about on spindly legs" (Appelfeld, 17). When Katerina leaves her village to work as a housekeeper in Jewish homes, she is quite akin to a science fiction explorer venturing to a new world. Katerina, who abandons her gentile culture, becomes the Jew — becomes the alien. This woman who defies categorization is also another science fiction stock character: the last of her kind on a post-Holocaust Earth. Polish gentile Katerina describes herself as the only Jew remaining in the world: "Now there are no Jews in the world, and I'm the only one, in secret, evoking the memory of their holidays in my notebook" (116). Katerina operates upon herself, re-creates herself as a Jew, and locates the last vestige of Jewish culture in her memory / text. Appelfeld responds to the Holocaust with the voice of a gentile woman who becomes a Jew; Katerina becomes a historian who authors the future's version of the lost Jewish world.

Katerina, who buries (or "immerses") herself in Jewish culture, can accurately create her memory / text. When interacting with her Jewish employers, Henni and Rosa, Katerina feels that there "were days when I had forgotten that I had been born to Christian parents, that I was baptized, and that I went to church, so immersed did I become in the Jewish way of life and their holidays, as if there were no other world" (Appelfeld, 66). She ventures outside her category, the niche that is her gentile village and family. Jews in Katerina's milieu also refuse to be categorized. This is an old Jew's response to the thugs who threaten him: " 'I'm not afraid,' said one of the old Jews, removing himself from a slit in the wall. . . . 'You're not a human being. You're a beast of prey,' said the Jew, and he didn't rush back to his hole" (64). He redefines the thugs as subhumans, as animals. When doing so, he removes himself from the anti-Semitism which recategorizes him as a subhuman animal.

Appelfeld questions the categories which emerge from prejudice. Katerina herself makes a fleeting attempt to assuage the erasure located within the Nazi oven: "Now there are no more Jews left in the world, but a little of them is buried in my memory, and I am afraid that that little bit will be lost" (205). Her memory is a place within which the idea of the Jew is buried.

Katerina's life undergoes a second transformation when she walks into an alley which resembles a hole: she "stepped in, as though out of a pit" (139). While within this alley, Katerina, the woman who changes from gentile to Jew, becomes a murderer. After a thug smashes her circumcised son Benjamin's head, she stabs the thug to death (140). She is the gentile / Jewish murderer of the gentile who murders her gentile / Jewish son. She is a new category, a composite Jew and gentile who is at once victimized by a gentile murder and the murder of this gentile. However, despite the genre fission which characterizes Katerina, people view her in terms of a fixed definition. Regardless of her shift from gentile to Jew, femaleness remains her most important marker.

Katerina, Jewish / gentile repository and author of Jewish culture, endures sexism: "In the villages they forgive murders but not murderesses. Murderesses have been regarded as a horror and a curse from time immemorial" (195). In a world characterized by the indescribable Holocaust atrocity that those outside the category human perpetrate, Katerina herself becomes uncivilized — a murderer. Blind to her recategorization as gentile / Jew, her community can only see her as Woman. Polish peasants who complacently watch trains en route to Auschwitz consider it important to define Katerina: "'There she is, the monster'" (200). Those who populate an environment of unearthly horror describe her as a stock science fiction character, a monster. She, ultimately, cannot pass as a Jew: she is called a monster because she is a woman, not because she calls herself a Jew.

HOW GERMAN IS WRAPPING THE REICHSTAG; HOW AMERICAN IS RAPPING RACISM: WALTER ABISH AND CHRISTO

Haizlip discusses the Jew as operated Jew. She describes a woman so disturbed "by the prejudice she experienced as a child" that she decided "never again to reveal her Jewish heritage. She would become a Gentile. She straightened her hair, bobbed her nose, changed her name, and left her . . . Jewishness behind . . . [t]he break did her more harm than good. She recanted her choice and returned to the bosom of her family and her religion. She could not 'pass' any longer" ("Passing," 51). Just as this woman tries to pass for gentile, contemporary Germany tries to pass for normal. As Walter Abish emphasizes in *How German Is It*,[2] in the manner of this woman's experience, Germany's charade does more harm than good.

According to Abish, Germans cannot escape their past: "Sooner or later, every German, young or old, male or female, will come across some description in a book, or newspaper, or magazine of those grim events in the concentration camps. . . . camps in the heart of Germany and neighboring Austria" (190). Abish goes so far as to portray the Nazi past literally seeping from a hole. One day, after a heavy rain, the ground in front of "the Karl-Mainz Bakery on the Geigenheimer Strasse" (136) ruptures and reveals a mass grave. Bodies and stench ooze from the hole in the ground in front of the bakery — the location of ovens which yield bread, the staff of life. The concentration camp oven is sharply contrasted with the bakery oven, the basis for Sundays spent in cafes, "the German *Sontag*. This is an introduction to the German tranquility and decorum" (156). Rather than positioning the bakery oven as the hole which most appropriately characterizes Germany, Abish attributes this position to the hole in the ground under the Karl-Mainz Bakery. The bodies and uncontrollable odor emanating from the hole emerge from a past which can cause the veneer of present civilized decorum to cave in. Just as the Jewish woman Haizlip describes cannot submerge her Jewish identity, Germany cannot eradicate the hole under the bakery. Attempting to fill in this sinkhole is as fruitless as Lady Macbeth's efforts to wash blood from her hands.

Categorical ambiguity characterizes the bodies discovered in the hole in front of the bakery. It is impossible to discern the corpses' identity: nor "can anyone really rule out the possibility, remote as it might appear, that these people were not inmates of the camp but Germans killed in air raids, or killed by Americans. . . . Hence, it could not be ruled out that the skeletons found in the mass grave were Germans" (Abish, 192). The categories "Jew" and "German" (which, of course, can be one and the same) will forever be indeterminate within the mass grave.

Abish's protagonist, Ulrich Hargenau, is also forever categorically undefinable. He is no longer married to a terrorist. And, close to the end of *How German*, Abish reveals that Ulrich is neither the son of the man who attempted to assassinate Hitler nor the brother of an architect. Ulrich will never know the identity of his father. Forever separated from the deconstructor / terrorist and the constructor / architect, Ulrich remains an ambiguity. He finds solace located in the space inside a hypnotic hallucination: the hypnotist says, "Every part of your body . . . [the following ellipses are in the original] is relaxed . . . you feel a pleasant listlessness . . . as if you were drifting in space . . . just drifting . . . deeper and deeper into a pleasant void . . . You are filled with well-being as you lie back" (252). Appelfeld's Jew crawls within a hole in a wall; Wright's blacks crawl into holes in the ground; Ulrich, to find peace in regard to Germany's past, crawls into a hole in hallucinatory space.

Drifting in hypnotic space is appropriate for Germans who locate their past in a "memory of a dream to end all dreams" (Abish, 252). Perhaps this dream state explains why, to me, crowds in German cities resemble Ira Levin's protagonists, the Stepford wives — eerily relaxed, nonboisterous automatons. This is a logical behavioral mode for Germans who must redeem themselves (and their new reunified democracy) by mourning and exhuming corpses. As Zipes explains, "What is new can never be new unless the dead are truly buried and mourned. . . . But redemption can only occur, I am convinced, if graves are turned over and ghosts exhumed" (3).

To my discussion of collapsing distinctions between blacks and whites, Jews and blacks, and Germans and Jews, I add a peculiar new juxtaposition: equating Jews with Nazis. Zipes refers to the "newest form of anti-Semitism, which conceptualizes the operated Jew as potential Nazi . . .

there is still a great tendency among Germans to operate on Jews as stereotypes, and this tendency has been exploited by anti-Semites to transform Jews into Nazis" (9, 23). Abish describes lack of distinction between Jews and Germans found in a mass grave; anti-Semites imagine that lack of distinction between Jews and Nazis is a fixed definition. Zipes recasts this particular anti-Semitic projection when he argues that, in terms of "operative processes in Germany that were preventing automonous development of individuality" (106), today's gentile German is an operated Jew: the "German as operated Jew remains in both Germanys today, despite the fact that little trace remains either of Jews themselves or of what they wanted to realize in their struggle for emancipation and acceptance" (106). Jews *are* a presence in today's Germany: gentile Germans, as Zipes suggests, themselves are Jews. And Gilman argues that there are even more unexpected Jews in Germany — that Turks now represent difference there: Turks enable "Jews more than ever to 'pass as Germans'—which they are by citizenship and culture — as they look and sound more like every other German than the new foreigners. Jews no longer define difference in Germany, while difference is still defined by the image of the Jew" (*German Culture*, 38). The Turks in Germany are Jews — and their presence turns German Jews into garden variety Germans. German reunification creates yet another category: the white German black. In other words, former West Germans position former East Germans as operated blacks — i.e., "niggers." [3]

Although lack of distinction between Jew and black does not apply to the gentile Haizlip, she does use blurred racial categorization to confront racism: "It comforts me to think there is a sea change in America. It is surely a new day when white Americans are willing to look at their roots and find that some of them are possibly colored. Perhaps some of us are beginning to do what one anthropologist suggested would be the first step in eliminating racism: separating our need to belong from the dangerous temptation to hate others" ("Passing," 54). The sea change that Haizlip advocates involves acknowledging the existing racial genre fission affecting the fixed definitions of black and white. As I explain, the first step she refers to has already been taken within science fiction texts about humans who transcend their humanity to become one new biological entity. In literary theory, this alternative body appears as Theresa de Lauretis' "excentric subject" and as Homi Bhabha's "hybridity." [4]

Imaginative and theorized visions of difference breaking down boundaries are not new. The 1953 film *Lili* portrays various selves emanating from a unified whole. In a dream sequence, four puppets, who each form an aspect of a puppeteer's personality, come to life, escaping from the boundaries of his psyche. When Lili visualizes the connection between the whole puppeteer and the various psychic components which comprise that whole, she realizes that she loves the differences which form his personality. At the film's conclusion, the puppets applaud Lili's decision to love the puppeteer. They approve of her acceptance of his differences. I describe how blacks and whites and Jews and Germans function in the same manner. They form, in words quoted from Cherrie Moraga's "Winter of Oppression, 1982" (words which appear in this chapter's title), "a colored kind of white people" (74). The image of the puppeteer's bodily boundaries dissolving to become the puppets who are the differing components of his whole self — a breakdown which reveals difference and leads to living happily ever after — is certainly pertinent to the epoch of late capitalism. Because multiculturalism does not threaten the economic order, world capitalism favors multiculturalism. In addition to the fact that capitalism has outgrown the nation state, the emerging world economic powers are Asian, not white. Racism might not flourish in a global environment which attributes more importance to economics (and its ties to diverse cultures) than to particular cultural identity. The antipathy between German and Jew and German and American is obsolete. World War II is over; Germany now contains more than a million Turks.[5]

If race is now a less specific category, the same holds true for the racist. Archie Bunker resides in Queens, not Mississippi. Michel Foucault explains racism's locational dispersal when he tells us that power, rather than being a unitary entity, is diverse and diffuse — that power is not wielded by a monolithic Big Brother. So too for racism. Neo-Nazis are not solely a German phenomenon. Nazism, of course, figures in the American as apple pie Ku Klux Klan and Aryan Nation. Skinheads, whose presence extends from New Zealand to South America, first emerged in England during the 1970s. Instead of positioning one charismatic figure as their major mouthpiece, instead of staging a Hitlerian rally, skinheads (postmodern racists) use music to spread their message. Individuals whose fused racial identities are as protean as computer users' potential multitudinous Internet personas currently encounter racists who, by imbedding hate messages within music, transcend fixed location. Music, which defies national boundaries, speaks to youth from diverse cultures. In the postmodern world, black is white, white is black, gentile is Jew, Jew is not white, Jew is called operated Nazi, and skinheads play to a global youth culture — i.e., become hypnotists.

Two hypnotized protagonists, Abish's Ulrich Hargenau and Poe's M. Valdemar, point to the potential assuaging of this racist trance. While hypnotized, Hargenau raises his hand: "And Ulrich, who felt pleasantly relaxed, slowly raised his arm, perhaps for no better reason than a desire not to impede the hypnosis . . . as he opened his eyes, with his right hand raised in a stiff salute" (Abish, 252). Valdemar, while in a state of mesmerism, at first raises his arm and later fails to do so. Poe's narrator explains that it "was now suggested that I should attempt to influence the patient's arm, as heretofore. I made the attempt and failed" (Poe, "Valdemar," 202). The raised arm is as categorically amorphous as Valdemar (the operated gentile / Jew / black) and Hargenau (fatherland resident whose father will forever remain unknown). The raised arm is at once a Nazi salute, the means Americans use to swear to the truth, and the Statue of Liberty's testament to freedom. Hargenau and Valdemar address this discrepant symbol: Hargenau, a German hypnotized to forget history, at once evokes the Nazi salute and the Statue of Liberty. Valdemar, who at first subversively raises his arm, ultimately cannot be made to do so. When Hargenau and Valdemar — operated sleepers — raise their arms, they conflate images of truth, justice, and the American way with Nazism — and with "stiff" phallic power. Phallic power is denied to most American Jewish men, to most American black men, and — regardless of their race or religion — to most women.

During the spring of 1995, when the artist Christo covered and uncovered the Reichstag, Germany signaled its intention to prepare for the time when the hypnotized sleeper wakes, to end historic forgetfulness, to revitalize the Reichstag. When Christo removes the sleeper's cover / shroud, when he wraps and unwraps the Reichstag, he inspires metamorphosis: transforming the Reichstag from an old regime's symbol to a new regime's symbol. Christo signals that the new and reunified is a more appropriate way to view Germany than the old and the divided — the East and the West, the Third Reich.[6] Skinheads counter Christo's efforts. Their musical rapping of the Reichstag — their efforts to re-ensconce the Reichstag's old symbolism — sends a different signal. Wrapping the Reichstag, like racial categories, is open to interpretation. Christo's wrapping encases the Reichstag. Whether his wrapping and his unwrapping are more powerful forces than skinheads' rapping remains to be seen.

9

PLAYING WITH TIME

The Holocaust as "A Different
Universe of Discourse"

Saul Friedlander describes Hitler in terms of time: "we are here
confronted with the two sides of Hitler: that of yesterday and that of today;
with the facts and with their reinterpretation; with reality and with its aes-
thetization. On the one hand, the approachable human being, Mr. Everyman enveloped in kitsch; on the other, that blind force launched into nothingness" (*Reflections*, 72). Yesterday's Hitler is a force forever ejected from
reality. Writers now use two methods to aestheticize today's Hitler: (1) they
invent alternative histories in which Hitler is less than heinous — even approachable — or (2) they play with time, imbuing the Holocaust with
myth. Sheila Finch's "Reichs-Peace" exemplifies the first method. Finch
casts Hitler as an almost nice guy whose supposed son, Wolfli Hitler, is an
astronaut stranded in moon orbit. Sherri Szeman's *The Kommandant's Mistress* exemplifies the second method. Her novel approaches the Holocaust
according to the chronologically chaotic alternative female and male viewpoints that *He Said, She Said* epitomizes.

Szeman divides *Kommandant* into three perspectives: the view of the
Kommandant, the view of his Jewish mistress, and biographical documents. She plays with time in that each section's narrative is temporarily
disordered. A sentence about postwar events might be followed by one
concerning events in the camp. Instead of encountering definitive history,
readers confront myths that two differing viewpoints convey. *The Kommandant's Mistress* conforms to David Stern's description of Holocaust
novels which "deliberately leave their readers in a state of uncertainty — is
what they depict real or fantasy or fiction? . . . many of the novels themselves resist aesthetic form: through their rough edges, the historical atrocity persistently seeps in" (49).

The persistent seeping Stern describes is a denotative necessity: it is impossible for any novel — or language itself — to communicate the whole

of Holocaust atrocity. This communicative difficulty is becoming even more difficult at the present moment, when those who were young adults between 1939 and 1945 are reaching advanced old age. When these people pass away, direct representation — eyewitness accounts of yesterday's Hitler — will pass away with them. Located at the brink of this disappearance, many novelists eschew reality when they grapple with the Holocaust. They play with time and aestheticize the Holocaust as myth, fantasy, story. Holocaust reality, then, is accessible to us via time travel fiction.

Since time travel is many science fiction writers' fictitious transportation of choice, I begin this chapter by analyzing two science fiction Holocaust stories: Jack Dann's "Timetipping" and "Camps." I then turn to four novels (all written after 1991) which, instead of focusing upon alternative histories or factual details, respond to the Holocaust by defying time or skewing chronological progression: Martin Amis' *Time's Arrow*, Alan Isler's *The Prince of West End Avenue*, Ellen Galford's *The Dyke and the Dybbuk*, and Tova Reich's *The Jewish War*. The Holocaust persistently seeps into these works which neither focus upon the historical Holocaust nor adhere to realistic time. These novels either mention the Holocaust in passing or describe a Holocaust which differs from the one that history documents. Finally, I argue that E. L. Doctorow's *The Waterworks*, categorized as mystery and thriller, is a Holocaust novel. *The Waterworks*, silent about the Holocaust, evokes the past to describe a different holocaust. At the present moment, when eyewitness accounts become a blind force launched into nothingness, the authors I discuss relegate history to that which is gone with the wind. They skew time, bringing science fiction and fantasy to bear upon the Holocaust's temporal representation.

Lawrence Langer illuminates their objectives when he explains that Holocaust history restrains Holocaust fiction: "When the Holocaust is the theme, history imposes limitations on the supposed flexibility of artistic license. We are confronted by the perplexing challenge of the reversal of normal creative procedure: instead of Holocaust fictions liberating the facts and expanding the range of their implications, Holocaust facts enclose the fictions, drawing the reader into an ever-narrower area of association, where history and art stand guard over their respective territories, wary of abuses that either may commit upon the other" (75–76). Facts enclose the fictions—position the fictions as surrounded spaces. Fiction, then, is placed in a hole. To escape this limitation, to find a route out of the hole, fiction becomes more fantastic. Hence, authors generate plots such as these: Amis' version of time moving backward from the present to the

Holocaust and beyond; Isler's Holocaust novel as a World War I reminiscence; Reich's Holocaust perpetrated by Jews in a future Israel; and Galford's defiant response to Hitler (and to patriarchy) accomplished via Jewish lesbians who use the fantastic to bring ancient Jewish tradition to the present.

These novels are akin to generic science fiction and fantasy — and *The Waterworks* is akin to them. The novelists juxtapose "Holocaust novel," "science fiction," and "fantasy" to confront a problem (the impending absence of eyewitnesses) that Langer associates with time: "the problem is not exclusively the reader's or the author's. Essentially, the problem is time's, and eventually time will solve it. What will happen, for example, when the specific details of the atrocities at Babi Yar and Auschwitz are forgotten. . . . In time, in other words, the boundaries separating the historical moment from its imaginative rendition will be blurred, and it will no longer matter so much whether fictional facts, tied to the actual deeds of history, have become factual fictions, monuments to artistic vision that require no defense or justification, but stand or fall on the strength of their artistic mastery of material" (75, 76). The authors emerge from the enclosing hole of history by burying themselves in aesthetics — by imagining fantastic Holocausts. They reject chronological reality to solve a temporal problem.

Early 1990s Holocaust novels solve "time's" problem by moving from chronological time to what Langer calls "durational time":

> Simulated recovery belongs to the realm of chronological time. In the realm of durational time, no one recovers because nothing is recovered, only uncovered and then recovered, buried again beneath the fruitless struggle to expose "the way it was." Holocaust memory cannot be used to certify belief, establish closure, or achieve certainty. Hence chronological time is needed to intrude on this memory by those who insist on rescuing belief, closure and certainty from testimonies about disaster. Durational time resists and undermines this effort . . . and this is what I call duration, which exists *this side* of the forgotten, not to be dredged from memory because it is always, has always been there — an always present past that in testimony becomes a presented past, and then, in narrative forms other than testimony, a represented past." (15)

Now, when the fruitless struggle to expose the way it was becomes (with each passing day) more fruitless, authors move from chronological time to durational time. Durational time solves the problem of history enclosing and stifling fiction. Now is the time for a kind of time which exists *"this side* of the forgotten." At a time when firsthand memories are ceasing to exist, durational times resists and undermines the efforts to dredge memories. Even the most sophisticated dredging machines cannot recover material from a hole whose existence is rapidly becoming more and more impossible. Durational time enables Holocaust novels to leap out of the rapidly enclosing hole of chronological Holocaust time. In Langer's words, "the duration of Holocaust time, which is a constantly re-experienced time, threatens the chronology of experienced time. It leaps out of chronology, establishing its own momentum, or fixation" (15). I understand this leap as a move to the fantastic, to science fiction.

I do not mean to imply that realistic portrayal of the Holocaust is no longer appropriate.[1] Rather, I believe that extremely elderly eyewitnesses (the only remaining eyewitnesses) necessitate looking toward a new form of representation — and science fiction provides this new form. Recognizing this point, Geoffrey Hartman describes the Holocaust in terms of science fiction imagery: "The SS became 'blade runners,' and turned into the very androids from which they thought they were saving mankind. . . . The proliferation in science fiction of a manichean war against uncanny robotic enemies that no longer wear uniforms but have the metamorphic power to infiltrate as look-alikes may express in new coloration a very ancient fear. . . . Lyotard and also Wallace Stevens would like to believe that art makes things a little harder to see, yet the present, popular exploitation of Holocaust themes suggests instead a repetition of the imaginative and ethical error that defamed the victims" (331). Hartman's turn toward science fiction imagery evokes the often expressed concerns regarding Holocaust representation and respect for its victims.

Many critics assert that realistic Holocaust portrayals (such as the television drama *Holocaust*) are exploitative. These critics insist that people inside gas chambers should not be depicted between McDonald's commercials. They believe that silence is preferable to such portrayals. It is impossible to represent the entirety of the Holocaust realistically or to broadcast commercial television sans commercials. While I am sympathetic to both sides of the argument about realistic representation, I insist that bringing science fiction to bear upon the Holocaust is not disrespectful. Science fiction is a new representational mode appropriate for educating a new generation. While Hitler may be of no concern to today's youth, androids do command their attention. Darth Vader does not bore young people. And my reading of no less an eminence than George Steiner implies that Hitler has much in common with science fiction authors. Steiner's *The*

Portage to San Cristobal of A. H. includes these words: "It was Adolf Hitler who dreamt up the master race. Who conceived of enslaving inferior peoples. Lies. Lies" (161). Science fiction writers routinely dream up master races and imagine that aliens will enslave inferior Earthlings. Hitler lied about an entire category of people in order to make his science fiction vision real. Science fiction provides a basis for calling Hitler a lying, monstrous invading body snatcher. Science fictional time travel — entering a different universe of time — enables the past historical Holocaust atrocity to seep into the now.

"TIME AND SPACE WERE *MESHUGGEH*": "TIMETIPPING" AND "CAMPS"

Jack Dann's "Timetipping" presents time travel as a specifically Jewish transportational mode. Time traveler Moishe Hodel, who eventually merges with his fellow time traveler Paley Litwak, announces that "time and space were *meshuggeh*. . . . Let the goyim take the trains" (18). Present-day rational transportation, the exceedingly functional German trains running on tracks once used for transporting Jews to concentration camps, can no longer carry people to the Holocaust. Confronted with this problem of time and space, writers depict the Holocaust via *meshuggeh* time and space. They play with time to create literary transport modes to "a different universe of discourse" (Langer, 20) — Langer's words which appear in this chapter's title. Authors of Holocaust fiction echo Litwak's assertion that "[t]ime is a hole. . . . He could feel its pull" ("Timetipping," 21). Their work pulls readers into a temporal hole, depicting what is beyond depiction by positioning readers and protagonists as time travelers. While war is now routinely televised, the Holocaust can currently be experienced only via "timetipping," *meshuggeh* time. "Timetipping" is a precursor to the early 1990s Holocaust novels which play with time.

The force which emanates from *meshuggeh* time and space is at once infinitely expansive and compressed. For example, mirroring the Borgesian infinite, Litwak's wife Golde appears in many varieties: "Golde kept changing as her different time lines met in Litwak's kitchen. . . . So for every sizzling Golde with blonde-dyed hair, he suffered fifty or a thousand Goldes with missing teeth and croaking voices" ("Timetipping," 20). Collapsing times and locations accompany the changing Goldes. Litwak experiences unexplained distinctions between periods, religions, places, and individuals. An "Egyptian named Rhampsinitus" (21), for instance, becomes "Rabbi Rhampsinitus" (22) and randomly blips in and out of "Timetipping." Does an Egyptian who becomes a rabbi exemplify *meshuggeh* characterization? Not necessarily: "Things change" (23). Egyptians no longer enslave Jews. Nazis no longer exterminate Jews en masse.

Things will never change for Jews the Nazis murdered, Jews exterminated because they were caught in the wrong place at the wrong time. For a Jew in Europe, time is all. In 1995, I was invited to be a visiting professor in Austria. If my parents had resided in Austria during the Nazi era, I might not have been born. Time and place imbued with caprice have an impact upon Litwak. When he appears in an American western town whose jail is a pyramid, a xenophobic sheriff tells him to "timetip or slip or flit somewhere else. There's no other way out of this depository" ("Timetipping," 23). Sheriffs "deposited him in a narrow passageway and dropped the entrance stone behind him. It was hard to breathe. . . . It was completely dark" (23). Litwak is inside a passageway resembling a gas chamber located in a place where ancient Egypt, Nazi Germany, and the American West converge. This convergence is logical. The *Führer* and the pharaoh enslave Jews. American death camp liberators were so many Moses figures. The Holocaust can be categorized as a Western: Jews were captured, transported in cattle cars, branded, and slaughtered — after the Nazis informed them that "in dieser Stadt ist nicht genügend Platz für uns beide" (there's not enough room in this town for both of us).

Fairy tale is also applicable to the Holocaust as Western that Dann evokes. Until the clock struck the moment of 1945 liberation, Jews could not legally escape the Nazis' camp / depository. It was necessary for imprisoned Jews to await this moment; they lacked the means to take the sheriff's aforementioned advice to "timetip or slip or flit somewhere else." When the clock reaches the liberating moment, when the Allies remove the entrance stone from the camp / depository, timetipping provides the only re-entry mode to the Holocaust occurrence. Authors now avail themselves of this mode. In order to return to the camp / depository, their texts chronologically slip and their protagonists flip and blip; authors imagine slippage between time and space.

"Litwak was a survivor" ("Timetipping," 19). He escapes from the depository. He might, if our world seeped into his, have lived to the time of liberation, to the first moment beyond the *meshuggeh* time and space that was Nazism. It is not certain whether or not Stephen, the protagonist of Dann's "Camps," is survivor Stephen / Sholom. Stephen is a young contemporary hospital patient. Stephen / Sholom, who is subject to alternative temporal laws, is at once a camp survivor and Stephen. Stephen / Sholom, in terms of our world, is EveryJew: Stephen "understood that *he* was Sholom. He was a Jew in this burning, stinking world" ("Camps," 103). If Stephen is Sholom, his particular time machine (no usual science fiction mechanism) functions via cyborg imagery. Stephen, the patient who must be attached to tubes to survive, might use pain as the time portal enabling him to become Sholom the camp survivor. Dann's idea of an appropriately Jewish time machine to return to the Holocaust is pain and a cyborg life-support apparatus.

While lying in his hospital bed, Stephen "can think only of pain. . . . [H]e enters pain's cold regions as an explorer, an objective visitor. It is a country of ice and glass . . . crystal pyramids and pinnacles . . . block upon block of painted blue pain. Although it is midafternoon, Stephen pretends it is dark" ("Camps," 101). Here *Kristallnacht* is juxtaposed with ancient Egypt and prison blocks. Pain might enable Stephen to become an explorer, to time travel back to the Holocaust — the cold dead place of piled (or pyramided) gassed bodies and Jewish slavery. In the present's midafternoon, Stephen might imagine that he enters the dark hole that was the Nazis' depository for Jews. Or he might really flit between the pain he experiences in his hospital room and the pain of camp internment. Josie, Stephen's hospital nurse, who appears in the camp as an American army nurse (in both reality and Stephen's potential time travel), states that this travel is "only a dream. Somehow, you're dreaming the past" (112). Stephen feels that he is "being sucked into" this dream (113). The sucking force is another version of Litwak's notion that time is a hole whose pull can be felt. Dann positions language to indicate that this force might be part of reality. Stephen / Sholom, who insists that he does not speak English, speaks "American" (118) to his fellow inmate Viktor — and he refers to Josie before he meets her. In addition, Stephen, who states that he does not speak German, speaks German in a slang "patois" (112). Stephen's dream of the past might be a direct experience.

In the camps, nightmares are real. "'Here we learn to trust our dreams,' Viktor said. 'They make as much sense as this. . . .' He made the gesture of rising smoke and gazed toward the ovens, which were spewing fire and black ash" ("Camps," 117). Viktor, witnessing the black Holocaust volcano, fuses nightmare with reality — and Josie stands at this fusion's convergence point. She enters the camp in real time, the moment of liberation, and provides medical assistance for the *Musselmänner*, "the walking dead. Those who became ill, or were beaten or starved before they could 'wake up' to the reality of the camps. . . . *Musselmänner* could not think or feel. They shuffled around, already dead in spirit" (104). *Musselmänner* are at once real and analogous to science fiction's living dead.

Musselmänner are unable to define camp reality (which is logically unreal) as real. Inhabitants of a nightmare, they refuse to wake up, to acknowledge seepage between nightmare and actuality. Real science fiction characters, they lack time machines to escape the night of the living dead. *Musselmänner* are living art forms: yellow stars deposited in "Van Gogh's *Starry Night* . . . [in which] everything seems to be boiling and writhing˙ as in a fever dream. A cypress tree in the foreground looks like a black flame, and the vertiginous sky is filled with great, blurry stars. It is a drunkard's dream. The orderly smiles" ("Camps," 109). Van Gogh's painting addresses the Nazi sick fever dream of constructed pain, the order of turning Jews into ash. The "black flame" Van Gogh paints might represent emission from the thruster which propels Stephen / Sholom to Mr. Sammler's planet.

Like Bellow's Artur Sammler, Stephen / Sholom (and his fellow inmates Viktor and Berek) survive internment in a mass grave. While located inside the grave, where he converses with Viktor and Berek, Stephen / Sholom is "amazed that there could be speech and reason inside a grave" ("Camps," 123). The hole they inhabit is filled with both murder and survival. It is, for them, a birth canal, a place from which three people emerge and experience a new life. Signs of this new life are immediately apparent. When the men crawl out of the grave and reenter the camp, they encounter Americans. They have reached the moment of paradigm shift, the time when camp hospitals heal and when camp inmates are defined as humans. Josie is present to explain the moment of liberation to the men. When Stephen / Sholom calls out to Josie the camp nurse, Josie the hospital nurse immediately answers Stephen.

While Josie's temporal experience in the camps adheres to reality, the same does not hold true for Stephen / Sholom. Josie tells Stephen that Viktor emerged from the grave before Stephen was "even born" ("Camps," 125). Stephen denies that he is the young man standing between Viktor and Berek in a picture: " 'That's not me,' he says, certain that he will never return to the camp. Yet the shots still echo in his mind" ("Camps," 125). The ambiguous echo resounds with this story's unstable time and language. It is impossible to discern whether the "shots" are rifle shots fired at those buried in the mass grave or photographs of the camp. While readers cannot know whether or not Stephen is Stephen / Sholom, one fact is certain: the Holocaust is now a place of no return. Nazis' rifle shots now exist only in pictures (snapshots preserving a moment). The trajectory of Amis' *Time's Arrow* provides the only way back to the Holocaust. When Otto Korner, protagonist of Alan Isler's *The Prince of West End Avenue*, aims his narrative arrow back to the Holocaust, he overshoots his mark. He lands during World War I.[2]

HAMLET AND THE HOLOCAUST: THE PRINCE OF WEST END AVENUE

A counterpart to Dann's Josie appears in *Prince*: a woman functions as a catalyst to transport a man from America to a European past. When Korner meets Mandy Dattner, a young physical therapist his retirement home employs, she evokes his youthful passion for the deceased Magda Damrosch. Josie appears both in the camp and in the present; Korner is initially certain that Dattner is Damrosch. His memory casts a female doppelgänger as a time machine. Remembrances of past passions transport Korner back to his World War I Zurich interactions with Damrosch.

Prince is a Holocaust novel which, with very few exceptions, positions its protagonist in the present and in the World War I era. Korner, the "Prince" of West End Avenue who participates in the retirement home's *Hamlet* production, shares something in common with Shakepeare's Prince Hamlet: Korner hesitates. Isler's readers and Korner's interlocutors must wait to learn about Korner's life in Nazi Germany. Shakespeare seeps into Isler's Holocaust novel: the retirement home residents' antics stemming from their efforts to stage *Hamlet* textually integrate comedy and revenge tragedy. When readers wonder which resident stole Korner's letter from Rainer Maria Rilke, mystery also enters this novel's genre juxtaposition.

This Holocaust novel's obsession with World War I is no mystery. It is, instead, logical: Korner survives the camp because he disassociates himself from it by mentally relocating himself in his past. He retains his future because he goes back to his past, playing with time. Readers are not immediately made aware of this circumstance. "Hamlet does not appear before scene two" (Isler, 246); Korner's close encounters with the Nazis are not revealed until near the novel's conclusion. He says of his first wife, who died on her way to the camp: "Of my first wife, poor Meta, I cannot write" (44). Almost one hundred pages later, Korner still hesitates: "Of Meta, his first wife, he still chooses not to speak" (130). *Prince*, a novel concerning textuality within textuality (*Hamlet*, Rilke's letter, and resident-authored sonnets pervade the narrative), is a Holocaust novel whose protagonist recalls the Holocaust with silence and writer's block.

Korner's involvement with *Hamlet* underscores that he cannot avenge the deaths of his entire family. His efforts to achieve revenge would constitute futile meta-efforts, beyond the time of Holocaust occurrence and probably beyond the lifetime of the perpetrators. Revenge is impossible because, like the Nazis, Korner himself is responsible (due to his journalistic writing) for the deaths of his family and other Jews. For Korner to contemplate revenge — in the manner of Hamlet and his sister Lola (who hangs herself) — he would have to contemplate suicide.

Korner embodies flouted classifications: he is a well-intentioned Jew who is at once victimized by Nazis and causes other Jews to be victimized by Nazis. The Nazis author words which result in Jewish death. So does Korner, author of newspaper articles which argue that Jews should remain in Nazi Germany. Hitler stages the Holocaust. Korner, in his present, stages *Hamlet*. In his past, his writing helps to stage the Holocaust. In his past and present, Korner is a director who influences people's movements. When Korner announces cast changes for *Hamlet*, he says that "a director should not be confused with a dictator" (163). The impact of his writing contradicts this statement.

Korner survives the camp because of his ability to direct his own chronological position. He creates what he calls "a radical shift in temporal perception" (227). Within the camp "signposts of civilization, the countless unrecognized details of ordinary life through which we . . . gain our sense of time and place and personhood," (225) are absent. To counter this absence, Korner repositions himself within his past world of normal civilized markers, becoming a time traveler. Korner explains his self-authored survival method:

> My solution was simple: I re-entered the past. Time, of course, does not exist in Hell, but before the camps there had been time. . . . To put it plainly, then, I chose a day from the past and relived it. . . . I relived whole days, then weeks. . . . For me, however, the normal relationship between yesterday and today was reversed. Where I *was* the past, what I seemed only to "remember" was the present. It was a deliberate effort of the will, and it saved my life.
>
> Here is how I did it. I would select a date — for example, July 17, 1914. (226–227)

He thus describes the logic of how, during World War I, he survived a Nazi death camp.

Korner's time travel experiences are presented in place of details about his life as a camp inmate. Readers are forever ignorant of "the countless unrecognized details" (225) regarding what he suffered in the camp. His relatives never experience those details. They form an unusual genre, Holocaust victims who never enter camps: his parents commit suicide in their home; Meta dies on the transit train; his sister Lola (who emigrated in 1934) commits suicide in America; his son dies on the train platform outside the camp. In addition to *Hamlet*, Isler brings another classic text to bear upon *Prince*: "Abandon all hope all ye who enter here." Although the sign Dante places outside his Inferno never appears in *Prince*, it is nonetheless applicable to Isler's novel. Within *Prince*, readers do not encounter Hitler's hell. Hope is retained.

The past world which readers do enter, Korner's life during World War I, is imbued with hope. When Korner time travels back to World War I Zurich, he turns Hitler's hell into a world of youth, art (Korner meets James Joyce and joins a group involved with Dada), and potential love. *Prince* also silences the hell which, for some, characterizes the World War I era. The normalcy of Korner's World War I past is ensconced within worldwide hellish cataclysm. According to Korner's point of view, generic extremes — such as heaven and hell — overlap. A pin that retirement home resident Lottie Grabscheidt wears can be understood to represent this generic fission. The pin is set "in silver filigree, a mask of comedy superimposed upon a mask of tragedy, a blotched design that from the slightest distance looks like a grinning skull" (6). Such superimposition of comedy and tragedy pervades *Prince* — and our lives. Life, after all, is a death camp in which time is the Hitler who will kill us all. Or, in Isler's words, "[t]ime . . . first traps us and then at length devours us" (141). Tragedy (both personal and historical), then, appropriately permeates the roles passion and art play in Korner's past. His passion for Magda is forever unconsummated. His potential as a poet, which Rilke's letter acknowledges, is never realized. Magda goes up in smoke; Korner's journalism is partly responsible for the fact that other Jews go up in smoke.

Even though Korner's retirement home is replete with comedic aspects, it is a tragic death camp to which we are all sentenced. Residents are aware of this point. They refer to their affable and responsible chief doctor as the "Kommandant." Selma, the employee who sits near the home's front door to record residents' exits and entrances, is called a "guard." When Selma changes her status from employee to resident, she becomes an "inmate." Korner describes old age as analogous to Nazi dehumanization of Jews:

"How defenseless we are, we 'old folk' in the world of the young. To them I was not a man, equipped with intelligence and feeling" (22). Establishing a further link between retirement home and death camp, Korner tries to solve the mystery of who stole his Rilke letter. He proceeds by resolving to "wheedle out of Selma in Personnel a complete list of all residents and staff. . . . From Selma's list I shall produce one of my own" (62). Nazi transport lists, the list of cloned Hitlers in Ira Levin's *The Boys from Brazil*, Schindler's list, Selma's list, and Korner's list are texts all.

It is not necessary for readers to abandon all hope when they enter the retirement home articulated as a death camp. The home yields new life — new hope — when Mandy becomes pregnant with a child fathered by one of the home's residents or doctors. This pregnancy finally causes Korner to differentiate between Mandy and Magda. "From this house of dying was to spring forth new life. . . . What has she [Mandy], poor child, to do with Magda Damrosch, now spiraling for more than thirty years, a wisp of smoke in the air" (179). Because Magda was never a mother, she is not Mandy. Magda represents past death; Mandy represents the hope of future life. Acting in terms of this future hope, Korner — who lost his child — plays father when he draws up "the papers" (241) which will place his estate in trust for Mandy's child. Unlike his newspaper articles, these papers are life-promoting texts.

While Korner seems relieved to sever the connection he establishes between Mandy and the deceased Magda, he regrets disconnecting the present and past: "I was wrong to sever the present from the past, for the past has no imperatives that the present cannot refuse. What can we do but grasp the fleeting moment? For me, in this now, that moment is our play. I want to be Hamlet. And I care not a whit for the comical figure I shall cut" (241). Rather than exemplifying the unkindest cut of all, for Korner, equating comedy with tragedy signals an openness to difference. He wishes to be Hamlet, to be a fiction. Wanting not to be Hitler's "propaganda" (225) — another fiction — he resorts to time travel. His decision shows that, like time, identity is fleeting and involves change.

Korner recasts himself as "another Otto Korner" (33), an Otto Korner whose name presently lacks an umlaut. His brother-in-law Kurt, who is "transformed" (48) in America, becomes Kenneth there. Meta's beloved Toto (her pet name for Korner) becomes her estranged Otto. The Lenin and Joyce Korner encounters in Zurich are not their later, famous selves. Gerhardt Kunstler, Korner's fellow retirement home resident whose father was his father's employee, is now his social equal. This emphasis upon transitory identity is, like *Prince* as a whole, about juxtaposition. It is "about past and present mingling, time dissolving, between hope and despair" (29). It is about Korner cutting a comedic Hamlet who is drawing a sword to cut down others while he himself escapes Hitler's attempt tragically to cut him down.

Another contradiction: Korner — who defines his past, present, and identity as mingling entities — attempts to enclose his past camp inmate identity within a shut box. He keeps old family photographs in a shirt box he places on a closet shelf, his "closet of the mind" (228). Korner, who never hides from the Nazis in an enclosed space, escapes his past by enclosing it within a closet. The shirt box is a container which absorbs his past, defining his past as a genre of containment. It is also a Pandora's box: "But once the box was opened, the contents tumbled out, uncontrolled, uncontrollable, revealing folly upon folly. The last pitiful truths demand to be told" (229). Korner's past refuses to be contained. At the moment when it spills out and acquires a life of its own, Isler's Holocaust novel is finally set in World War II, rather than World War I.

Surrounded by his tumultuous, tumbling memories, Korner, who survives the Nazis by resituating his life story's chronology, inadvertently causes others' deaths because he misinterprets the story of his culture. In *Prince* — a novel written by an English professor whose imaginative vision continually emphasizes the importance of word, text, and interpretation — Korner directs his family toward a tragic end. The author of the aforementioned newspaper articles which urge Jews to remain in Nazi Germany, Korner is a bad cultural studies critic. Rilke's letter praising Korner's poetry book (called *Days of Darkness, Nights of Light*) states that his poetry "promises an abundant harvest: 'the roots dig deep'" (144). The contents of Korner's Pandora's box indicate an appropriate way to interpret Rilke's comment: because Korner does not understand Jews in terms of genre fission, he is an inadvertent destroyer of Jews. Korner's roots reveal that he has played the part of the gravedigger: "What were we if not Germans? We sprang from the German soil" (232). Nazis allow no seepage between the genres "Jew" and "German." Nazis cut Jewish roots out of the fatherland and define Jews as those who soil Germany. Echoing Sander Gilman (whose comments are discussed in chapter 8), Korner retrospectively realizes that Nazis classify Jews as diseases: "We refused to recognize that they saw us as maleficent bacteria in the bloodstream of an otherwise

healthy body politic. . . . Meanwhile, stupidly, some of the bacteria cre-
ated committees, held meetings . . . fought over words and phrases" (234).
Jews who cast themselves as literary critics did not save Jewish lives. In
relation to the body politic, bacteria lack illocutionary force. Korner,
who once insisted that Jews are German, now argues that he will act in
Shakespeare's *Hamlet*, not retirement home resident Tosca Dawidowicz's
Hamlet. He of all people should acknowledge the validity of Dawidowicz's
Hamlet, the point that fixed definitions should not be valorized. Korner,
after all, redefines the Nazi's Jew-as-bacteria image in terms of permanence: "she lurks within me yet, my Magda, like a bacillus in the bloodstream" (154).

"The rest is silence" describes Magda's fate. Korner never reveals what
happens to her, exactly how she becomes a swirl of smoke. The details
of the demise of his second wife (called "the Contessa") are quite explicit,
however. This woman who "could not bear to think of being sealed in
a coffin and buried beneath the earth" (95) constructs an alternative plan
which is, in contrast to Nazi ovens, a positive and dignified burial method
for Jews. For her first husband, the Contessa designs a headstone containing a niche for a Torah scroll. Her version of Korner's Pandora's box is
a Chinese box enclosing Jewish ashes infused with Jewish creativity: "My
idea was, when I died . . . that Torah scroll, in the niche, should be un-
screwed, and this Torah scroll, with me in it, should be screwed in instead"
(97). She creates a death symbol for Jewish permanence.

Although *Prince* emphasizes art and life, the Contessa focuses upon art
and death. And so does *Hamlet*. Hamlet dies with staged dignity. "Let four
captains / Bear Hamlet like a soldier to the stage." The Contessa acts as a
captain who stages her own death. Similarly, throughout *Prince*, the nursing home residents cause Jewish culture to have an impact upon *Hamlet*.
Lipschitz, for example, suggests equipping the praying Claudius with "a
tallis and tephillen" (42). Hamlet is imagined speaking in Lipschitz's voice:
"Like Lipschitz, Hamlet might well ask, 'How d'you think it feels to have
for a father a schlemiel?'" (156). This juxtaposition of *Hamlet* and Jewish
culture reflects the masks of comedy and tragedy superimposed on Lottie
Grabscheidt's pin.

Prince ends with the words "[t]he READINESS is all" (246). For Korner,
readiness involves letting interpretation out of its enclosed box / hole, turning the boxed fixed definition into an interpretive Pandora's box which
defies generic classification. To exemplify this Pandora's box, I offer the no-

tion that Fortinbras' description of Hamlet's death is applicable to Holocaust victims:

> Let four captains
> Bear Hamlet like a soldier to the stage,
> For he was likely, had he been put on,
> To have proved most royal; and for his passage
> The soldier's music and the rite of war
> Speak loudly for him.

Holocaust memorials speak for the passage of victims who were not fully put on, who had insufficient chance to prove themselves most royal.

Fortinbras continues:

> Take up the bodies. Such a sight as this
> Becomes the field, but here shows much amiss.
> Go, bid the soldiers shoot.

Korner plays Hamlet; Isler plays Fortinbras. Isler decides that the sight of Jewish bodies becomes the past Nazi killing field, not the contemporary world. He shields readers from the sight of these bodies. The retirement home resident who recites Fortinbras' last lines refers neither to Danish soldiers nor to Nazi murderers, but to a memorial. When, at the end of their lives, Korner and his fellows re-create *Hamlet*, they bear the Jewish body to the stage to present part of the body of the Shakespearean canon. Gentile art, then, merges with Jewish life and impending Jewish death. The "Hatikvah" (246) is their music and becomes a rite of World War II. Korner is "the 'star'" (246), a transcender of the yellow star's subhuman marking.

Prince's explanation of its own crux expresses Isler's interweaving of love, death, art, and life — his Jewish *Hamlet*: "*to achieve grandeur, art must descend to the level of palpitating humanity; obversely, to achieve grandeur, palpitating humanity must ascend to the level of art*" (132). *Hamlet* descends to West End Avenue; Korner ascends to *Hamlet*. His ascendance is grand. Nazi propaganda is a descent. Depicting Jews as palpitating unhumanity unworthy of life and art is "a case of fart for fart's sake" (148).

This case also applies to the retirement home residents' *Hamlet*. The answer to the question about what Shakespearean actor / nursing home resident Lipschitz is "doing in the stairwell" (148) combines high and low art, Shakespeare and mystery. Lipschitz goes to the stairwell "to pass wind. . . . with that stink, no one could get near him. He must've blown himself off the landing, a self-propelled rocket" (148). Because he is a survivor, Lipschitz can produce both art and fart. He is no victim of Hitler's science fiction story about how gas should propel stinking Jews off the face of the Earth.

Korner becomes a self-propelled star. Fully aware that "the past cannot be changed" (149), he reinterprets the yellow star. The yellow star is a text, Rilke's letter, which Korner carries with him throughout his life, "miraculously preserved even in the concentration camps, yellowed" (16). Rilke's yellowed text functions as a sun to illuminate Korner's *Days of Darkness*. Isler's *Prince* illuminates "promises" (144) of new art and life — the Jews who survive and who relocate Europe and *Hamlet* on West End Avenue. The world of the Holocaust — the transport to the East — can be replayed in World War I — and downplayed in Korner's 1978 Upper West Side. Isler presents *Hamlet* as a Jewish West Side story.

"I SEE AN ARROW FLY — BUT WRONGLY, POINT FIRST": *TIME'S ARROW*

Martin Amis presents the Holocaust as a time travel story. *Time's Arrow* concerns how one Tod T. Friendly (who becomes John Young and Oime'dilo Unverdorben and who has a doppelgänger imprisoned within him) moves backward in time (to Auschwitz and to his birth). Unverdorben arrives at an Auschwitz which differs from the historical Auschwitz. It is a life camp: after Jews are retrieved from heaven and gassed back to life, they are "deconcentrated . . . channeled back into society" (140). The world of this Other Auschwitz ignores temporal and biological reality and — in addition to time travel — embraces such science fiction tropes as alternative history and the notion that multiple consciousnesses can inhabit one body. Hitler changes the Jewish body by situating Jews outside the category "human"; Amis changes reality and the human body's place within reality. *Time's Arrow* is a power fantasy which accomplishes what is beyond readers' ability: travel to an imaginative Auschwitz where, upon arrival, Jews are revived. It is a revenge comedy aimed at Hitler as body snatcher.

Auschwitz as resuscitation center for Jews is a rewritten tale first told by the Allies, who, like Dann's protagonist Josie, turn camp hospitals into true healing centers. Time is the force which pulls Unverdorben and his doppelgänger back to Auschwitz as maternity hospital, the place of Jewish rebirth. Their ultimate destination, however, places birth within its proper context, moving it from the historical to the biological. Unverdorben and the doppelgänger eventually enter the body of the mother. Hitler eradicates the biological function of the Jewish mother: to give birth to Jews, to act as a force which expels Jews from within her body. Amis' Nazi doctor as Jewish resuscitator fuses with the body of the Jewish mother.

Amis couples a fantastic return to the inner body with emphasis upon defecation expelled from the body's inner space. Excretion is a frequent topic of conversation in the Auschwitz officers' club: "In the officers' club . . . where shit is constantly mentioned and invoked, we sometimes refer to Auschwitz as Anus Mondi" (124). The "Auschwitz universe was . . . made of shit" (123). In this Other Auschwitz, the *Scheissekommando* fills ditches. They "fill that hole. Dig it up again. Shift that" (124). This filling of the hole is "therapy" (124), or a fairy tale, for readers.[3] Fairy tale storks fly forward to protect children from directly encountering the facts of life; *Time's Arrow* flies backward from the facts of death in the concentration camp ditch. Amis' retold Holocaust tale recasts Nazi ovens as resurrection machines whose product turns Jews into Christ clones. Every Jew who passes through Amis' Auschwitz as life camp has been murdered and is resurrected. Blurring the distinction between Jews and Christ emphasizes that Christ was a Jew. Given the opportunity, Hitler would have killed Christ.

Amis continues relentlessly to obscure differences between "human" and two articles located within the human body: the doppelgänger and shit. The doppelgänger complains: "Maybe I'm tired of being human, if human is what I am. I'm tired of being human" (93). The doppelgänger, who may be human, is forever positioned inside the human body, in the location of shit. And this situation also holds true for his host, who is eventually reabsorbed within the mother's body. The doppelgänger's humanity is open to question, but not his unchanging position within a human body: his permanent resemblance to a turd is forever retained, forever constipated. The doppelgänger and its host newly ensconced within the mother — turds reabsorbed in a constipated body — are permanently within the body.

Time's Arrow emphasizes that humans who, during the Holocaust, define other humans as shit act like shit themselves—are shit. Hence, it is logical for a human sentience to speak from within a human body which is not its own and for an adult human body to return to the mother's body. Jewish victims in *Arrow* reemerge from heaven — which is certainly not an inner place of shit. Two fantastic reversals characterize these bodily absorptions and reemergences: the dead Jews get their bodies back and the Nazi doctor loses his body via birth rather than death. The doctor's second birth constitutes death (an untimely birth, due to backward temporal progression) for a Nazi who should never have been born. Death is birth for the Jews who should not have died untimely deaths. Amis redefines "birth" and "death" to deliver justice to the murderers and their victims.

The doppelgänger, whose birth and death are never described, desires to have a body of its own: "how I wish I had a body of my own, one that did my bidding. I wish I had a body, just an instrument to feel weary with or through, shoulders that slump . . . feet that drag, a voice that groans or sighs or asks hoarsely for forgiveness" (92). The doppelgänger sounds like one of Dorothy's Oz companions who bemoans the lack of a heart, brain, or courage. Amis' story is not about traveling down a fictitious yellow brick road, however. Rather, it is pertinent to the real roads Amis describes in his afterword: the *Reichsautobahnen*, "built to endure for a thousand years" (168). Unlike Dachau (which is now a museum) and Auschwitz (which has now been positioned as a point of contention between Jews and Polish gentiles), the autobahn exists in our time unchanged from the Nazi years. And so too for German train tracks. Amis emphasizes that these transportational arteries belong to the National Socialist body. He describes the Holocaust as "reptilian and 'logistical.' . . . The National Socialists found the core of the reptile brain, and built an autobahn that went there" (168). The autobahn and the German train tracks are arteries of the Nazi reptilian body which defy time, which exist unchanged in our time. These arteries — these remnants of the dead Nazi reptilian body — represent that body and, hence, indicate that there should be no forgiveness for surviving murderers. The murderers, who now ask "hoarsely for forgiveness," deserve to be reabsorbed into the dead Nazi body — deserve death.

Extant transportational arteries also indicate that there should be no forgiveness for the Allies' lack of action in regard to bombing the train tracks, allowing these tracks to exist in the future unchanged. Bombing the tracks, however, would not kill the Nazi reptilian body. Severed reptilian body parts regenerate. Past bombed tracks would not eradicate present Neo-Nazis. Some humans are shit. But Amis includes hope for change in regard to this statement. The doppelgänger, as I have mentioned, says, "I'm tired of being human" (93). Since this voice speaks from inside the body, the words can be interpreted as "I'm tired of being shit."

Neo-Nazis suffer from no such fatigue. Facing a situation in which Hitler almost completely eradicated the Jewish body from Europe, they separate anti-Semitism from the Jewish body, generating anti-Semitism which thrives where Jews are absent. When Neo-Nazi hatred requires a real Jewish body, they desecrate Jewish cemeteries. This desecration is a real world action in opposition to Amis' imagined resurrection of dead Jewish bodies. Amis casts the dead Jewish body as a newly born doppelgänger, a sentient entity given a body. Neo-Nazis, in contrast, revictimize dead Jewish bodies, causing them to conform to Harlan Ellison's title "I Have No Mouth and I Must Scream."

Why do Neo-Nazis target dead Jewish bodies? Needing an Other in order not to attack themselves, they attack dead Jews anew. Those who overturn Jews' headstones wish to leave the genre Other intact, to avoid locating the Other within themselves. The dead Jewish victim ensures that hatemongers will not position a doppelgänger of difference within the white gentile national body. Turks function in kind. Within Germany, Turks are guest victims as well as guest workers. Because they have Jewish cemeteries to vandalize and Turks' houses to burn, German skinheads do not have to turn upon themselves. However, even though East Germans and West Germans are not burning each other's houses, Austrian and German youth are smoking themselves to death. While young American blacks are not heavy smokers, the same does not hold true for young Austrians and Germans. Why do citizens of welfare states which emphasize cleanliness and precision compromise their own welfare? Are young Austrians and Germans assaulting their bodies to mourn the Jewish bodies their grandparents assaulted? Do they imagine themselves to be, like the doppelgänger Amis creates, sentiences without bodies?

A HOLOCAUST OF ISRAEL'S OWN: *THE JEWISH WAR*

Young Austrian and German smokers damage themselves. So do the protagonists of Tova Reich's *The Jewish War*. They are American Jews, who become Israeli Jews, who become Other than Israeli Jews, who create a Holocaust in the Cave of the Machpelah, "the original Jewish graveyard . . . purchased by Abraham . . . as a resting place for his wife, Sarah" (Reich, 58). When Reich plays with time by locating a Jewish war in the near future, by directing time's arrow forward, the events she describes are quite feasible. Reich's Jerry Goldberg becomes Yehudi HaGoel, and his close friend Herbie Levy becomes Hoshea HaLevi. Amis' Unverdorben returns to his mother's body; Goldberg and Levy are born again in Israel. HaGoel, the leader of a fanatic sect who creates an underground concentration camp, differs markedly from summer camp counselor Jerry Goldberg. HaGoel provides another reason for Israel, the place where all Jews are citizens, to become a place of Jewish difference. *The Jewish War* is especially poignant in light of an event which occurs in the near future in relation to this novel's publication date: the November 4, 1995, assassination of Prime Minister Yitzhak

Rabin by an Israeli extremist (the first instance in Israeli history of a Jew assassinating an Israeli prime minister). With regard to the assassination, Reich's alternative history, "The Battle of the Brothers," "when Jews shoot at Jews"(242), becomes historical reality. In both Reich's novel and Israel, Jews turn their homeland into a location where the same becomes different and does not belong together. Reich evokes the Holocaust to call for bridging this schism. She echoes Erica Jong's and Sander Gilman's points about the fixed nature of Jewish identity, which position the Holocaust as a force to create Jewish unity (discussed in chapter 8). Hence, like Amis, Reich recasts the Holocaust in terms of healing. While Amis makes Holocaust victims whole, Reich stresses that Israel should function as a whole — not as warring factions who destroy themselves.

As opposed to this wholeness, HaGoel, leader of the Kingdom of Judea and Samaria, invents a new cultural genre: Jewish "Palestinians" who try to establish their own state within Israel. HaGoel motivates people to join him because he is charismatic and cosmic: "All of the morning sunlight seemed to collect in his person, to be sucked up and absorbed by the oil with which he had been polished and set apart, to mass in him and bounce out from him, to radiate. . . . Those who came into his orbit were sucked in by the compelling force and drive of his personality. Around Yehudi things happened, or seemed at any moment about to happen" (10, 31). He is a force whose personality has an impact upon his followers' trajectories. HaGoel's attempt to reconfigure Israel as a Chinese box — an Israel within Israel — results in a decidedly un-Jewish tragedy, a Jewish Jonestown disaster. HaGoel, inciter of crowds (33), acts as an American Israeli Hitler. Schicklgruber moves from Austria to Germany, becomes Hitler, and causes Jews to die. Goldberg moves from America to Israel, becomes HaGoel, and causes Jews to die. HaGoel, a polygamous (and, hence, Muslim-like) Jewish Hitlerian figure, defies categories and perpetrates a new (and recently made real) category pertinent to Israel: the Jewish war.

HaGoel, Rabin's assassin, and the Nazi murders that Dann depicts are quite congruent with each other. The point to be garnered from recent history and Reich's novel is that no Jew should categorize other Jews as vermin. No Jew should view other Jews as a character in Reich's novel, Israeli army officer Uri Lapidot, views HaGoel and his followers. Lapidot echoes Sander Gilman's aforementioned points about equating Jews with disease: the army officer describes HaGoel and his kingdom as "this infestation . . . the germ . . . a tumor" (137). Lapidot, while looking at HaGoel's compound, does not see humans: "these were not his own people . . . but a highly predetermined, programmed colony of insects, say" (238). Reich, who breaks down distinctions between some Jews and Nazis, is, of course, not part of the new anti-Semitism which equates Jews with Nazis. Rather, she rightly emphasizes that divisiveness among Jews does not serve Jews well. *The Jewish War* proclaims that genre fission in the form of Jew fighting Jew is an abomination. In contrast to this point, Lapidot positions HaGoel's compound outside unified Israeli convergence. He sees the compound as a despised black hole force: he observes "the convergence from every corner of the Compound toward what appeared to be this black hole that sucked everything in, this irresistible black force on the bench in the courtyard" (238). There is no place for murder within the community of Jews that the force which is the state of Israel propels into the Arab-dominated Middle East.

Reich emphasizes this point when she equates HaGoel's entire enterprise with death — and Shelley, one of his wives, articulates this connection: "everything we've been struggling for and killing ourselves for here in Hebron is connected to a couple of tombstones in the Machpelah and the people we believe are buried under them" (192). HaGoel's group's struggles are connected to a graveyard which will become their burial place. Emunah, HaLevi's wife, believes that the "whole of Israel is one big cemetery" (244). Reich's novel as a whole counters Emunah's opinion. *The Jewish War* defines Israel as a place of rebirth, a place for recategorizing victims as citizens, a place which should not become a cemetery for Jews who die at the hands of Jews.

Three important either humorous or tragic plot events in *Jewish War*, which can be understood according to imagery relating to enclosure, point to the necessity of Jewish solidarity within Israel: (1) HaGoel's first appearance in Israel accomplished via a flying casket, (2) the descent of his daughter into the Cave of the Machpelah, and (3) his followers' underground demise.

HaGoel's arrival in Israel is rather extraordinary. When he and HaLevi hide inside coffins being transported by plane from America to Israel, they are at once enclosed and seemingly outside time: "Enclosed within the coffin, it seemed to Yehudi that he had been bracketed out of time" (52). The men *are* bracketed out of time: they share their coffins with Holocaust survivors' corpses en route to burial in Israel. The dead Jews are given a belated chance literally to have an impact upon Germany: flying corpses hit German soil. HaGoel describes this occurrence: "When these two dead

Jews . . . hit that polluted ground, with their blue numbers tattooed on their forearms, those Nazis will know that we haven't finished with them yet. . . . [T]hey'd better watch their heads. Dead Jews will come pouring down upon them from the sky. . . . [L]ike the evildoers of the generation of Noah, they will perish in the deluge" (54).

Amis describes a viable consciousness without a body: Reich describes a viable body without a consciousness. She imagines the dead Jewish body inside a coffin, a flying contained space, which acts like a bomb. The dead Jewish body, recast by Reich as no target for cemetery desecrators, becomes an object of vengeance which targets Germany. The coffins rain genre fission (the dead Jewish body as active vengeful agent) upon Germany. Upon arrival in Israel, the coffin containing HaGoel resembles the ones which "bomb" Germany. It is thought to be "a bomb of some sort, a time bomb maybe, which, when planted deep in the Hebron soil, would explode cataclysmically" (61). HaGoel is a time bomb who eventually explodes Jewish solidarity.

HaGoel uses his daughter At'halta D'Geula to enlarge his chink in the Israeli world machine. Upset because Jews can only approach the Cave of the Machpelah "like contaminated lepers into the cave through a hole in the wall—a chink, a crack, a miserable crack" (126), HaGoel uses a harness and rope to lower his daughter into this hole. He simultaneously stages an opposition to the pervasive story about rescuing a child who falls into a well and creates something new under the sun: the Israeli female astronaut. In order to calm At'halta D'Geula, HaGoel tells her that her trip inside the cave is "a scientific experiment . . . no different from the kind that are performed by the astronauts . . . when they go up into outer space, only she was going down into inner space. . . . [HaGoel] lowered her through the hole. . . . She was pretending . . . that this was a game and that she was an astronaut" (127–128). When lowered into the cave's inner space, At'halta D'Geula acquires the right stuff to fuel a myth about how she sees the Messiah in the cave.

HaGoel does not see that her descent portends her impending permanent loss. One day At'halta D'Geula simply disappears. This is how Emunah reacts to her disappearance: "At'halta D'Geula's essence had been sucked back into the soil . . . the child had become one with the landscape, a landscape different, surely, from the low, marshy coast of Guyana, where she had spent her two years in the Peace Corps" (177). All the children in HaGoel's group will eventually disappear. When HaGoel turns his underground compound into Jonestown, all the children will be pulled back into the soil. HaGoel, inventing a new geographical category, fuses death, Hebron, and Guyana.

When HaGoel begins his war against Israel, he recategorizes Jews. First he directs the children in his group to brandish rocks and slingshots, to become indistinguishable from Intifada fighters. Then the children move from imitating the Intifada to imitating Anne Frank: they gather in "The Annex" (243), an underground gallery. Finally, HaGoel "operates" (Jack Zipes' term discussed in chapter 8) upon himself to recast himself as a Christ figure who emerges from a coffin and who will emerge from a grave. He puts "into effect the second stage of their *operation* [italics added] . . . they would all move underground. . . . Underground, their lives would go on exactly as they had above. . . . Yehudi . . . had endured a similar ordeal before, and he had risen then out of his coffin" (246). This "operation" fails. There is no second coming for HaGoel. No Christ, HaGoel is a Hitler, a charismatic figure who causes Jewish death. Emunah writes, "I am buried alive" (247). Unlike Bellow's Mr. Sammler and the protagonists of Dann's "Camps," she will die in a hole / grave. HaGoel and his followers never emerge from "their little burrows and holes" (255).

HaLevi desires to instruct the children waiting out the war against Israel underground, the children "stuck under the earth in this black pit" (251). He believes that the besieged and contained children can experience the Holocaust "firsthand" (252). HaLevi's pedagogical plan fails. The children believe that one of the best things about the Holocaust was that tedious routines (such as school) were interrupted (252). Even if these children were more scholarly, regardless of their dire situation, it would be impossible for them to reexperience the Holocaust "firsthand." While Reich can imagine a near-future Israel, her protagonists, who inhabit a reality-based world, cannot go back in time.

Adults invent a contest to channel the energies of the encapsulated children, "the first annual great Holocaust Contest of the Kingdom of Judea and Samaria" (254). First prize: a gratis trip for two to Auschwitz (254). Winners, of course, will not reexperience the Holocaust. HaLevi explains that, in order to win this contest, it is necessary to "stick to the facts" (256). When the children do so, they will — despite their desire to avoid school — learn something. They will learn the crux of *The Jewish War* — and what Israel should learn in the wake of Rabin's murder. HaLevi explains the lesson: "every single type of Jew without exception was hunted down . . . no Jew was excused, the artificial divisions between Jew and Jew would then instantly fall away . . . it would follow naturally that we have no choice but to love each other, to love all Jews . . . in the end, all Jews are created equal, as they say in America, at any moment we Jews might find ourselves herded together without discrimination in the same cattle car, or packed naked together without distinction in the same gas chamber, our nameless ashes mixed up randomly together in the same ash heap" (257). HaLevi implies that Hitler chose the Jews to be the people who are denied genre fission (i.e., factionalism that tears the fabric of Jewish community). In the world of past Holocaust — and potential future Holocaust — it is time for Jews to learn to act as a cohesive force.

HaLevi tells the children that, in order to win the contest, they should turn themselves "into little Germans . . . savor the details, suck on the facts" (258). HaGoel turns them into little victims, children who ingest poison and die, in the manner of Jonestown victims. God will never "lift them [the children] out of the pit" (263). HaGoel's followers die entombed within the Cave of the Machpelah, the first Jewish cemetery. HaGoel perpetrates a Holocaust against Jews, acting in opposition to Amis' fairy tale about murdered Jews being put back together again. Because HaGoel is a force who instigates genre fission among Jews in Israel, his followers become things which fall apart. They are Jews herded together without distinction into an underground mass grave.

NONTRADITIONAL LESBIAN
BODIES AND JEWISH TRADITIONS:
THE DYKE AND THE DYBBUK

Ellen Galford's *The Dyke and the Dybbuk* applies a feminist perspective to writers' recent combinations of time, the Holocaust, and disembodied thought. After being imprisoned inside a tree for two hundred years, dybbuk Kokos ensconces herself within the descendant of a woman she haunted centuries ago: lesbian taxi driver Rainbow Rosenbloom. The second sentence in *Dyke* associates Rainbow with outer space imagery. Galford's narrator says, "If we are smacked by a rogue asteroid, ingested by a black hole, or poisoned by something dripping through our tattered ozone canopy, feel free to lay it at her [Rainbow's] door" (1). The narrator, to indicate that Rainbow chooses not to be a mother, evokes the Holocaust as a hole in history. Rainbow "has done nothing to replace the legions that have lately fallen through a hole in history" (2). Although a medieval Jewish dybbuk escaping from within a tree and haunting an irreverent contemporary lesbian is rather unorthodox, Galford emphasizes matters at the heart of contemporary Jewish experience: continuity and survival. Jewish female continuity leads Kokos to Rainbow.

Rainbow emanates from a line of women who, lacking the advantage of a hole in time, still manage to survive the Holocaust: "In some chink of time between pogrom and cholera and Holocaust, Gittel-plus-five [Rainbow's ancestor] packs up husband, baby and a pair of brass Shabbos candlesticks and conveys the family genes — via wooden wagon, railway carriage and passenger steamer — to London. The Jews who have come before — Hispanic and Iberian grandees, German bankers . . . who, by their manners and education, could pass as Christian whites — are not particularly thrilled to see her" (26). Here Galford evokes Jewish schism, the damaging emphasis upon difference among Jews, which pervades *The Jewish War*. She responds to this schism by asserting that postmodern emphasis upon multicultural difference upstages both difference among Jews and Jewish difference. A CEO in the "dybbuk corporation" which employs Kokos asks her, "What would you do, say, with a subject whose mother was a Polish Catholic, whose father was an atheist from Nigeria, and who herself has embraced some Californian amalgam of Taoism, cabbalism, science fiction and Polynesian cargo cult?" (48). This cultural conglomeration underscores that Rainbow is not different because she is Jewish. Rainbow is different because, as a lesbian taxi driver, she exists somewhere over the rainbow of usual patriarchal structures.

Rainbow, who chooses not to have children, is the last of her line because of her free choice — not because of Hitler's choice. The Jewish world of her ancestors, the world from which Kokos springs, is, of course, gone from contemporary Europe. When fantasy and time travel enable Kokos to merge with Rainbow, the lost European Jewish world reappears.

Rainbow and Kokos form a double defiance of Hitler; they signify that Jewish people and tradition endure — even though a haunted lesbian provides a very untraditional way to symbolize tradition. Kokos, a feisty dybbuk, has a long history of colliding with patriarchy. Hundreds of years ago, when she battled a sage / patriarch, she was defeated. He captured her and imprisoned her in a tree. The sage / patriarch "crouches down, and a hole opens in the bark . . . they [his disciples] are deafened by [Kokos'] shrieks and roars from inside the box, and a seepage of foul vapours. . . . A mere 200 years later, lightning bisects the oak. Together with a stream of bewildered refugees — outraged crows, some squirrels . . . I am flung out into the open air" (12–13). Galford and Amis echo each other: both skew time to create a fairy tale of Jewish rebirth. Although Kokos experiences a traumatic and lengthy imprisonment, unlike Jews forced into gas chambers, the dybbuk forced into the tree can reemerge. In the manner of the inmates of Amis' restorative concentration camp, after time passes, Kokos leaves a hole / prison, joins refugees, and begins a new life unscathed.

Despite Galford's emphasis upon fantasy, she makes important points about lack of Jewish solidarity and anti-Semitism. Kokos articulates this comment when Rainbow enters a Hasidic neighborhood in London: "To Hitler and his henchmen . . . you'd be Jewish. . . . But, in the Jewish-ness stakes, sweetheart, the kosher ayatollahs who run this neighbourhood would place you somewhere between a Tibetan lama and the fairy on top of the Christmas tree" (119). The kosher ayatollahs would certainly catego-rize a Jewish lesbian as something Other than themselves. Galford stresses that, in a world replete with anti-Semitisim, even divisions between Jewish ayatollahs and Jewish lesbians are not in Jews' best interest. She includes realistic anti-Semitism within her fantasy: Rainbow encounters vandals who, when spray-painting a large blue swastika on a Jewish cemetery, write "DEAD YIDS INSIDE" (148). Galford asserts that Jewish resistance to such acts is no fantasy. Teenage yeshivah boys attack the vandals (148). Such re-sistance is also a part of Kokos' fantastic world: "ragged shadows" (148) come over the Jewish cemetery wall to murmur their resentment. The dead Jewish bodies and living boys fight back.

In addition to bringing ancient Jewish tradition to bear upon the pres-ent, Galford redefines Jewish tradition and continuity in terms of lesbian-ism. Rainbow, the lesbian who chooses not to reproduce, carries Kokos, a vestige of Jewish tradition, within her body. Further, in addition to Kokos, Anya (the first Gittel's lover) appears in Rainbow's world. Anya describes herself as being outside gender categorization: "Not quite a woman — be-cause I wanted to do things with Gittel that only a man was supposed to want to do; not quite a man — because I wanted Gittel to do the same things back to me" (223). Anya also describes a new category. She believes that, in addition to graveyard shadows and dybbuks, lesbians are also ghosts. Lesbians "walk like ghosts through a world that tries not to see us" (225). Lesbians are relegated to a supernatural realm; they become invisible women deprived of their bodies. Flouting this invisibility, Anya continues to defy categorization. When Rainbow asks if she is a dybbuk, she replies, "'I'm neither one thing nor the other" (226). Anya at once represents Jew-ish continuity and lesbian presence. When Anya and Rainbow make love, they epitomize Jewish survival and continuity of Jewish tradition. Again, Galford emphasizes Jewish tradition in a very nontraditional manner. A contemporary Jewish lesbian who defies patriarchal imperatives makes love to a Jewish lesbian who made love to her ancestor. Their lovemaking concerns "survival" (244).

Galford underscores that survival is about adaptation. Time's passage, as well as Hitler, is responsible for the old Jewish world's demise. In other words, the "world has changed. Jews have changed. Women have changed. Sex has changed" (106). Change is necessary for survival — even for patriarchy's survival. Kosher ayatollahs have no place in a postmodern world where patriarchal master narratives no longer reign supreme. Patriarchy must open its eyes to see the lesbian body clearly (the Jewish lesbian body or otherwise). This is Galford's message for a world in which Hitler no longer threatens Jewish women: Jewish lesbians should not be cast out from the Jewish community in a manner which is (in spirit) analogous to Hitler casting Jews out from the human community.

PROTESTANT PATRIARCHS AS HOLOCAUST VICTIMS: THE WATERWORKS

If Jewish lesbians can represent Jewish tradition, then why not imagine Protestant patriarchs portrayed as Holocaust victims? E. L. Doctorow contributes his own meta-category — the Protestant patriarch experiencing Holocaust-like victimization — to Galford's nontraditional traditional Jews, Amis' resurrected Holocaust victims, Reich's Jews who destroy Jews, and Isler's tale about Nazi concentration camp internment during World War I. Doctorow locates *The Waterworks* in New York City's past and depicts Protestant patriarchs who evoke the Holocaust. The blurbs for *The Waterworks* describe it as a thriller and detective fiction. I argue that Doctorow's novel is, in addition, Holocaust literature. Doctorow indirectly tells a Holocaust story from the point of view of rich Protestant men who seek life. Like Amis and Isler, Doctorow presents reversals. *Waterworks*, written by a Jew, describes exorbitantly wealthy Protestant men who voluntarily intern themselves in a concentration camp. Their Kommandant is Dr. Wrede Sartorius, a mad scientist Naziesque doctor whose medical talent can prolong the relationship of their consciousness to their bodies — i.e., prolong their lives.

Doctorow suggests that his mystery can be read as a Holocaust narrative. His text directly announces that Dr. Sartorius might be German: "The name Sartorius is Latin, of course, but it comes out of Germany. . . . I [McIlvaine, the narrator] reasoned then that our Latinated German doctor could have come over in the great immigrations after the failed democratic revolutions of 1848" (183). *Waterworks* brings readers back to McIlvaine's time (1871 becoming 1872) and McIlvaine back to Martin Pemberton's search for his "dead" father, Augustus Pemberton (who supposedly expires in 1870). *Waterworks* seeps between nineteenth-century New York and Nazi Germany. Martin indicates that Sartorius behaves like a Nazi doctor: "What I saw in him was an aristocratic dominance over men like my father. He was supreme . . . indifferent to everything but his work. . . . I saw him with a hypodermic tube inject cellular matter into deadened brains. I saw first one, than another, of the orphan children begin to age, like leaves turning yellow" (274). The children Sartorius experiments upon and harms could appropriately be described in terms of yellow stars as well as yellow leaves. Hitler uses death camps to try to eradicate Jews; Sartorius uses a life camp to dominate patriarchy — to control powerful men. No one volunteers to enter Amis' life camp. Not so for Pemberton and his fellows in relation to Sartorius' life camp. They submit to Sartorius because he is their only hope to defy impending death. Augustus Pemberton is a Jew in relation to Sartorius as Nazi doctor.

Wealthy Protestant men voluntarily enter Sartorius' life camp located under the New York City waterworks. Relinquishing control of their bodies, they live in a semi-conscious state analogous to the *Musselmänner* Dann describes. When McIlvaine and police officer Edmond Donne find Martin Pemberton, they encounter someone who resembles a concentration camp victim: "And there, on a pallet, something moved. . . . scragglybearded, weak-eyed and blinking, lifting a skeletal arm against the light. . . . a poor soul, nothing but rags and bones . . . whom I had . . . difficulty recognizing. . . . The diagnosis was that Martin was suffering from starvation and dehydration and the attendant breakdowns of function" (229, 231). In addition to this allusion to Holocaust victimization, Martin's stepmother Sarah and half-brother Noah, who are forced to leave the Pemberton mansion, become displaced persons.

Doctorow's description of Sartorius could appropriately appear in *Time's Arrow* to describe Unverdorben's activities: Sartorius "was recomposing their [the Protestant patriarchs'] lives piece by piece, swaddling them like infants . . . schooling them in an assemblage of life's cycles, and with his emollients, and powders, and fluid injections from the children, reconstituting them metempsychotically as endless beings" (277). Unverdorben recomposes and reconstitutes Jewish victims to defy history; Sartorius recomposes and reconstitutes powerful patriarchs to defy time. Both undertakings are equally fruitless.

ONCE UPON A TIME "TILL THE CLOSE OF TIME"

Time and history cannot be defied. Amis makes this point when he describes a painted stage set clock located at Treblinka's prop railway station: the clock's "hands hadn't moved to an earlier time. How could they move? They were painted, and would never move to an earlier time. Beneath the clock was an enormous arrow, on which was printed: Change Here For Eastern Trains. But time had no arrow, not here. Indeed, at the railway station in Treblinka, the four dimensions were intriguingly disposed. A place without depth. A place without time" (143). The artistic artifact — the painted arrow or the printed word — at once represents the past and does not cause direct experience of the representation. No humans can alter the temporal movement that *Time's Arrow* describes — not even powerful Protestant patriarchs.

Human powerlessness in relation to time is most pertinent to the Holocaust. Although death camps were different human-made universes — places with different discourses, dimensions, and depths — they were not places without time. The victims reached an eastern terminus; time marched on. In the universe of the Holocaust, time's arrow flew through the universe according to its own trajectory. Time is a force which exists independently of all human genres. All that people can do in regard to this fact is to recall the past — experience the Holocaust as a "once upon a time." After all, as McIlvaine announces at the conclusion of *The Waterworks*, time stops only within art: "Of course it was Sunday, the day of rest. But my illusion was that the city had frozen in time. . . . And let me leave you with that illusion . . . though in reality we would soon be driving ourselves up Broadway in the new Year of Our Lord, 1872" (348–349). "Sunday," "the day of Rest," and the passage from 1871 to 1872 are constructions, illusions of control regarding humans' inability to stop time. Time is a genre-free waterworks, a continuously leaking faucet which seeps as it sees fit. Humans can control only their own discourse — imbue words with power.

Doctorow, Jewish writer, knows that Sunday is no day of rest for him. Doctorow, Jewish writer, knows that 1872 is not the year of *his* lord. Doctorow knows that positioning the temporarily gentile as an all-encompassing genre is an illusion, a once-upon-a-time discourse sleight of hand. Once upon a time, linguistic illusion removed Jews from the genre human. Once upon a time (which is now the past and could become the future) hate discourse pulled Jews into the abyss that was the Holocaust.

Hitler forced Jews to play for time; only writers can play with time. Only writers can control the flow of time in the manner of engineers controlling the flow of water. Writers can dam time, contain time. A post-1945 Holocaust narrative, then, is analogous to a waterworks; a post-1945 Holocaust narrative is a flow of time contained. Hence, Doctorow appropriately places the 42nd Street reservoir—which eventually becomes the 42nd Street Library's location— in his Holocaust novel which never mentions the Holocaust. The reservoir (which controls and contains water) is a hole covered, filled in, and eradicated by a depository for discourse (the library). Ironically, within the vast 42nd Street Library, there are no words able to describe the Holocaust adequately. Langer describes this lack of language in terms of current, flowing, overflowing, and a reservoir: "in Holocaust discourse . . . we are . . . baffled by the lack of language to confront the difference between the chronological current, which flows until we channel it between the permanent banks of historical narrative, and durational persistence, which cannot overflow the blocked reservoir of its own moment and hence never enters what we call the stream of time" (15–16).

The Waterworks represents Holocaust discourse's durational persistence as a blocked reservoir of its own time, time which cannot flow to our time. Once upon a time there was a 42nd Street reservoir. Once upon a time there was a Holocaust. Both are gone. Both are described in the library by language that our temporal position "afterward" now makes inadequate. We cannot drink the life-giving 42nd Street reservoir water. We cannot enter the death-giving Nazi camp. We can only reside in our "different universe of discourse" (Langer, 20) in which these no longer existent realities can only be represented. As Langer explains, "Just as the Nazis and the Jews inhabited different universes of discourse . . . so we who come 'afterward' inhabit a different universe of discourse from the ones that the victims lived and died in. . . . Just as there was no common idiom between the victims and the killers, there is no common idiom between the killed and ourselves. . . . Only through the invention of a mythic narrative 'afterward' can we reconstruct an idiom to change their death from a 'forgettable' (because unbearable) occasion into a memorable one. But this only grafts speech onto silence, it does not illuminate the silence" (20).[4] *The Waterworks* grafts speech onto Holocaust silence — and calls attention to the silence.

The writers I discuss in this chapter engineer the flow of time, presenting time as a waterworks / reservoir which contains a mythic narrative afterward. Their Holocaust stories are artistic time's arrows pointing to an east of the past and containing the sign REST IN PEACE. Since I cannot go back to the Holocaust, I defer to someone who was alive during its time. George Steiner explains why the rest is silence "till the close of time": "we can imagine the cry of one, the hunger of two, the burning of ten, but past a hundred there is no clear imagining . . . take a million and belief will not follow nor the mind contain, and if each and everyone of us . . . were to rise before morning and speak out ten names that day, ten from the ninety-six thousand graven on the wall in Prague, ten from the thirty-one thousand in the crypt at Rome . . . ten out of six million, we should never finish the task, not if we spoke the night through, not till the close of time nor bring back a single breath" (49). "The rest is silence," says Otto Korner.

Discourse as Black Hole —
and as Liberated Light

Genre Fission: A New Discourse Practice for Cultural Studies
concerns merging race, class, and gender boundaries to challenge fixed
definitions that the patriarchal cultural hegemony perpetuates. I concen-
trate upon forces which bring disparate categories together, enabling categories to exist in the same point or space. These forces bring to mind an
image which figures in the conclusion to my *Feminist Fabulation: Space /*
Postmodern Fiction: Ad Reinhardt's cartoon *How to Look at Space* (1946). In
this epilogue, rather than looking at terrestrial space, I look toward outer
space. I designate the black hole to serve as an emblem for juxtaposing routinely discordant discourses. After positioning the black hole as an appropriate postmodern metaphor for genre fission, I use this placement to explore various cultural instances. These instances (in which the disparate
are pulled together) include subjects which have never appeared together
in an epilogue: Bill Clinton's sex scandal, selling books, and the Star Wars
missile defense system. Finally, to avoid generic rigidity, I release light from
its place within discourse as black hole through my discussion of these
(as I understand them) liberated light scenarios: *The Sound Of Music*,
Karen Joy Fowler's feminist science fiction story "Game Night at the Fox
and Goose," and artist Noritoshi Hirakawa's *A Temptation to Be a Man*.

THE POSTMODERN BLACK HOLE

When Michael D. Lemonick, writing in *Time*, explains that Johns Hopkins University researchers use the Hubble telescope to examine a gas disk
spinning at 1.93 km/h at the center of galaxy M87 (a galaxy located far,
far away: 50 million light-years from Earth), he links seepage with a black
hole. The gas disk spins because "the gas is funneling, like water down a
drain, into the gravitational pit of a black hole as massive as 2 million suns"
(Lemonick, 51). Lemonick uses a simile to compare a gas disk to water

pulled within a black hole. Despite his figure of speech, he mentions a real black hole. And so does this epilogue. Although I refer to the actual body in outer space, I position the black hole as protean entity which itself defies categorization. In my chapters, black holes, among other things, represent such disparities as bestial mouths, prostitutes' windows, garages, and holes in walls and in the ground. Although black holes seep between genres throughout this book, within the epilogue the black hole is a black hole is a black hole. The black hole, for example, is not a vagina. Unlike Michele Wallace, I do not position the black hole as a metaphor to discuss race.[1] Astronomers who use the Hubble telescope to look toward space see no political incorrectness. I hope readers will have a similar view of discourse as black hole.

Since my audience consists of humanities types (who are apt to argue that a rose is a rose is a rose is a clitoris) rather than astronomers (who look at black holes sans the eyes of psychoanalytic or culture critics), I offer a standard definition to make readers comfortable: a black hole is

[o]ne of the end points of gravitation collapse, in which the collapsing matter fades from view, leaving only a center of gravitational attraction behind. General relativity predicts that, if a star of more than about three solar masses has completely burned its nuclear fuel, it should collapse to a configuration known as a black hole. The resulting object is independent of the properties of the matter that produced it and can be completely described by stating its mass and spin. The most striking feature of this object is the existence of a surface, called the horizon, which completely encloses the collapsed matter. The horizon is an ideal one-way membrane; that is, particles and light can go inward through the surface, but none can go outward. As a result, the object is dark, that is, black, and hides from view a finite region of space (a hole). (Peters, 42)

With this description of light pulled into a black hole in mind, I see fixed definitions as rather analogous to roach motel inhabitants: when genre seepage pulls fixed definitions together, they check in, but they can't check out.

The black hole appears in the grand mix characterizing critical discourse about postmodernism. Jean Baudrillard, for example, discusses postmodern "implosion," and David Harvey coins the term "time-space compression."[2] Fredric Jameson describes postmodernism as a new space, a submerging and filled volume which absorbs postmodern bodies and deprives them of space and distance: "distance in general (including 'critical distance' in particular) has very precisely been abolished in the new space of postmodernism. We are submerged in its henceforth filled and suffused volumes to the point where our now postmodern bodies are bereft of spatial coordinates and practically (let alone theoretically) incapable of distantiation" (87). Jameson views political interventions as at once part of the system and pulled into the system — "reabsorbed" by the system as black hole: "political interventions . . . are all somehow secretly disarmed and reabsorbed by the system of which they themselves might well be considered a part, since they can achieve no distance from it" (87). Hans Bertens responds to Jameson by directly mentioning a black hole: "'a political form of postmodernism'" (Jameson, 92) is needed "if we do not want our critical faculties to disappear in a postmodern black hole" (Bertens, 172).

For Bertens, Don Delillo's *Ratner's Star* is the postmodern novel par excellence. Endor, the novel's mathematician protagonist, meditates within a hole he digs for himself. He might be responding to this fact characterizing his world: all forms of representation will end when the Earth enters a "mohole." Bertens connects Delillo's mohole / black hole to postmodern theoretical discourse: "there are those, like Lyotard, who actively seek to contribute to the demise of representation and for whom the mohole is a form of the sublime with emancipatory potential. . . . At this level of abstraction, that of postmodernity as mohole, postmodernism is a resurfacing of the anti-representationalism that has its source in the self-reflexivity of modernity" (Bertens, 240, 242). Instead of advocating the demise of representation, Bertens calls for the need to honor both anti-representationalism and representationalism: "After an overlong period in which Enlightenment universalist representationalism dominated the scene, and a brief, but turbulent period in which its opposite, radical anti-representationalism, captured the imagination, we now find ourselves in the difficult position of trying to honor the claims of both, of seeing values of both representation and anti-representation, of both consensus and dissensus" (248). *Genre Fission* honors the claims of both representation and antirepresentation, consensus and dissensus. Genres, after all, must exist and be intact before fission can occur. Representation converging with antirepresentation is a fitting image for the present world, which is at once characterized by homogenous Western capitalism and heterogeneous regionalism (such as the movement within Quebec to separate from Canada). The emphasis upon race, class, and gender within *Genre Fission* exemplifies a political form of postmodernism. This book, then, attempts to overcome two major difficulties in current postmodern theory: (1) incorporating the heterogeneous

and homogeneous and (2) including the political from a feminist perspective. I turn to specific cultural genre fission scenarios which, when understood in terms of my discourse as black hole and liberated light metaphors,
are simultaneously heterogeneous and homogeneous — and reflect my
feminist perspective.

One Reader Randomly Reading the New York Times

Genre fission pervades postmodern culture. My attention to three texts
which I arbitrarily encounter while perusing the January 14, 1999, *New York
Times* — articles about *60 Minutes*, book selling, and an advertisement for
the televised version of Tom Brokaw's *The Greatest Generation* — illustrates
this point. *60 Minutes* originator Don Hewitt states that he created the program by "breaking up the old hourlong documentary into three separate
stories, all packaged 'like Hollywood packages fiction'" (Bumiller, B2). *60
Minutes*, born as a new, segmented form of the monolithic documentary,
was packaged in the manner of a category (fiction) which differs from
its own category. Now, thirty years after *60 Minutes* first appeared, the
show spawns a new newness: *60 Minutes II*, a program different from and
in competition with *60 Minutes*. (Hewitt calls this competitor "our kid
brother" [Bumiller, B2], not our clone.)

60 Minutes, when presented as "Hollywood packages fiction," crosses
generic boundaries. The same is true regarding a new packaging trend for
novels. Major publishing houses (such as HarperCollins, Penguin, and
Doubleday) now place novel excerpts on supermarket shelves tucked inside Diet Coke cartons. The book manifests "shaky status . . . as a bedrock
cultural artifact . . . [and] is a less definite object than it once was" (Jacobs,
F2). It is logical to develop a marketing strategy which combines diet soda
and novels. Books are commodities, so many cereal boxes in drag. "Actually, what's disturbing about the Diet Coke promotion is not that it seems
‚wrong. It's that it seems exactly right. Walk into a Barnes & Noble super-
store and you'll notice that the long role of new releases, book jackets facing out, could just as easily be a supermarket cereal aisle" (Jacobs, F2*).
Cap'n Crunch and Captain Ahab become one within the supermarket.
Cereals and "books are products for a mass market" (Jacobs, F2). "Snap
crackle pop" at once describes Rice Krispies and novels.

And books now resemble the television documentary format that
60 Minutes superseded. A full-page *New York Times* advertisement (appearing on January 14, 1999, E12) announces that Tom Brokaw's bestseller
The Greatest Generation will be a *Dateline NBC* special (televised on Janu-

ary 15): "Tom Brokaw's Number 1 Bestseller Is Now an NBC News Special." *The Greatest Generation, Dateline,* and the pre-*60 Minutes* documentary share one format. If CBS and NBC merge, Don Hewitt could feature Brokaw's sequel to *The Greatest Generation* on the imagined show I call *Dateline/60 Minutes III.* This hypothetical television program, like my reading of texts appearing in the January 14 *New York Times,* does not provide a clear answer to this question: What is it? What exactly is "is"? The most infamous example of President Clinton's verbal hairsplitting is *the* question of the early 1999 cultural moment.

President Clinton's "Sexual Incontinence" as Genre Fission

This crucial question relates to other "is" questions which reverberate through the American cultural ear: Is it a bird? Is it a plane? No, it's Superman. The definitive "no" constitutes a fixed definition. True, the strange visitor from another planet *is* Superman. But here the definition of what "is" is needs to be expanded; "no" can be contradicted. In the sense that Fevvers, the protagonist of Angela Carter's *Nights at the Circus,* is a bird/woman, Superman is a bird/alien. Superman is also a plane: when Lois Lane flies while situated in Superman's arms, she is transported as comfortably as any Concorde passenger. In fact, the sexist airline advertisement which announces "fly me" is applicable to Superman transporting Lois in the sky. Superman — at once bird, plane, alien, and Clark Kent — is characterized by juxtaposed categories. And so is Bill Clinton. Clinton participates in a scandal story devoid of conclusion. In an article called "Over Time; The End Was a Mirage. The Scandal Lives On," Francis X. Clines comments that "[f]or sheer durability, the story is beginning to resemble a toxic waste dump of fetid ingredients and methane energies" (1). The sex scandal story seeps into affinity with Love Canal.

Clinton — who leaps over the Republican House of Representatives impeachment trial managers in a single bound and bends their steely accusations in his bare hands — is Superpresident, a.k.a. the Comeback Kid. Superpresident Clinton is the genre seepage president. What *New York Times Magazine* contributing writer Jacob Weisberg calls Clinton's "sexual incontinence" (35) and the media saturation accompanying the president's personal conduct are replete with genre seepage leakages.[3] "The president" used to have one explicit meaning: moral hero. During the last sixty years or so, the United States experienced what Weisberg calls "the heroic phase" (30) of the American presidency in which presidents were measured against their roles in the Depression, World War II, and the Cold War. Currently, during peaceful and prosperous times, the president's role is "diffuse and bewildering" (Weisberg, 30). "President" no longer automatically means heroic leader. Harry Truman guided America through the end of World War II; Clinton, like the protagonist of *The Truman Show*, stars in a seemingly endless lack of distinction between entertainment and government. Clinton inhabits a real-life soap opera, an indistinct genre. "Clinton has not failed to keep his public entertained. To some it has seemed like a tragedy, to others a sitcom" (Weisberg, 30). He blurs distinctions between real-world White House drama and television humor.

How to characterize this president who defies characterization? At the New York University rally to support the president held immediately before his impeachment trial began, Mary Gordon called him "the first woman president" and Toni Morrison called him "the first black president." Gordon's and Morrison's descriptions have not as yet been realized. And Weisberg views Clinton in terms of another nonexistent category: the "governor-president."[4] According to Weisberg, a governor-president recasts the White House as something other than itself: "Bill Clinton is the President who, for better or worse, turned the White House into a governor's mansion" (31). I add that Clinton acts as a literary critic–president who turns the White House into an English Department. Literary critics, as we are all aware, spend their professional lives trying to discern "what the meaning of 'is' is." Clinton informs the country that "I did not have sexual relations with that woman" because, in the manner of postmodern literary critics, he does not subscribe to fixed definitions. His at once heterogeneous and homogeneous definition of "sexual relations"—his simultaneously open and fixed definition of "sexual relations"—includes intercourse and excludes oral sex.

Weisberg's conclusion is just as contradictory as Clinton's strained legalisms. This writer's appraisal of Clinton-haters at once establishes separate genres and eradicates overlapping genres. "I think there are three separate psychological profiles of Clinton-hating, which have blurred together at times" (Weisberg, 65). His discussion of simultaneously separate and blurred profiles includes liberals who derive their hatred from the 1960s, the Washington establishment, and conservative Clinton-haters (who, according to Weisberg, are related to liberal Clinton-haters). Weisberg believes that Clinton-hating is beyond category: "The question of Clinton-hating finally transcends conventional political analysis" (52). Clinton does not perpetuate the presidency as a separate and heroic genre.

His troubles have "humanized him like no previous President. . . . [A]s with other celebrities Clinton's screw-ups are a comforting reminder that he isn't any better than the rest of us and doesn't think that he is" (52, 65). Toys "Я" Us. Clinton is America's boy toy, the country's most interesting plaything, a compelling entertainment. Clinton Is Us. That's what the definition of "is" is.

Bombing and Speaking

August 21, 1998 (when the American military bombed the Sudan and Afghanistan), and January 19, 1999 (when Clinton delivered his State of the Union Address), are days which will live in genre fission infamy. Discourse relating to these examples of Clinton bombing and speaking blurs distinctions between fiction and reality. In relation to the decision to bomb, the media associated the "Lewinsky matter . . . [with] the bombing coverage almost immediately because of the similarity between the recent movie 'Wag the Dog,' in which a fictional American President fabricated a war to divert attention from reports that he had propositioned a girl in the White House" (Mifflin, A13). The president's decision was understood in terms of this movie. No wonder *Wag the Dog* inspired a *New York Times* article about the alleged lack of distinction between Hollywood fiction and presidential action: "Wagging Tongues in 'Incredibly Cynical Times'" (Bruni, A12). The article describes people's sense "that life was imitating art," that the bombing reflected "the bizarre parallels between fiction and fact" (Bruni, A12). Those interviewed were struck by "the odd ways in which Hollywood and Washington commingled." "*Wag the Dog* . . . [e]verybody at the office was talking about it" (Bruni, A12). The entire country was talking about genre fission.

At the official Pentagon briefing, Secretary of Defense William S. Cohen was asked "whether he had seen *Wag the Dog*" (Purdum, A11). While Cohen refused to answer, none other than Newt Gingrich defined the appropriate genre in which to place the president's action. During a conference call with Republican leaders, Gingrich said, "I simply start by saying if you saw the TV coverage of the two embassy bombings and the caskets come home to America, you know that this is real" (Purdum, A11). Gingrich insists that the president acts according to Washington reality, not Hollywood fantasy. He offers a fixed definition of Clinton's decision to bomb: the decision is "real." The public, in contrast, responds by interpreting what Cohen calls Clinton's "absolute obligation to protect the American people from terrorist activities" (Purdum, A11) in terms of fiction: the *Wag the Dog* conspiracy. Equating the president's intentions with *Wag the Dog* exemplifies generic disparity as that which unleashes cynicism.

On January 19, Clinton was presented as a dual personality. That evening's *NBC Nightly News* described him as "the defendant on trial by day and the president by night." White House Counsel Charles Ruff, like the newscast, also split Clinton. Ruff's January 19 presentation before the Senate included this idea: disagreement with Clinton the man (the husband and father) should not encompass the office of president. But Clinton, known for his ability to compartmentalize, is a whole encompassing many aspects, not a living example of compartmentalization. Superman is at once Clark Kent and an alien from Krypton; America's present leader is both President William Jefferson Clinton (a designation hardly ever used before the impeachment trial) and regular guy Bill Clinton. Superman and Superpresident are simultaneously homogeneous and heterogeneous. Ruff, however, argued for a clear distinction between the office of president and the human foibles characterizing the office's holder. According to Ruff, Bill Clinton's private actions do not rise to the level of removable offense for President William Jefferson Clinton. Although Ruff correctly asserted that impeachment is not a remedy for private wrongs, Bill Clinton and William Jefferson Clinton are one.

Despite this fact, while delivering his State of the Union Address, Clinton denied genre seepage when he split himself into two separate and distinct categories: he played the presidential role to the hilt and ignored his role as trial defendant. President Clinton was flying high in the House of Representatives chamber (then devoid of House managers' accusations) as surely as Superman, devoid of Clark Kent's glasses, flies high above Metropolis. During the January 19 *News Hour with Jim Lehrer*, commentator Mark Shields stated that Clinton's State of the Union Address performance conveyed "no sense that this is not a man at the top of his game." Shields' colleague Paul Gigot cast Clinton's bravado in literary terms: he characterized the address delivery style as "a suspension of disbelief." Gigot went on to describe Clinton's performance as creating "an alternative world view . . . an alternative vision of reality" which constituted "an alternative universe . . . an unreality." Add science fiction writer to Clinton's numerous roles. Clinton's State of the Union Address, in addition to omitting the obvious (he never referred to his status as defendant) and creating an alternative universe, also predicted the future. Clinton used "he or she" to describe the person who will be president a century from now. Evoking a woman president elected during a future far far away drew the most sustained applause from Clinton's audience, consisting of his accusers, defendants, and judges. Clinton, the first elected president to be impeached, is the first president to speak in the predictive manner of a feminist science fiction writer.

His State of the Union Address delivery blurs boundaries between fiction and reality. Or, in the words of New Jersey's Senator Robert Torricelli, "You couldn't make this stuff up" (*Charlie Rose*, January 19, 1999). Torricelli's comment also pertains to Clinton's decision, immediately before his trial began, to bomb the Sudan and Afghanistan. Knee-jerk responses to this decision position Clinton both as a real president acting in the nation's best interest and as a *Wag the Dog* protagonist. Clinton was once impugned for causing traffic jams when he went to a barber on a bad hair day. Now, when he wields presidential power to make fundamental leadership decisions, people wonder: does he or doesn't he have the nation's best interest in mind? Only Clinton knows for sure.

Star Wars

Juxtaposing fact and fiction in relation to government extends beyond Clinton's actions. Ronald Reagan, as we are all aware, envisioned a Star Wars program to protect America from nuclear attack. The ancestor of Reagan's *Star Wars*, a more limited defense system, also combines fact and fiction. This is apparent in the photo which accompanies the *New York Times* article on the new Pentagon missile defense system. Despite the new system's more modest scope, it would still do Princess Leia and her empire proud: "The new defense would use space-based sensors, early warning radars and missiles based in North Dakota or Alaska to shoot down no more than a handful of missiles from rogue states or terrorists" (Myers, 4:16). The following caption describes the photo (accompanying the article) of light beams aimed at Earth's surface from an orbiting "USA"-emblazoned space craft: "It's not a movie poster. This vision of the destruction of nuclear missiles came from the Defense Department." In other words, like Clinton's decision to bomb Afghanistan and the Sudan, the Defense Department vision of light rays from outer space hitting Earth came from Washington, not from Hollywood.

LIGHT LIBERATED FROM WITHIN THE BLACK HOLE

I began this epilogue by mentioning light pulled into a black-hole focal point. Now, in closing — and in the spirit of generic flexibility — I liberate light, releasing it from within my metaphorical postmodern black hole. Or, in the manner of the Defense Department poster, I highlight freely traveling light. I emphasize that light, in addition to repelling missiles, can zap sex-role stereotypes.

Casting Light on "How Do You Solve a Problem Like Maria?"
or Climb Ev'ry Laser Beam?

Science fiction and adventure tales are replete with swashbuckling male heroes who wield or confront laser beams. Agent 007, for example, is understandably nervous when strapped to a table as Goldfinger aims a laser beam at his groin. His experience epitomizes an instance where light is of paramount concern to a male hero. Even god, played by Charlton Heston, proclaims, "Let there be light." Joanna Russ offers an anecdote about heroes who have less control over light. Russ says, "I remember Harlan Ellison recounting how he nearly throttled a [science fiction movie] producer who insisted he could get a character out of a tight spot by having him *climb a laser beam*" (*To Write Like a Woman*, 172).

A male hero trying to climb a laser beam certainly subverts gender roles: the hero (when eliciting the laughter evoked by slipping on a banana peel) appears more silly than heroic. One of the most popular films of all time, *The Sound of Music*, positions light similarly. I do not mean to imply that the film proclaims "climb ev'ry laser beam." However, while singing "How Do You Solve a Problem Like Maria?" the nuns allude to light when contemplating how to cope with Maria, the "unpredictable headache" who "can outpester any pest." The Mother Superior, in reference to Maria, asks, "How do you hold a moonbeam in your hand?" To do so, of course, is impossible. Woman-as-light cannot be held, taken in hand. The nuns can neither control Maria nor answer this question: "How do you find a word that means Maria?" There is no word to describe the woman who hears a new discourse practice: the musical sound / language of living hills. The nuns cast out Maria, whose famous circular motion, enacted at the start of *Sound*, functions as a vortex which moves her beyond patriarchal language. They expel the would-be nun located in the wild zone (Elaine Showalter's term), the uncontrollable moonbeam. Contrary to light pulled into black holes, Maria, described as uncontrollable light, is jettisoned from the abbey's inner space.

It is true that many aspects of *The Sound of Music* are analogous to *Pretty Woman*, transferred from Beverly Hills to Salzburg. (The hills are alive with the sound of shopping?) In both films, a lower-class woman marries a rich man and lives happily ever after. I maintain, however, that *Sound* is subversive. Maria tells Baron von Trapp exactly what is on her mind. Behaving as she sees fit, she brings a behavioral paradigm shift to the von Trapp household. Her feminine attention to nurturing and music wins the day against masculine militarism. Maria epitomizes femininity at its best. Scarlett O'Hara uses drapes to adorn herself; Maria uses drapes to liberate children — to make play clothes for them.

The Baron ultimately responds to Maria as uncontrollable moonbeam by embracing her — by holding her torso in his hands. When he rejects the Baroness, his female social equivalent, and marries the obstreperous governess — the woman so far outside his class and notion of protocol — he personifies genre fission. Further, he evades the Nazis by acting in a manner equally as incongruous for a male hero as climbing a laser beam: he behaves in terms of his wife's femininity — he sings. (Indiana Jones, Agent 007, and Charlton Heston / god do not sing.) He takes refuge within an abbey, within Maria's female community. The von Trapps can climb mountains and find safety because, like the Baron, the nuns deviate from their usual role. They sin: they sabotage cars belonging to Nazis. These women control technology. The Baron, who transcends class and gender, is the new male hero of a new social story.

Although he is certainly no Nazi sympathizer, the Baron acts as a Kommandant within the household that he controls according to a military model. His children, clad in gray uniforms, must march to "line up" when he blows a whistle. Maria will have none of his whistle signals. She says, "I could never answer to a whistle. Whistles are for dogs and cats and other animals but not for children and definitely not for me. It would be too humiliating." She evokes the difference between the humiliation she censures and the humiliation that Jews, reduced to subhuman status by Nazis, endure. Hence, issues about race — as well as class and gender — all indirectly slip into this Hollywood musical. Maria combats the particular fascism she encounters with a guitar case, not a gun. And she herself plays the Kommandant when she informs von Trapp, "Excuse me sir, I don't know your signal." His answer: "You may call me captain." Although von Trapp is no Captain Kirk, Maria turns his domestic space into her own *Enterprise*. Her orders are followed. "At ease," she tells the children when von Trapp leaves the room. Her "at ease" forever replaces von Trapp's military commands.

Karen Joy Fowler's "Game Night at the Fox and Goose"

A film classic can be read as feminist discourse; feminist discourse can become old hat. Allison, the protagonist of Karen Joy Fowler's feminist science fiction story "Game Night at the Fox and Goose," faces this fact when she encounters a supposed woman described in terms of light. The "woman's" "face was shadowed by an Indiana Jones–type hat, but the candle on the table lit up the area below her neck" (235). Throughout Fowler's story, unreliable light surrounds the "woman." For example: "the woman's face remained shadowed. . . . The candle flame was casting shadows which reached and withdrew and reached at Allison over the table. In the unsteady light, the woman's face flickered like a silent film star's. Then she pulled back in her chair and sank into darkness beyond the candle" (237, 239). The woman's face, not the light, flickers. This unusual illumination portends that Fowler's feminist science fiction story will also flicker — i.e., change genres in mid-narrative. "Game Night" is feminist science fiction which becomes a horror story. "Game Night" opposes Tobin Siebers' notion of the romantic couple (discussed in the introduction). "Game Night" concerns how a woman's desire to be rescued by a strong extraterrestrial woman (cut from central casting as feminist science fiction alternative-universe denizen) becomes a close (and potentially irrevocable) encounter with man as monster. The "woman," who pulls back her chair and sinks into darkness, is a male alien who persuades Allison to pull herself into an alternative universe — which might be a darker place for women than our own universe. The moral of "Game Night at the Fox and Goose": women should not put all their eggs in one generic basket — including the feminist science fiction genre. Allsion is not a protagonist of James Tiptree, Jr.'s "The Women Men Don't See." Unlike Tiptree's Ruth and Althea Parsons, benign aliens do not rescue Allison from patriarchal Earth. "The feminine force" (239) is not with Allison.

Fowler's protagonist's "woman's" discourse affects feminist readers as well as Allison. These readers want "Game Night" to remain a feminist science fiction story. They want Allison to find an improved alternative to patriarchal reality. When Allison tells the "woman," "I'll follow you. Which way?" (242), she casts herself as a feminist science fiction protagonist. For her, this role is as ineffective as the aforementioned rescue via attempted laser beam ascension. No eventual Baron von Trapp–like good guy, the "woman" / male alien malevolently convinces Allison to agree to locate "the door that says Women and go on through it" (242). Feminist science fiction slips into horror fiction when Allison enters the men's restroom, "the small bathroom that apparently fronted two universes" (243). Here feminist science fiction, a fantastic didactic version of Marilyn French's *The Women's Room*, negates itself in the men's room.

When Allison finds herself in a bathroom larger than the one she entered, which contains "a row of urinals" (243), she knows she has not reached a feminist utopia. The urinals are Allison's genre fission focal point, the place where her hoped-for feminist utopia goes down the drain and emerges as nightmare. Allison, would-be refugee from patriarchy, is propelled into an unknown and potentially meta-patriarchal universe from which there may be no return. Because she is a literal believer in feminist fairy tales, Allison voluntarily flushes her life down the toilet, which is her white black hole. She learns that feminist fantastic narrative is discourse which lacks fixed definition. When this woman, located in an unknown men's room, sees her supposed female feminist science fiction rescuer remove his breasts and toss them "into a wire wastebasket" (243), she encounters the evil twin of Bontecou's *Untitled* (discussed in the introduction), the liberatory wire black-hole artwork.

The alien's explanation for his cross-dressing charade (which seems to anticipate Clinton's verbal hairsplitting): "I never lied. . . . You just translated wrong. . . . He tipped his hat to her" (243). Allison mistakenly translates his verbal *Untitled* as Russ' "When It Changed." Instead of journeying to Whileaway, Allison relocates to the universe of the literal female man — not "for a while." The alien is the male monster Allison initially does not see. Instead of interpreting feminist discourse as a fixed definition, she would have done better, while using bright light, to ask her rescuer to tip his Indiana Jones hat — a black hat. Or, according to the language of my introduction: Allison, when translating, mistakenly resorts to the clichés from outer space rather than the grand mix. No Barbie Liberation Organization rescues her after she has been pulled into the toilet which becomes a urinal.

Noritoshi Hirakawa's A Temptation to Be a Man

What is a woman to do when she is cast in a patriarchal spotlight in which "her face flickered like a silent film star's" (Fowler, 239) — in which her head is unfocused and her mouth is shut. Noritoshi Hirakawa's *A Temptation to Be a Man* (1993), an artwork in the form of a projected slide, sheds light on this question. *Temptation*, exhibited in Frankfurt's Museum for Modern Art, projects a picture of a white woman, with legs spread, lying on a white sheet. This image of woman is sexually screened on the sheet,

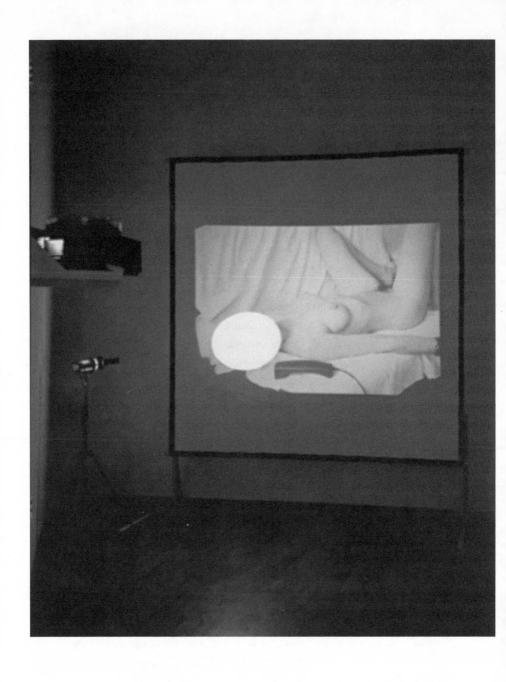

Noritoshi Hirakawa, A Temptation to Be a Man, *1993. Museum for Modern Art, Frankfurt. Photo: Axel Schneider.*

literally projected by light emanating from a phallic mechanistic orifice. The female image's head is not flickering; it is obliterated. Another projected entity, a round white light, appears in place of her head. The head behind the white light is obscured in the manner of objects located in a black hole. The female image's head appears as a round white hole.

Hirakawa, who uses light to portray headless sexualized Woman, also pictures technology: a telephone and a watch appear on his slide. I echo my introduction: who is this headless woman gonna call? I suggest time check — a particular time check whose mechanistic recorded voice announces that it is time to see beyond fixed definitions. In the manner of subversive nuns pulling wires out of Nazis' automobiles, Woman can pull the plug out of her hole in the wall, her "chink in the world machine" (Tiptree, "Women Men Don't See," 154). Woman can turn off projectors which at once obscure her head by highlighting it as a hole and spotlight her genital hole. Woman can become a Connecticut Yankee who tells her own story of shadow and light and gravitational force to suit herself — to eclipse patriarchal stories. Woman can author a new discourse practice which appropriates the force, enabling the force to be with her. Woman can have the balls to place balls in her own court, not in some version of King Arthur's court. Genre fission, after all, reveals that Maria is not the problem. Maria's new discourse practice is the solution.

THE EPILOGUE'S EPILOGUE

"How do you hold a moonbeam in your hand?" Arthur Miller expresses himself in a manner akin to this question. Charlie Rose, when discussing the Broadway revival of *Death of a Salesman*, asks Miller if his present 83-year-old self can equal the achievement of the play's young author. Miller replies, "If I am lucky enough to catch the lightning I can do it" (*Charlie Rose*, February 25, 1999). Hold the moonbeams. Catch the lightning. These impossibilities are possible in generating a new discourse practice. Why? Tom Wolfe discusses what I perceive to be Marshall McLuhan's answer. Wolfe states that McLuhan told General Electric Company executives that "light is information with no message" (Wolfe lecture). Information with no message is analogous to a black hole devoid of light. Discourse can be something other than discourse.

Kaboom! Or Genre Fission Means Never Having to Say You're Sorry
Light can illuminate discourse. How? Genre fission emits liberated light emanating from an explosion which blows up fixed definitions. I conclude

by unleashing this energy via explaining my understanding of "fission." I do so with the awareness that it is certainly unconventional directly to explain a book's title in its final sentences. My decision reflects a different approach which resists categorizing this book and itself exemplifies my premise about resisting categorization.

"Fission," the act of cleaving or splitting into parts, is defined in a manner which signals opposition. This opposition is connoted by "cleave," which at once means to adhere closely (i.e., to stick or cling) and to split or divide as if by a cutting blow (i.e., to cut off or sever). Fission, then, resists being pinned down categorically. Genre fission involves both a black hole's convergence and liberated light's reemergence, both cohesion and explosion. Intact genres burst out of their usual categorical boundaries; critics generate new interpretations by bringing together the resulting scattered shards. Critics working under the genre fission rubric explode fixed definitions and conservative notions.

Genre fission is the ultimate culture wars weapon with which to counter the plethora of heinous "ism"s. Abbie Hoffman famously declared: "Steal this book." Re *Genre Fission*: throw this book. Why? The fantastic has real counterparts. Pierre Boulle imagined a planet of the apes, and Monique Wittig gave us *Les guérillères*. Real Guerrilla Girls, who may not have read Boulle and Wittig, fight discrimination clad in gorilla masks. Using the Girls' affinity to Boulle's and Wittig's fantastic visions as an inspiration, why not equate "book" with "hand grenade"? Hence: throw this book. Blow up, for example, the Right Wing's appropriation of the American flag and "family values."

Why the bomb image? Bombs were implanted in my childhood consciousness, as a baby boomer who attended elementary school during the height of the Cold War. Reading, writing, and arithmetic lessons were routinely interrupted by shelter drills, the duck and cover exercise which, in the event of nuclear attack, would ensure that children would die in an orderly fashion. It was, then, normal for my classmates routinely to practice genre fission, to merge the disparate, to associate bombs with texts. In other words, one minute I focused upon *Fun with Phonics* while intoning "See Dick see Jane see Spot see Puff." During the next minute, after a bell sounded, I was required to crouch under a desk with my hands placed over my head.

Unlike schoolchildren, words cannot be controlled. My first grade teacher never imagined that when I grew up I would read "see Dick" as a reference to the Dick / prick Geiger Counter I describe in my contribution to the 2000 critical anthology *Future Females, the Next Generation: New Voices and Velocities in Feminist Science Fiction Criticism*.[5] She never imagined that "See Spot see Puff" could refer to the trail of smoke emanating from the spot — ground zero — which marks a genre fission explosion.

Make the evil "ism" empire duck and cover. Throw this book at 'em. See what then happens to conservative Dicks — and Janes. Go, Guerrilla Girl. Go, little book, now liberated from the expected generic doings of the usual category "book." Or: Kaboom!

NOTES

INTRODUCTION

1. Nichols posits new directions for the study of visual culture by exploring deci-
sive moments when the traditional boundaries separating fiction from nonfiction and truth from falsehood blur. He offers important departures from prevailing trends by altering interpretive frameworks of psychoanalysis and
neoformalism.

2. This is how Siebers describes his "vision of 'heterotopia,' of mixed places and
themes": "I mean to evoke his [Gianni Vattimo's] idea that postmodernism
views utopia in terms of multiplicity. I am also insisting on my idea that postmodernism defines utopia through the metaphor of the romantic couple,
where individuals must overcome their differences (the most threatening being
sexual difference) to attain happiness (the most sought-after being sexual happiness)" (Siebers, 20).

3. Joann Loulan, during a *20 / 20* interview, insisted that the term "lesbian" still applies to her (ABC television, April 17, 1998).

1. BRIDGING THE DEAD FATHER'S CANONICAL DIVIDE

1. I have said that "antipatriarchal fabulation is authored by men who bash manhood even though they are ensconced within patriarchy's powerful positions.
Antipatriarchal fabulation involves different behavior patterns, not the different
worlds Robert Scholes refers to in his definition of fabulation" (Barr, *Lost*, 111).

2. For a story which emphasizes Poe's relationship to his mother and, by giving the
story power to act upon the author, questions distinctions between author and
story, see Angela Carter, "The Cabinet of Edgar Allan Poe," in *Women of Wonder: The Contemporary Years*, ed. Pamela Sargent, 103–113 (San Diego: Harcourt
Brace, 1995).

3. See my discussion of "Dunyazadiad" in *Feminist Fabulation*, 235–240.

4. Chapter 8 discusses killing corpses as an analogue for anti-Semitism.

2. "ALL GOOD THINGS"

1. David Gerrold is the author of "The Trouble with Tribbles," the single most
popular *Star Trek* episode.

3. SHUTTING THE BESTIAL MOUTH

1. See my *"Thelma and Louise*: Driving towards Feminist Science Fiction." In *Lost in Space*, 21–29.

2. Fuss says: "The relentless shot / reverse shot movement of these intimate face-offs [between Starling and Lecter], the sustained back-and-forth rhythm of the camera's head-on, level gaze, creates a structure of symbolic exchange whereby the two heads eventually become interchangeable, substitutable, switchable. . . . The technique of the cinematic close-up, which Demme relies upon so heavily to figure the identification between Lecter and Starling, in effect decapitates the subject, reducing it in scale to the level plane of the face by simultaneously enlarging the face to fill the screen's entire visual field. The face, the surface upon which subjectivity is figured, is also the zone of bestiality and primoridal hunger, the overinvested corporeal of not just an ocular but an oral identification" (190–191).

3. In this regard, Alf explains that the seventies are over. We no longer live in a time when "gentle and knowing defloration had been understood by some of the younger, less married faculty gallants as an extracurricular service they were being salaried to perform" (Updike, *Memories*, 82).

4. Piercy explains that, when creating Becky, she "was actually drawing on a number of criminal cases in which women had taken violent actions usually reserved for men, but in support of their own women's goals. . . . I called her Becky because I was thinking of Thackeray's Becky Sharp. I was interested in how different it is now for an ambitious working class kid like Becky who wants to climb out of her class after the loss of book culture and its replacement by mall culture and TV. Becky is as much a child of the media as she is her own parents' child" (Marge Piercy, letter to Marleen Barr, September 18, 1996).

5. LOS YORK / NEW ANGELES

1. To a New Yorker, the name "New York" means "Manhattan." For example, a Queens resident who intends to travel to "the city" might say, "I am going to take the subway to New York." In accordance with this practice, I often use "New York" as a synonym for "Manhattan."

2. Los Angeles also has a voluptuous art museum. Jo-Anne Berelowitz, in "L.A.'s Museum of Contemporary Art and the Body of Marilyn Monroe," explains that Arata Isozaki, "by his own admission, designed the body of Monroe into the museum. . . . Isozaki directly projects a human body onto a building. . . . The museum, in other words, IS an erotically projected female body. . . . [T]he Monroe metaphor has come to dominate the whole building. . . . And so they filled the body of Marilyn with monuments to male potency" (22, 28, 29, 35).

3. Kunstler's following description of Tomorrowland is akin to my description of Wright's Guggenheim spiral as mall and theme park: "Tomorrowland looks strikingly like the first great shopping malls of the early sixties, all parabolic woggle architecture and space-rocket imagery. The rides and attractions have mostly to do with worship of vehicles: cars. . . . the 'people mover' eliminates the need to walk" (226).

4. The *New York Times* describes the private gated community as a new American phenomenon: "The fastest-growing residential communities in the nation are private and usually gated. . . . By some estimates, nearly four million Americans live in these closed-off, gated communities. . . . What is different now is that a big portion of middle-class families, in nonretirement, largely white areas of the country, have chosen to wall themselves off. . . . Critics worry that as homeowners withdraw into private domains, the larger sense of community spirit will disappear. . . . The private towns seek to create an idealized America, and their business is booming. . . . The developers of these communities sell security, predictability, and open space. . . . 'The issue is the extent to which Americans are becoming a country of separate communities walled off inside their fortresses.'. . . These private communities are totally devoid of random encounters. So you develop this instinct that everyone is just like me, and then you become less likely to support schools, parks or roads for everyone else" (Egan, 1, 22).
5. See Fredric Jameson, "Postmodernism, or the Cultural Logic of Late Capitalism," *New Left Review* 146 (1984): 53–92.
6. When Jo-Anne Berelowitz describes the land surrounding Los Angeles as a "veld," she seems to reflect the analogy I draw between Los Angeles and Johannesburg. Berelowitz says that immigrants to Los Angeles "transformed the vast veld around L.A. into a concatenation of sprawling suburbs" (32).

6. AMERICAN MIDDLE-CLASS MALES MARK THE MOON

1. Erica Jong says this about Apollo's lack of attention to womankind: "Nineteen sixty-nine was the year sex was discovered. . . . It was the year of the moon shot, of male astronauts walking on the female moon and planting their spikes in what was called 'one small step for a man, one giant leap for mankind.' Womankind was not much thought of in all that phallic blasting, phallic thrusting. We were an afterthought" (125).
2. Ursula K. Le Guin's "Sur," a story about women explorers journeying to the South Pole and electing to leave no mark of their arrival, contrasts sharply with the behavior of the Apollo astronauts.
3. John Varley, in *Steel Beach*, imagines that this is not the case. He describes how fraternity brothers on Luna destroy the sight of the first moon landing. Museum curators re-create the original: "When Armstrong and Aldrin came in peace for all mankind, it was envisioned that their landing site, in the vacuum of space, would remain essentially unchanged for a million years, if need be. Never mind that the exhaust of lift-off knocked the flag over and tore a lot of the gold foil on the landing stage. The footprints would still be there. And they are. . . . [T]hings are often not what they seem. . . . Nowhere in the free literature or the thousands of plaques and audio-visual displays in the museum will you hear of the night . . . when ten members of the Delta Chi Delta fraternity, Luna University Chapter, came around on their cycles. . . . Their cycles wiped out most of the footprints. . . . [T]wo guys went out there and tromped around with replica Apollo moon boots. . . . Presto! An historical re-creation passing as the real thing. This is not a secret, but very few people know about it" (Varley,

212–213). The absence of women in the Hayden Planetarium exhibit is akin to the Luna museum's silence about the fraternity brothers.

4. John Noble Wilford comments upon the "eclipse" of the moon race: "But the wonder now evoked by the lunar landing is that the United States so recently had the optimism to conceive such a grand undertaking . . . and then so readily abandoned the enterprise" (1).

5. Jim Lovell and his co-author Jeffrey Kluger describe the cardboard and duct tape solution devised by Ed Smylie (NASA'S chief of the Crew System's Division): "In order to make the oversized command module cartridges work in the inhospitable LEM, what Smylie envisioned doing was inserting the back half— the outflow half— of the bulky lithium hydroxide box into a plastic bag and taping the bag in place with heavy, airtight duct tape. An arched piece of cardboard taped inside the bag would hold it rigid and prevent it from collapsing against the outflow vents. Smylie would then punch a small hole in the bag and insert the loose end of one of the pressure-suit hoses into it, making this connection airtight with tape as well" (Lovell and Kluger, 251). Holes saved the astronauts.

7. WOMEN "CHURTENING" VIA THE CHA CHA

1. Space exploration has often linked science and narrative. Ronald Reagan, the movie star president, derives his Star Wars from the movies. *Apollo 8* astronauts read from Genesis as they circle the moon at Christmas. In addition, the film *Air Combat* mentions connections between fiction, science, and outer space: Robert Goddard read *War of the Worlds*. After Wernher von Braun served as a consultant for Fritz Lang's *Frau im Mond*, the Nazis, who felt that the film's design for a rocket was too real, confiscated the film. The countdown so much associated with launching space vehicles originally appeared in *Frau im Mond*. When *Apollo* and *Soyuz* docked in space, American and Russian astronauts conversed in terms of "knock knock" jokes. After the Russian knocked on the *Apollo* capsule, the American asked, "Who's there?"

2. See Marleen S. Barr, "*Searoad Chronicles of Klatsand* as a Pathway toward New Directions in Feminist Science Fiction: Or, Who's Afraid of Connecting Ursula Le Guin to Virginia Woolf?" *Foundation* (Spring 1994): 58–67.

3. Here Alvarez addresses the "who wears the pants?" quandary that my introduction discusses.

4. A recast John F. Kennedy also figures in chapter 2.

5. Esperanza, who has an extraordinary mother and experiences the death of a sister, resembles a fantastic version of Cokie Roberts.

8. WRAPPING THE REICHSTAG VS. RAPPING RACISM

1. In "Jews Are Not White" Michael Lerner states that the "degree to which people buy into being 'white' is the degree to which people are willing to forget their roots and their past. . . . No wonder, then, that ruling elites in the U.S. have best succeeded in offering the designation 'white' to those whose material existence is one of deprivation and oppression. . . . Herein lies the liberatory potential of

multiculturalism: To reject the fantasized concept of 'whiteness' . . . Jews must respond with an equally determined insistence that we are not white, and that those who claim we are and exclude our history and literature from the newly emerging multicultural canon are our oppressors" (33). Sander Gilman calls a chapter in *The Jew's Body* "The Jewish Nose: Are Jews White? Or, the History of the Nose Job" (170). He asks, "[A]re Jews white? And what does 'white' mean in this context?" (Gilman, 170). And he repeats his question: "[A]re Jews white? Or do they become white . . . acculturate into American society, so identifying with all its evocation of race, that they — at least in their own mind's eye — become white?" (238). See also Ruth Frankenberg, *White Women, Race Matters: The Social Construction of Whiteness* (Minneapolis: University of Minnesota Press, 1993).

2. Following the example of Abish's title *How German Is It*, I do not include question marks in my subtitle.

3. There is another new categorical distinction. Rafael Seligmann describes German Jews as the "Indians of Germany," the non-African "vanished American" who is more present in myth than in reality (Gilman, *German Culture*, 19).

4. According to Bhabha, "This interstitial passage between fixed identifications opens up the possibility of a cultural hybridity that entertains difference without an assumed or imposed hierarchy. . . . the theoretical recognition of the split-space of enunciation may open the way to conceptualizing an *international culture*, based not on the exoticism of multiculturalism or the *diversity* of cultures, but on the inscription and articulation of culture's *hybridity*. To that end we should remember that it is the 'inter'— the cutting edge of translation and negotiation, the *inbetween* space — that carries the burden of the meaning of culture. It makes it possible to begin envisaging national, anti-nationalist histories of the 'people'" (Bhabha, 4, 38–39).

5. Gilman describes how Turks present in Germany affect the dichotomy between Jews and Germans: "But their [Jews who are German and reside in Germany] notion of 'Germany' is defined in terms of their self-identified Jewishness. . . . Thus their Germany is peopled by 'Germans'— a rather risky generalization given the fact that there are over a million and a half people of Turkish descent in contemporary Germany who may or may not be included in any legal definition of the 'German' but who certainly complicate the simple dichotomy of 'German' and 'Jew.'. . . it is this complexity that makes the new visible invisibility of the Jew in German culture possible" (*German Culture*, 19).

6. While wrapping the Reichstag suggests the positive and new, clashing cultures still pose problems in Berlin. The *Guardian* indicates that Berlin authorities do not view Turks openly displaying their culinary culture as a picnic: "The Tiergarten on a weekend is a mass barbecue: the air is thick with the smoke of a thousand sizzling roasts. . . . In a city noted more for its darker side of past decadence, and current turmoils, the Tiergarten appears a wholesome and peaceful counterpart. This is lost on the Berlin authorities. . . . According to Volker Liepelt, chief whip of Berlin's governing Christian Democrats, the grill parties in the Tiergarten are a stain on one of the 'calling cards of our city' and he wants

them banned. . . . Most of those grilling in the Tiergarten are of Turkish origin and, although Liepelt would never say it, this seems to be the problem. . . . While events like the Reichstag wrapping suggest a new spirit intending to catch the international eye, rows such as that over Tiergarten . . . show that the cozy provincialism produced by decades of isolation is alive and well" (Studemann, 11).

9. PLAYING WITH TIME

1. Hayden White addresses the issue of realistic portrayal: "This is not to suggest that we will give up the effort to represent the Holocaust realistically but rather that our notion of what constitutes realistic representation must be revised to take account of experiences that are unique to our century and for which older modes of representation have proven inadequate" (52).

2. Alan Isler is quite concerned with time. When he read from *Prince* at a New York Barnes & Noble (August 9, 1995), he mentioned that many reviews state that he is sixty years old. He read three chapters outside of their chronological order.

3. Philip Roth also creates a Holocaust fairy tale for readers in *The Ghost Writer*. He imagines that Anne Frank survives, comes to America, and now lives there in disguise.

4. Szeman's *Kommandant's Mistress* shows the lack of common idiom between victim and killer of differing nationality and gender. When the Jew murders the Nazi, Jew and Nazi assume each other's categories.

EPILOGUE

1. Michelle Wallace uses the black hole metaphor to argue that black feminist creativity subverts the racist status quo: "I used a black w/hole as a metaphor — a hole in space which appears empty but is actually intensely full — to portray a black feminist creativity that appeared to authorize a 'negative' view of the black community but was, in fact, engaged in reformulating black female subjectivity as the product of a complex structure of American (US) inequality" ("Negative Images," 125).

2. See Jean Baudrillard, "L'Effet Beaubourg: Implosion et dissuasion," *October* 20 (1982): 3–13, and "The Implosion of Meaning in the Media and the Implosion of the Social in the Masses," in *In the Shadow of the Silent Majorities: Or, the End of the Social and Other Essays* (New York: Semiotext(e), 1983). See also David Harvey, *The Condition of Postmodernity: An Enquiry into the Origins of Cultural Change* (Oxford and Cambridge, Mass.: Blackwell, 1989).

3. I originally wanted to call this book *Genre Seepage*. However, I was advised not to do so because "seepage" evokes body fluid images. With regard to my discussion of President Clinton's "sexual incontinence," I appropriately retain "genre seepage."

4. Weisberg explains that "Clinton has recast the Presidency on the more modest model of his previous job. Unlike Presidents, governors have few opportunities to be visionaries. Instead, they do what Clinton has done — a job of crisis management, political accommodation and governmental reform" (32).

5. See Marleen S. Barr, "Post-Phallic Culture: Reality Now Resembles Utopian Feminist Science Fiction," in *Future Females, the Next Generation: New Voices and Velocities in Feminist Science Fiction Criticism*, ed. Marleen S. Barr, 67–84 (Boulder, Colo.: Rowman and Littlefield, 2000). I refer to what I call a Dick/prick Geiger Counter to describe Mary Anne's response to her former husband, Dr. Dick, in the CBS sitcom *Cybill* (1995–1998).

WORKS CITED

Abish, Walter. *How German Is It: Wie Deutsch Ist Es*. New York: New Directions, 1979.

Aikath-Gyaltsen, Indrani. *Daughters of the House*. New York: Ballantine, 1991.

Air Combat. 1993. U.S. News Productions. Perpetual Motion Films. Produced by Stuart Rakant and Michelle Feroux. Edited by Eytan Sternberg. Written by Robert J. Litz. Narrated by Monte Markham.

Alexander, Christopher. *The Timeless Way of Building*. New York: Oxford University Press, 1979.

Alf. September 22, 1986 – June 18, 1990. NBC. Lorimar Television. Produced by Bernie Brillstein and Tom Patchett. Created by Paul Fusco. With Max Wright and Anne Schedeen.

Alvarez, Julia. *How the Garcia Girls Lost Their Accents*. New York: Plume, 1992.

Amis, Martin. *Time's Arrow or the Nature of the Offense*. New York: Crown, 1991.

Appelfeld, Aharon. *Katerina*. Trans. Jeffrey M. Green. New York: Random House, 1989.

Apple, Max. "Bridging." In *The Granta Book of the American Short Story*, ed. Richard Ford, 546–554. New York: Viking, 1992.

Applebome, Peter. "A Sweetness Tempers South's Bitter Past." *New York Times*. July 31, 1994, 1, 20.

Artist's Choice Modern Women. 1995. Manhattan Media Projects. Produced by Gail Jensen and Jeffrey Owne Jones. Edited by Amanda Zinoman. With Elizabeth Murray and Kirk Varnedoe.

Asimov, Isaac. *Fantastic Voyage*. New York: Bantam Books, 1988.

———. *I, Robot*. New York: Gnome, 1950.

Atwood, Margaret. *The Handmaid's Tale*. New York: Fawcett, 1986.

———. *Lady Oracle*. New York: Fawcett, 1987.

———. *The Robber Bride*. New York: Doubleday, 1993.

Aubl, Eileen. Letter. "We're Losing Ground to the Kitsch Culture." *New York Times*. June 12, 1994, 27.

Austin, J. L. *How to Do Things with Words*. Cambridge, Mass.: Harvard University Press, 1962.

Ballad of Little Jo. 1993. Rank / Fire Line / Polygram / Ioco. Produced by Fred

Berner and Brenda Goodman. Written and directed by Maggie Greenwald. Photography by Declan Quin. Music by David Mansfield. With Suzy Amis, Bo Hopkins, and Ian McKellan.

Barr, Marleen S. *Feminist Fabulation: Space / Postmodern Fiction*. Iowa City: University of Iowa Press, 1992.

———. *Lost in Space: Probing Feminist Science Fiction and Beyond*. Chapel Hill: University of North Carolina Press, 1993.

———, ed. *Future Females, The Next Generation: New Voices and Velocities in Feminist Science Fiction Criticism*. Boulder, Colorado: Rowman and Littlefield, 2000.

Barrie, James M. *Peter Pan*. 1911. Reprint: New York: Scribner's, 1980.

Barth, John. *Chimera*. New York: Fawcett, 1972.

———. *The End of the Road*. New York: Avon, 1958.

———. "The Literature of Exhaustion." In *The Friday Book: Essays and Other Nonfiction*, 62–79. New York: G.P. Putnam, 1984.

———. "Night-Sea Journey." In *Lost in the Funhouse*, 3–13. Garden City, N.Y.: Doubleday, 1968.

———. *Once upon a Time: A Floating Opera*. Boston and New York: Little, Brown, 1994.

———. Reading. Barnes & Noble Union Square. New York City. March 1994.

———. "Teacher: The Making of a Good One." *Harper's* 273 (November 1986): 58–65.

Barthelme, Donald. *The Dead Father*. New York: Farrar, Straus and Giroux, 1975.

Barthes, Roland. "Myth Today." In *Mythologies*, 109–159. New York: Farrar, Straus and Giroux, 1957.

Bellow, Saul. "The Bellarosa Connection." In *Something to Remember Me By*, 5–89. New York: Signet, 1991.

———. *Mr. Sammler's Planet*. New York: Viking, 1969.

———. "Something to Remember Me By." In *Something to Remember Me By*, 187–222. New York: Signet, 1991.

Bennet, James. "US Cruise Missiles Strike Sudan and Afghan Targets Tied to Terrorist Network." *New York Times*, August 21, 1998, 1, A10.

Berelowitz, Jo-Anne. "L.A.'s Museum of Contemporary Art and the Body of Marilyn Monroe." *Genders* 17 (Fall 1993): 22–40.

Bertens, Hans. *The Idea of the Postmodern: A History*. New York and London: Routledge, 1995.

Betsky, Aaron. "Riding the A Train to the Aleph: Eight Utopias for Los Angeles." In *Heterotopia: Postmodern Utopia and the Body Politic*, ed. Tobin Siebers, 96–121. Ann Arbor: University of Michigan Press, 1994.

The Beverly Hillbillies. CBS. September 26, 1962–September 7, 1971. Produced by Al Simon. Music by Perry Botkin and Curt Massey. With Buddy Ebsen, Irene Ryan, Donna Douglas, Max Baer, Raymond Bailey, and Nancy Kulp.

Bhabha, Homi K. *The Location of Culture*. London and New York: Routledge, 1994.

Birnbach, Lisa. "Meet the New Neighbors." *New York Magazine*, February 20, 1995, 38–44.

Blade Runner. 1982. Warner / Ladd / Blade Runner Partnership. Produced by
Michael Deeley and Ridley Scott. Directed by Ridley Scott. Written by
Hampton Fancher and David Peoples. From the novel by Philip K. Dick.
Photography by Jorden Cronenweth. With Harrison Ford, Sean Young, and
Edward James Olmos.

Blair, Linda. "Jackie O, Who Lived a Mini-Series." *New York Times*, May 29, 1994,
1, 25.

Borges, Jorge Luis. "Pierre Menard, Author of *Don Quixote.*" In *Ficciones*, 45–55.
New York: Grove Press, 1962.

Boulle, Pierre. *Planet of the Apes.* Trans. Xan Fielding. New York: Vanguard Press,
1963.

Boyer, Peter J. "We're Not in Camelot Anymore." *New Yorker*, May 23, 1994, 39–45.

The Boys from Brazil. 1978. ITC Entertainment Circle Production. Executive
Producer, Robert Fyer. Directed by Franklin J. Schaffner. With Gregory Peck
and Laurence Olivier.

Bradbury, Ray. *The Martian Chronicles.* Garden City, N.Y.: Doubleday, 1958.

Brantenberg, Gerd. *Egalia's Daughters.* Seattle: Seal Press, 1985.

Bruck, Connie. "Hillary the Pol." *New Yorker*, May 30, 1994, 58–96.

Bruni, Frank."Wagging Tongues in 'Incredibly Cynical Times.'" *New York Times*,
August 21, 1998, A12.

Bumiller, Elisabeth. "30 Years As Grand Old Man of *60 Minutes.*" *New York Times*,
January 14, 1999, B2.

Butler, Octavia E. *Parable of the Sower.* New York: Four Walls Eight Windows, 1993.

———. Reading. Barnes & Noble Astor Place. New York City. April 1996.

Cairns, John, Jr. "Global Coevolution of Natural Systems and Human Society."
Revista de la Sociedad Mexicana de Historia Natural 47 (1997): 217–228.

Calvino, Italo. "All at One Point." In *Cosmicomics*, 43–47. New York: Harcourt
Brace Jovanovich, 1968.

———. *Invisible Cities.* San Diego: Harcourt Brace Jovanovich, 1972.

Carlson, Margaret. "Female Chauvinist Pigs?" *Time*, December 12, 1994, 62.

Carter, Angela. *Nights at the Circus.* New York: Viking Press, 1993.

Castillo, Ana. *So Far from God.* New York: Plume, 1994.

Cavalli-Sforza, Luigi Luca, Paolo Menozzi, and Alberto Piazza. *The History and
Geography of Human Genes.* Princeton: Princeton University Press, 1994.

Chaikin, Andrew. *A Man on the Moon: The Voyages of the Apollo Astronauts.* New
York: Viking, 1994.

Charlie Rose. WNET. Rose Communications Inc. in association with Bloomberg
television news.

Charnas, Suzy McKee. *Walk to the End of the World.* London: Women's Press, 1989.

Cixous, Hélène. "The Laugh of the Medusa." In *New French Feminisms: An
Anthology*, ed. Elaine Marks and Isabelle de Courtivron, 245–264. New York:
Schocken Books, 1981.

Clarke, Arthur C. *Childhood's End.* New York: Harcourt Brace, 1963.

Clines, Francis X. "Over Time; The End Was a Mirage. The Scandal Lives On."
New York Times, February 28, 1999, section 4, 1.

Corwin, Miles. "High-Tech Facility Ushers in New Era of State Prisons." *Los Angeles Times*, May 1, 1990.

Crichton, Michael. *Disclosure: A Novel*. New York: Knopf, 1994.

Dallas. April 2, 1978–April 30, 1978; September 23, 1978–May 3, 1991. CBS. Lorimar Productions. Produced by Philip Capice and Leonard Katzman. Created by David Jacobs. With Larry Hagman, Barbara Bel Geddes, Linda Gray, Patrick Duffy, and Victoria Principal.

Dances with Wolves. 1990. Guild / Tig Productions. Directed by Kevin Costner. Written by Michael Blake. Photography by Dean Semler. Music by John Barry. With Kevin Costner, Mary McDonnell, and Graham Greene.

Dann, Jack. "Camps." In *Timetipping*, 101–125. Garden City, N.Y.: Doubleday, 1980.

———. "Timetipping." In *Timetipping*, 18–27. Garden City, N.Y.: Doubleday, 1980.

Davis, Erik. "Space: 1994." *Village Voice*, July 26, 1994, 24–25.

Davis, Mike. *City of Quartz: Excavating the Future in Los Angeles*. London and New York: Verso, 1990.

Delillo, Don. *Ratner's Star*. New York: Vintage, 1980.

Dennis, Patrick. *Auntie Mame: An Irreverent Escapade*. 1955. Reprint: Thorndike, Maine: G. K. Hall, 1994.

Dillard, R. H. W. "Who Is the Man in the Boat?" *New York Times Book Review*, July 3, 1994, 13.

Doane, Mary Ann. *Femmes Fatales: Film Theory, Psychoanalysis*. New York and London: Routledge, 1991.

———, Patricia Mellencamp, and Linda Williams. "Feminist Film Criticism: An Introduction." In *Re-Vision: Essays in Feminist Film Criticism*, ed. Doane, Mellencamp, and Williams, 1–15. Frederick, Md.: University Press of America, 1984.

Doctorow, E. L. *The Waterworks*. New York: Signet, 1995.

Dr. Jekyll and Mr. Hyde. 1932. Paramount. Directed by Rouben Mamoulian. Screenplay by Samuel Hoffenstein and Percy Heath. With Fredric March, Miriam Hopkins, and Rose Hobart.

Duggan, Dennis. "For Filmmakers New York, New York Is a Wonderful Town." *New York Newsday*. Special Public Affairs Section: "A Day at the Movies Starring . . . New York, New York." June 19, 1994, 3.

Echevarría, Roberto González. "Sisters in Death." *New York Times Book Review*, December 18, 1994, 28.

Egan, Timothy. "Many Seek Security in Private Communities." *New York Times*, September 3, 1995, 1, 22.

Ellison, Harlan. "I Have No Mouth and I Must Scream" (1967). In Eric S. Rabkin, *Stories: An Anthology and Introduction*, 388–399. New York: HarperCollins, 1995.

Europa, Europa. 1991. France / Germany. Les Films du Losange / CCC Film Kunst / Perspektywa. Directed by Agnieszka Holland, Margaret Menegoz, and Artur Brauner. Written by Agnieszka Holland from the book by Salomon Perel.

Photography by Jacek Petrycki. With Marco Hofschneider, Julie Delpy, and
Andre Wilms.

Everything You Always Wanted to Know about Sex But Were Afraid to Ask. 1972.
United Artists. Produced by Charles H. Joffee. Directed by Woody Allen.
Screenplay by Woody Allen after a book by David Reuben. With Woody Allen,
John Carradine, Lou Jacobi, and Anthony Quayle.

Fein, Esther B. "Philip Roth Sees Double: And Maybe Triple Too." *New York
Times*, March 9, 1993, section C, 13.

Feirstein, Bruce. *Real Men Don't Eat Quiche.* New York: Pocket, 1982.

Fiedler, Leslie A. *Love and Death in the American Novel.* New York: Stein and Day,
1966.

Finch, Sheila. "Reichs-Peace" (1986). In *Women of Wonder: The Contemporary
Years*, ed. Pamela Sargent, 172–190. San Diego: Harcourt Brace, 1995.

Firestone, David. "While Barbie Talks Tough, G.I. Joe Goes Shopping." *New York
Times*, December 31, 1993, A12.

The Flight of Apollo 11: Eagle Has Landed. 1969. NASA. Produced by Clayton
Edwards. Directed by Ted Lowry.

Fowler, Karen Joy. "Game Night at the Fox and Goose" (1989). In *Women of
Wonder: The Contemporary Years*, ed. Pamela Sargent, 233–243. San Diego:
Harcourt Brace, 1995.

"Frank Lloyd Wright's Masterwork." *Architectural Forum* (April 1952): 141–144.

French, Marilyn. *Our Father.* New York and Boston: Little, Brown, 1994.

———. *The Women's Room.* New York: Jove Books, 1977.

Friedan, Betty. *The Feminine Mystique.* New York: Norton, 1963.

Friedlaender, Salomo (Mynona). "The Operated Goy" (1922). In *The Operated
Jew: Two Tales of Anti-Semitism*, trans. Jack Zipes, 75–86. New York and
London: Routledge, 1991.

Friedlander, Saul, ed. *Probing the Limits of Representation: Nazism and the Final
Solution.* Cambridge, Mass.: Harvard University Press, 1992.

———. *Reflections on Nazism: An Essay on Kitsch and Death.* New York: Harper
and Row, 1982.

Friedman, Ellen G. "Where Are the Missing Contents?: (Post)Modernism,
Gender, and the Canon." *PMLA* 108 (1993): 240–252.

Fuss, Diana. "Monsters of Perversion: Jeffrey Dahmer and *The Silence of the
Lambs.*" In *Media Spectacles*, eds. Marjorie Garber, Jann Matlock, and
Rebecca L. Walkowitz, 181–205. New York and London: Routledge, 1993.

Galford, Ellen. *The Dyke and the Dybbuk.* Seattle, Wash.: Seal Press, 1994.

Garcia, Cristina. *Dreaming in Cuban.* New York: Ballantine, 1992.

Gerrold, David. "The Kennedy Enterprise." In *Alternate Kennedys*, ed. Mike
Resnick, 52–68. New York: Tor Books, 1992.

Gilligan's Island. September 26, 1964– Sepember 3, 1967. CBS. Directed by Charles
Norton and William D'Arcy. Created by Sherwood Schwartz. Produced by
William Froug and Sherwood Schwartz. Music by Sherwood Schwartz. With
Alan Hale Jr., Bob Denver, Tina Louise, Jim Backus, and Natalie Schafer.

Gilman, Sander. *The Jew's Body.* New York and London: Routledge, 1991.

————. *Jews in Today's German Culture*. Bloomington: Indiana University Press, 1995.

The Gods Must Be Crazy. 1980. South Africa. New Realm / Mimosa / CAT. Directed, produced, and written by Jamie Uys. Photography by Buster Reynolds. With N'xau, Lena Farugia, and Hans Strydom.

Goldstein, Richard. "*Schindler's List*: Myth, Movie and Memory." *Village Voice*, March 29, 1994, 24–31.

Gordimer, Nadine. "Once upon a Time." In *Jump and Other Stories*, 23–30. Cape Town and Johannesburg: David Philip, 1991.

Gottlieb, Sherry. *Love Bite*. New York: Warner Books, 1994.

Green Acres. September 15, 1965–September 7, 1971. CBS. Produced and created by Jay Sommers. Directed by Richard L. Bare. Music by Vic Mizzy. With Eddie Albert and Eva Gabor.

Guare, John. *Six Degrees of Separation*. New York: Vintage Books, 1994.

Gurganus, Allan. *White People*. New York: Ivy Books, 1990.

Haizlip, Shirlee Taylor. "Passing." *American Heritage*. (February / March 1995): 46–54.

————. *The Sweeter the Juice*: New York: Simon and Schuster, 1994.

Haldeman, Joe. *The Forever War*. New York: St. Martin's Press, 1974.

Hamilton, William. "New Yang and Los Yingeles." *Buzz* (March 1995): 120.

Handy, Bruce. "Fly Me to the Moon." *New York Times Magazine*, July 10, 1994, 62.

Hartman, Geoffrey H. "The Book of Destruction." In *Probing the Limits of Representation: Nazism and the "Final Solution*," ed. Saul Friedlander, 318–334. Cambridge: Harvard University Press, 1992.

Hassan, Ihab. "Pluralism in Postmodern Perspective." In *The Postmodern Turn*: *Essays in Postmodern Theory and Culture*, 167–187. Columbus: Ohio State University Press, 1987.

Havel, Václav. "The New Measure of Man." *New York Times*, July 8, 1994, A27.

"Helicopter Rescue Is Planned for Robot." *New York Times*, August 7, 1994, section 1, 31.

Herman, Jerry. "The Man in the Moon." In *Mame*, 39–40. New York: Random House, 1967.

He Said, She Said. 1991. Paramount. Directed by Ken Kwapis and Marisa Silver. Produced by Frank Mancuso, Jr. Written by Brian Hohlfeld. With Kevin Bacon, Elizabeth Perkins, and Nathan Lane.

Hevesi, Dennis. "Fire Damages a Landmark Hotel in Brooklyn." *New York Times*, August 27, 1995, 31, 33.

Hoffman, Abbie. *Steal This Book*. New York: Grove Press, 1971.

Holland, Norman N. *5 Readers Reading*. New Haven: Yale University Press, 1975.

Holocaust. April 16–20, 1978, September 1979. NBC. Titus Productions. Produced by Herbert Brodkin. Written by Gerald Green. Created by Marvin Chomsky. Produced by Robert Berger. With Michael Moriarty, Meryl Streep, Joseph Bottoms, and Rosemary Harris.

hooks, bell (Gloria Watkins). "Third World Diva Girls: Politics of Feminist

Solidarity." In *Yearning: Race, Gender, and Cultural Politics*, 89–102. Boston: South End Press, 1990.

Isler, Alan. *The Prince of West End Avenue*. New York: Penguin, 1995.

Jacobs, Karrie. "Next, the Drink 'n' Read." *New York Times*, January 14, 1999, F2.

Jameson, Fredric. "Foreword." In Jean-François Lyotard, *The Postmodern Condition: A Report on Knowledge*, trans. Geoff Bennington and Brian Massumi, vii–xxi. Minneapolis: University of Minnesota Press, 1984.

———. "Postmodernism, or the Cultural Logic of Late Capitalism." *New Left Review* 146 (1984): 53–92.

Janowitz, Tama. *The Male Cross-Dresser Support Group*. New York: Crown, 1992.

The Jeffersons. 1975–1985. CBS. Tandem Company. Directed by Jack Shea. Produced by Norman Lear. Music by Jeff Berry and Ja'net DuBois. With Sherman Hemsley, Isabel Sanford, Marla Gibbs, and Roxie Roker.

Jong, Erica. *Fear of Fifty: A Midlife Memoir*. New York: HarperCollins, 1994.

Jungle Fever. 1991. Forty Acres and a Mule Filmworks / Universal Pictures. Directed, produced, and written by Spike Lee. With Wesley Snipes, Annabella Sciorra, and Spike Lee.

Junior. 1994. Northern Lights Entertainment / Universal Pictures. Directed and produced by Ivan Reitman. Written by Kevin Wade and Chris Conrad. Photography by Adam Greenberg. With Arnold Schwarzenegger, Danny DeVito, and Emma Thompson.

Kakutani, Michiko. "Of a Roth within a Roth within a Roth." *New York Times*, March 4, 1993, C17.

Kaplan, Sam Hall. *Los Angeles Times*, November 4, 1978, x, 13.

Kessler, Carol Farley. "Consider Her Ways: Cultural Work of Charlotte Perkins Gilman's Stories, 1908–1913." In *Utopian and Science Fiction by Women: Worlds of Difference*, ed. Jane L. Donawerth and Carol A. Kolmerten, 126–136. Syracuse: Syracuse University Press, 1994.

Kunstler, James Howard. *The Geography of Nowhere: The Rise and Decline of America's Man-made Landscape*. New York: Simon and Schuster, 1993.

Langer, Lawrence L. *Admitting the Holocaust: Collected Essays*. New York: Oxford University Press, 1995.

Latham, Rob. "Subterranean Suburbia: Underneath the Small Town Myth in the Two Versions of *Invaders of Mars*." *Science-Fiction Studies* 22 (1995): 198–208.

Leary, Warren E. "Newts and Metal Projects Ride Columbia into Space." *New York Times*, July 9, 1994, 10.

Le Guin, Ursula K. "The Day before the Revolution" (1974). In *Stories: An Anthology and Introduction*, ed. Eric S. Rabkin, 859–869. New York: HarperCollins, 1995.

———. *A Fisherman of the Inland Sea: Science Fiction Stories*. New York: HarperPrism, 1994.

———. "For Hélène Cixous." In *Discontented Discourses: Feminism / Textual Intervention / Psychoanalysis*, ed. Marleen S. Barr and Richard Feldstein, frontispiece. Urbana: University of Illinois Press, 1989.

———. "Is Gender Necessary?" (1976). In *The Language of the Night: Essays on*

Fantasy and Science Fiction, ed. Susan Wood, 135–147. London: The Women's Press, 1989.

———. *The Left Hand of Darkness*. New York: Harper and Row, 1969.

———. *Searoad: Chronicles of Klatsand*. New York: HarperCollins, 1991.

———. "Sur." In *The Norton Anthology of Literature by Women*, ed. Sandra M. Gilbert and Susan Gubar, 2007–2022. New York: Norton, 1985.

———. "Why Are Americans Afraid of Dragons?" In *The Language of the Night: Essays on Fantasy and Science Fiction*, ed. Susan Wood, 39–45. New York: G. P. Putnam, 1979.

Lem, Stanislaw. "Prince Ferrix and the Princess Crystal" (1967). In *Stories: An Anthology and Introduction*, ed. Eric S. Rabkin, 870–877. New York: HarperCollins, 1995.

———. *The Star Diaries*. Trans. Michael Kandel. New York: Harcourt Brace, 1985.

Lemonick, Michael D. "Cosmic Close-ups." *Time*, November 20, 1995, 44–53.

Lerner, Michael. "Jews Are Not White." *Village Voice*, May 18, 1993, 33–34.

———. *Tikkun's Politics of Meaning: A Brief Summary*. Undated pamphlet.

Levin, Ira. *The Boys from Brazil*. New York: Random House, 1976.

———. *The Stepford Wives: A Novel*. New York: Random House, 1972.

Lili. 1952. MGM. Directed by Charles Walters. Produced by Edwin H. Knopf. Music by Bronislaw Kaper. Story by Paul Gallico. Screenplay by Helen Deutsch. With Leslie Caron, Mel Ferrer, and Zsa Zsa Gabor.

Littmann, Mark. *Footsteps: In Honor of the Apollo Moonflights*. Salt Lake City: Hansen Planetarium, 1979.

Lovell, Jim, and Jeffrey Kluger. *Lost Moon: The Perilous Voyage of Apollo 13*. Boston and New York: Houghton Mifflin, 1994.

Lyotard, Jean-François. *The Postmodern Condition: A Report on Knowledge*. Trans. Geoff Bennington and Brian Massumi. Minneapolis: University of Minnesota Press, 1984.

Mame. Book by Jerome Lawrence and Robert E. Lee. Music and lyrics by Jerry Herman. New York: Random House, 1966.

McCarthy, Mary. *The Group*. New York: New American Library, 1963.

McHale, Brian. *Postmodernist Fiction*. New York and London: Methuen, 1987.

Mifflin, Lawrie. "What a Difference the News Makes: Clinton as Commander in Chief." *New York Times*, August 21, 1998, A13.

Moraga, Cherrie. "Winter of Oppression, 1982." In *Loving in the War Years*, 73–76. Boston: South End Press, 1983.

Mr. Ed. October 1, 1961–September 4, 1966. Directed by Arthur Lubin. Produced by Al Simon and Arthur Lubin. Music by Jay Livingston and Ray Evans. With Alan Young and Connie Hines.

Mulvey, Laura. "Visual Pleasure and Narrative Cinema." *Screen* 16 (1975): 6–18.

Mumford, Lewis. *The City in History*. New York: Harcourt, Brace and World, 1961.

Muschamp, Herbert. "On West 57th, a Confederacy of Kitsch." *New York Times*, June 5, 1994, 2:4.

Myers, Steven Lee. "Rethinking a Treaty for a New Kind of Enemy." *New York Times*, January 24, 1999, 4:16.

The Nanny. 1993–. CBS. Sternin / Fraser Ink Inc. in association with Tristar Television. Produced and written by Robert Sternin, Prudence Fraser, and Peter Marc Jacobson. Directed by Lee Shallat. Created by Sternin, Fraser, Jacobson, and Drescher. Music by Timothy Thompson. With Fran Drescher, Charles Shaughnessy, and Lauren Lane.

"New Englanders 'Killed' Corpses, Experts Say." *New York Times*, October 31, 1993. 1:36.

"New York, New York, It's a Helluva Town!" 1944. Words by Betty Comden and Adolph Green. Music by Leonard Bernstein.

Nichols, Bill. *Blurred Boundaries: Questions of Meaning in Contemporary Culture.* Bloomington: Indiana University Press, 1994.

Oates, Joyce Carol. *Blackwater*. New York: Dutton, 1992.

——. *Foxfire*. New York: Dutton, 1993.

——. *Them*. New York: Fawcett, 1984.

On the Town. 1944. Book by Betty Comden and Adolph Green, based on the idea by Jerome Robbins. Directed by George Abbott. Musical director Max Goberman. Music by Leonard Bernstein. Choreography by Jerome Robbins. Scenery by Oliver Smith. Costumes by Alvin Cott. With Cris Alexander, John Battles, Robert Chisholm, Betty Comden, Adolph Green, Sono Osato, Alice Pearce, and Nancy Walker.

Oz, Amos. *To Know a Woman*. Trans. Nicholas de Lange. San Diego: Harcourt Brace Jovanovich, 1991.

Panizza, Oskar. "The Operated Jew" (1893). In *The Operated Jew: Two Tales of Anti-Semitism*, 47–74. New York and London: Routledge, 1991.

Papashvily, George, and Helen Waite. *Anything Can Happen*. New York: Harper and Bros., 1940.

Peters, Philip C. "Black Hole." In *McGraw Hill Encyclopedia of Astronomy*, ed. Sybil Parker, 42–44. New York: McGraw-Hill, 1983.

Piercy, Marge. *He, She, and It*. New York: Knopf, 1991.

——. *The Longings of Women*. New York: Ballantine, 1994.

——. "Marleen Barr's Lost and Found." In Marleen S. Barr, *Lost in Space: Probing Feminist Science Fiction and Beyond*, ix–xi. Chapel Hill: University of North Carolina Press, 1993.

——. *Woman on the Edge of Time*. New York: Fawcett, 1985.

Poe, Edgar Allan. "The Facts in the Case of M. Valdemar" (1845). In *The Science Fiction of Edgar Allan Poe*, 194–203. New York: Penguin, 1976.

——. "The System of Dr Tarr and Prof. Fether," (1845). In *The Science Fiction of Edgar Allan Poe*, 175–193. New York: Penguin, 1976.

——. "The Thousand-and-Second Tale of Scheherazade" (1845). In *The Science Fiction of Edgar Allan Poe*, 135–153. New York: Penguin, 1976.

——. "The Unparalleled Adventure of One Hans Pfaall" (1840). In *The Science Fiction of Edgar Allan Poe*, 12–64. New York: Penguin, 1976.

Pretty Woman. 1990. Buena Vista / Touchstone. Produced by Arnon Milchan and Steven Reuther. Directed by Garry Marshall. Written by J. F. Lewton. Photography by Charles Minsk. With Richard Gere, Julia Roberts, and Ralph Bellamy.

Purdum, Todd S. "Critics of Clinton Support Attacks." *New York Times*, August 21, 1998, A1, 11.

Pynchon, Thomas. *Vineland*. New York: Little, Brown, 1990.

Quindlen, Anna. "The Fourth Wall." *New York Times*, July 19, 1992, 17.

Rauber, Marilyn. "Hillary for Prez? Friends Want First Lady in Office." *New York Post*, May 23, 1994, 2.

Raven P. H., and G. B. Johnson. *Biology*. St. Louis: Times Mirror / Mosby College Publishing, 1986.

Reich, Tova. *The Jewish War*. New York: Pantheon, 1995.

Revkin, Andrew C. "Once Glamorous, a Grande Dame Had Fallen on Hard Times." *New York Times*, August 27, 1995, 33.

Richards, David. "On Stage, Survival of the Fizziest." *New York Times*, June 12, 1994. 2:1, 32.

Roland, Alex. "How We Won the Moon." Review of *A Man on the Moon* by Andrew Chaikin and *Moon Shot* by Alan Shepard and Deke Slayton. *New York Times Book Review*, July 17, 1994, 1, 25.

Rosemary's Baby. 1968. Paramount / William Castle. Directed and written by Roman Polanski. Based upon the novel by Ira Levin. With Mia Farrow, John Cassavetes, and Ruth Gordon.

Roth, Philip. "The Breast." In *A Philip Roth Reader*, 445–483. New York: Farrar, Straus and Giroux, 1980.

———. *The Ghost Writer*. New York: Farrar, Straus and Giroux, 1979.

———. *Operation Shylock: A Confession*. New York: Vintage, 1994.

Rush, Norman. *Mating*. New York: Knopf, 1991.

Rushdie, Salman. *Haroun and the Sea of Stories*. New York: Penguin, 1991.

Russ, Joanna. "Amor Vincit Foeminam: The Battle of the Sexes in Science Fiction." *Science-Fiction Studies* 20 (1980): 2–15.

———. "The Clichés from Outer Space." In *Dispatches from the Frontiers of the Female Mind*, 27–34. London: Women's Press, 1985.

———. *To Write Like a Woman: Essays in Feminism and Science Fiction*. Bloomington and Indianapolis: Indiana University Press, 1995.

———. "When It Changed." In *The Norton Anthology of Literature by Women*, ed. Sandra M. Gilbert and Susan Gubar, 2262–2269. New York: Norton, 1985.

Said, Edward. *The World, the Text, and the Critic*. Boston: Harvard University Press, 1983.

Sargent, Pamela. *Earthseed: A Novel*. New York: Harper and Row, 1983.

———. *The Shore of Women*. New York: Crown, 1986.

Schindler's List. 1993. Universal / Amblin. Directed by Steven Spielberg. Produced by Steven Spielberg, Gerald R. Molen, and Branko Lustig. Written by Steven Zaillian from the novel by Thomas Keneally. Music by John Williams. With Liam Neeson, Ben Kingsley, and Ralph Fiennes.

Scott, Jody. *I, Vampire*. London: Women's Press, 1986.

———. *Passing for Human*. London: Women's Press, 1986.

Self, Will. *Cock and Bull*. New York: Random House, 1992.

Shakespeare for My Father. Helen Hayes Theater. New York. 1993. By Lynn Redgrave. Directed by John Clarke. With Lynn Redgrave.

Shepard, Alan, and Deke Slayton (with Jay Barbee and Howard Benedict). *Moon Shot: The Inside Story of America's Race to the Moon*. Atlanta: Turner Books, 1994.

Siebers, Tobin. "Introduction: What Does Postmodernism Want? Utopia." In *Heterotopia: Postmodern Utopia and the Body Politic*, 1–38. Ann Arbor: University of Michigan Press.

The Silence of the Lambs. 1991. Orion. Directed by Jonathan Demme. Produced by Gary Goelzman. Screenplay by Ted Tally from a novel by Thomas Harris. With Jody Foster, Anthony Hopkins, and Scott Glenn.

Slonczewski, Joan. *A Door into Ocean*. New York: Avon, 1987.

Soja, Edward W. *Postmodern Geographies: The Reassertion of Space in Critical Social Theory*. London and New York: Verso, 1989.

The Sound of Music. 1965. Twentieth Century Fox. Directed by Robert Wise. Produced by Argyle Enterprises. Music by Richard Rodgers. Lyrics by Oscar Hammerstein II. Book by Howard Lindsay and Russel Crouse. With Julie Andrews and Christopher Plummer.

"Space Fantasy: Five Different Designs." United States Postal Service, 1992.

"Spiral Art Gallery." *Architectural Forum*. (April 1952): 141–144.

Staples, Brent. "Life in the Information Age: When Burma-Shave Meets Cyberspace." *New York Times*, July 7, 1994, A18.

Stark, Steven. "Weekend Edition." National Public Radio.

Starr, Kevin. *Southern California through the 1920's*. New York: Oxford University Press, 1990.

Stein, Gertrude. "Composition as Explanation." In *Selected Writings of Gertrude Stein*, ed. Carl Van Vechten, 511–553. New York: Random House, 1972.

Steiner, George. *The Portage to San Cristobal of A. H.* New York: Simon and Schuster, 1979.

Stern, David. "Imagining the Holocaust." *Commentary* (July 1976): 46–51.

Stimpson, Catharine R. "Female Insubordination and the Text." In *Where the Meanings Are*, 155–164. New York and London: Methuen, 1988.

———. "Nancy Reagan Wears a Hat: Feminism and Its Cultural Consensus." In *Where the Meanings Are*, 179–196. New York and London: Methuen, 1988.

Studemann, Frederick. "Berlin Diary." *Guardian*, July 17, 1995, 11.

Szeman, Sherri. *The Kommandant's Mistress*. New York: HarperCollins, 1993.

Tannen, Deborah. "Wears Jump Suit. Sensible Shoes. Uses Husband's Last Name." *New York Times Magazine*, June 20, 1993, 18, 52, 54.

10. 1979. Warner / Orion / Geoffrey. Produced by Blake Edwards and Tony Adams. Written and directed by Blake Edwards. Photography by Frank Stanley. Music by Henry Mancini. With Dudley Moore, Julie Andrews, and Bo Derek.

1071 Fifth Avenue: Frank Lloyd Wright and the Story of the Guggenheim Museum.

1993. Stella Films. Presented by Richard Rogers. Produced by Ultan Guilfoyle, Directed by Peter Lydon. Photography by George Tifflin. Music by Robert Lockhard. Narrated by Brendan Gill. With F. Murray Abraham and Claire Bloom.

Tepper, Sheri S. *The Gate to Women's Country* (1988). New York: Bantam, 1989.

Thelma and Louise. 1991. UIP / Pathé Entertainment. Directed and produced by Ridley Scott. Written by Callie Khouri. Music by Hans Zimmer. With Susan Sarandon, Geena Davis, and Harvey Keitel.

Theroux, Paul. *Chicago Loop.* New York: Ivy Books, 1990.

Thompson, J. N. "Patterns in Coevolution." In *Coevolution and Systematics*, eds. A. R. Stone and D. L. Hawksworth, 119–143. Oxford: Clarendon Press, 1986.

Tierney, John. "Earthly Worries Supplant Euphoria of Moon Shots." *New York Times*, July 20, 1994, 1, 15.

Tiptree, James, Jr. "Houston, Houston, Do You Read?" In *Aurora: Beyond Equality*, ed. Vonda N. McIntyre and Susan Janice Anderson, 36–98. Greenwich, Conn.: Fawcett, 1976.

———. "The Women Men Don't See." In *Warm Worlds and Otherwise*, ed. Robert Silverberg, 131–164. New York: Ballantine, 1975.

The Truman Show. 1998. Paramount Pictures. Scott Rudin Productions. Directed by Peter Weir. Produced by Edward S. Feldman. Written by Andrew Niccol. Music by Philip Glass. With Jim Carrey, Ed Harris, and Laura Linney.

Updike, John. *Bech: A Book.* New York, Knopf: 1982.

———. *Bech Is Back.* New York, Knopf: 1982.

———. *Couples.* New York: Knopf, 1968.

———. *Memories of the Ford Administration.* New York: Knopf, 1992.

———. "Recruiting Raw Nerves." *New Yorker*, March 5, 1993, 109–112.

———. *S.* New York: Knopf, 1988.

Varley, John. *Steel Beach.* New York: Berkley, 1992.

Vera, Hernán. "On Dutch Windows." *Qualitative Sociology* 12, no. 2 (Summer 1989): 215–234.

Verhovek, Sam Howe. "Myths Die with Their Boots On." *New York Times*, October 24, 1993, 4:1, 5.

Verne, Jules. *Around the Moon [Autour de la lune].* 1872. Paris: J. Hetzel.

———. *From the Earth to the Moon, and a Trip around It [De la terre à la lune].* 1865. Paris: J. Hetzel.

Vonnegut, Kurt. *Slaughterhouse Five.* New York: Delacorte, 1970.

Wallace, Michelle. "*Boyz N The Hood* and *Jungle Fever*." In *Black Popular Culture*, ed. Gina Dent, 123–131. Seattle: Bay Press, 1992.

———. "Negative Images: Towards a Black Feminist Cultural Criticism." In *The Cultural Studies Reader*, ed. Simon During, 118–131. London and New York: Routledge, 1993.

Wasserstein, Wendy. *Uncommon Women.* New York: Dramatist's Play Service, 1978.

Weisberg, Jacob. "The Governor President." *New York Times Magazine*, January 17, 1999, 30–36, 41, 52, 65.

Weldon, Fay, *The Life and Loves of a She-Devil*. London: Hodder and Stoughton, 1983.

"What's So Funny about NYC?" *New York Magazine*, February 20, 1995, 45.

White, Hayden. "Historical Employment and the Problem of Truth." In *Probing the Limits of Representation: Nazism and the "Final Solution,"* ed. Saul Friedlander, 37–53. Cambridge, Mass.: Harvard University Press, 1992.

Wilford, John Noble. "25 Years Later, Moon Race in Eclipse." *New York Times*, July 17, 1994, 1, 20–21.

Wittig, Monique. *Les guérillères*. Trans. David Le Vay. New York: Viking, 1971.

Wolf. 1994. Columbia. Directed by Mike Nichols. Produced by Douglas Wick. Written by Jim Harrison and Wesley Strick. Music by Ennio Morricone. With Jack Nicholson, Michelle Pfeiffer, and James Spader.

Wolf, Naomi. *The Beauty Myth: How Images of Beauty Are Used against Women*. New York: William Morrow, 1991.

Wolfe, Tom. "Marshall McLuhan." Lecture. Fordham University. February 25, 1999.

Wright, Richard. *Uncle Tom's Children*. New York: Harper and Row, 1936.

Zipes, Jack, trans. and commentary. *The Operated Jew: Two Tales of Anti-Semitism*. New York: Routledge, 1991.

Zoline, Pamela. "Instructions for Exiting This Building in Case of Fire." In *Despatches from the Frontiers of the Female Mind*, 93–110. London: Women's Press, 1985.

INDEX

Cold War, 125
Collins, Michael, 122, 123
Columbia (space shuttle), 119, 123
Coover, Robert, 48
Copley, Bill, xiii, 73, 74, 78, 80, 82, 84
Corwin, Miles, 112
Couples (Updike), 69
Crichton, Michael, xv
Crocker Center (Los Angeles), 108
cross-dressed texts, 3–19
The Crucible (Miller), 99

Dachau, 209
Dahmer, Jeffrey, 34
Dakota, 112, 149
Dallas (television program), 66
Dances with Wolves, xv
"Dancing to Ganam" (Le Guin), 143, 145, 146
Dann, Jack, xiv, 193, 196, 197, 198, 200, 207, 211, 214, 219
Dante II (robot), xvi
Dateline NBC, 226, 227
Daughters of the House (Aikath-Gyaltsen), 138, 148, 149–151, 164
Davis, Erik, 133
Davis, Mike, 105, 106, 108, 110, 114
"The Day before the Revolution" (Le Guin), 141
Dayan, Moshe, 55
De Beauvoir, Simone, 156–157
De Montaut, Henri, 130
The Dead Father (Barthelme), 4, 6
Death of a Salesman (Miller), 237
deconstruction, 40
DeLillo, Don, 225
Demjanjuk, John, 51–52, 54
Dennis, Patrick, 131
Derek, Bo, 99
Derrida, Jacques, 37
diasporism, 53
Dick, Philip K., 104
Dillard, R. H. W., 50
Disclosure (Crichton), xv
Disney World, 88

Doane, Mary Ann, 73, 80, 82
Doctorow, E. L., xiii, 193, 218, 219, 220, 221
A Door into Ocean (Slonczewski), 150
Douglas, Michael, xv
Dr. Jekyll and Mr. Hyde (film), 34
Dr. Jekyll and Mr. Hyde (Stevenson), 33, 34
Dreaming in Cuban (Garcia), 137, 148, 151, 152–155, 164
Drescher, Fran, 165–166
Drescher, Henrik, 126–127
Dubos, René, 126
"Dunyazadiad" (Barth), 9, 241n3
durational time, 194–195, 221
The Dyke and the Dybbuk (Galford), 193, 215–218

Eagle (spacecraft), 123, 126
"Easter Parade" (Berlin), 55
Echevarria, Roberto González, 151, 152
Egalia's Daughters (Brantenberg), 164
Eisenhower, Dwight, 22
Ellison, Harlan, 210
The Empire State Building, 96, 117, 118
Encounter in Space (Munch), xiv, xviii
The End of the Road (Barth), 47
Epicot Center, 88
Europa, Europa, 46
Everything You Always Wanted to Know about Sex But Were Afraid to Ask (film), xviii, 122

"The Facts in the Case of M. Valdemar" (Poe), 7, 10, 168, 191
Fairfax (Los Angeles), 105
Fantastic Voyage (Asimov), 103
Farrow, Mia, 149
Fear of Fifty (Jong), 166, 180
Feinstein, Diane, 28
feminist dystopia, 138
feminist fabulation, 14, 143, 145, 146, 147, 148, 159, 162
Feminist Fabulation: Space/Postmodern Fiction (Barr), x–xi, xviii